Learn What the Bible REALLY Says - Fast!

Robert M. Kelley

Kelley Bible Books
P.O. Box 293125 • Kettering, Ohio 45429-9125
www.kelleybiblebooks.com

ISBN 0-9767629-0-0

Printed in the United States of America

Published by Kelley Bible Books
P.O. Box 293125, Kettering, Ohio 45429-9125, U.S.A.

10   9   8   7   6   5   4   3   2   1

Cover design: Kimberly D'Angelo at bookcovers.com

To: The Honor and Glory of the
        One God

About the Author

Robert M. Kelley heads his own training and consulting business in Kettering, Ohio. He has conducted management training and consulting for thousands of executives, managers, and professionals for 93 major organizations in 15 countries on 6 continents for over 21 years. Customers include AT&T, the US Department of Defense, and the Westinghouse Savannah River Co.

Before beginning his business full-time in 1984, Bob worked 22 years in the information technology, automotive, and aerospace industries, working for companies such as the NCR Corporation, General Motors, and B.F. Goodrich Aerospace.

Kelley has spoken on management subjects in cities from Philadelphia to San Francisco, from Chicago to Miami, at seminars, conferences, and professional society meetings sponsored by organizations such as the American Management Association, the Association of Systems Management, the Association of Information Technology Professionals, and the Project Management Institute.

In 1988 Bob authored the 240 page hardcover book, *Planning Techniques (Basic & Advanced)*. This book has been on the *Dayton Daily News* Top Ten Best-Seller list for weeks. Thousands of volumes in five printings have been sold worldwide.

Kelley has authored 46 published articles, which have appeared in publications such as the *Dayton/Springfield Business Life*, *Dayton Business Reporter*, and *Business Life*.

Bob has studied the Bible for 40 years.

Kelley received a BS degree in mechanical engineering from Case Western Reserve University in Cleveland, Ohio, and a BA degree in liberal arts from Ambassador College in Pasadena, California.

Bob and his wife of 42 years, Beth, live in Ohio. Their four adult children (two daughters and two sons) live in California.

Contents

Introduction

What You Learn

Have you been *told* this is what the Bible says?
- "Good people go to heaven after death."
- "Bad people go to hell after death."
- "Heaven is now filled with good people."
- "Hell is now filled with bad people."
- "Hell is ever-burning."
- "Everyone has an immortal soul."
- "This is God's world."
- "God is a Trinity."
- "Today is the only day of salvation."
- "The many billions of people who have never even heard the name of Christ will all burn in hell."

Incredible as it may sound, what the Bible *really* says is that every single statement in the above list is *false*! The Bible shows that, in most cases, the truth about the above listed subjects is the exact *opposite* of this list!

In addition, the Bible reveals wonderful truth, of which you may never have heard:
- Every person who has ever lived will have the opportunity of the New Covenant.
- People who have lived on Earth in past ages will be physically resurrected to live again on Earth and have the opportunity of salvation.
- There are multiple days of salvation.
- Jesus Christ will return to Earth from heaven and rule Earth for 1,000 years.
- Successful Christians will rule with Christ.
- Christ and successful Christians will rebuild Earth.
- Earth will never be destroyed.
- All life on Earth will never be destroyed.
- Earth will become the center of the universe.

How You Learn *Fast*

The first way you learn fast deals with how the Bible is written. In the Bible, information on a given subject is *scattered* throughout its 66 constituent books. Without *Learn What the Bible* Really *Says -- Fast!* you would have to perform a great deal of research to identify the appropriate Bible verses for a given subject. However, I have *already* performed this research for you and have organized Bible verses on different subjects into separate chapters. This book contains thirty-two chapters. A single chapter contains the key Scriptures on a given subject. Using one chapter you can quickly look up the key Bible verses on that subject.

A second way you learn fast deals with how Scriptures are identified in a chapter. In each chapter key Scriptures are identified. The three most important Scriptures on a subject are in **bold** type and the next seven most important Scriptures on this subject are underlined. (Some chapters have less than ten key Scriptures.) The Bible is a big book, but you *can* learn it, subject by subject, chapter by chapter, Scripture by Scripture, day by day.

A third way you learn fast deals with God's Master Plan. God's Master Plan is a "road map" of the Bible, a palpable framework of overview Bible knowledge. If you *first* know God's Master Plan, specific Bible study will simply add detail to an already known Bible knowledge framework. *Without* knowledge of God's Master Plan I have seen Bible students become confused and quit. *With* knowledge of God's Master Plan I have seen Bible students progress rapidly. God's Master Plan is covered in chapters 9-12.

Using *Learn What the Bible* Really *Says -- Fast!* enables you to learn essential Bible truth as quickly as possible.

Why You Need to Learn the Bible Fast

The Bible shows that immediately before Christ's return to rule Earth for 1,000 years, Earth will be ruled by a Satanic one-world government. People have given this coming ugly political and governmental entity different names. I choose to call it Satan's One-World Government (SOWG). (See chapter 29 to learn about SOWG.) When Satan's One-World Government takes control over Earth, those who seek God will be persecuted and put to death. It behooves all people to take Christ's warning seriously:
> "As long as it is day, we must do the work of him who sent me. Night is coming, when no one can work." (John 9:4 *NIV*)

Christ had a limited amount of time -- three and one-half years -- to carry out his mission from God. Every living human being has a limited amount of time.

How to Use *Learn What the Bible* Really *Says -- Fast!*

You can use the chapters in any order. You may choose to study specific chapters of interest or go through them in the order in which they appear. (The contents page and subject index can aid you in selecting a specific chapter.) Using a chapter, perform these steps: (1) Open your Bible and verify that the Scripture quotations in the chapter are correct. (2) Write or type pertinent

Scriptures on paper or on a computer file. Writing or typing slows down your mind to better absorb Scripture. Your goal should be to learn the Word of God, the Bible: Writing or typing facilitates this goal. (3) Ask God (via prayer) for the Holy Spirit to reveal to you the meaning of Scripture. (4) After having received Biblical understanding, thank God for it.

Why I Wrote *Learn What the Bible* Really *Says -- Fast!*

Today religion and organized Christianity present a Babylon of confusion. In addition, some church denominations have totally abandoned the Bible, replacing it with secular humanism. In addition, today there are cults. The Watchman Fellowship publishes an annual *Index of Cults*. It lists over 1,000 cults active in the US. There are Eastern religious cults, New Age cults (they aren't new; they have ancient origins), and "Christian cults" (an oxymoron if there ever was one).

Two major concerns motivated the writing of *Learn What the Bible* Really *Says -- Fast!* First, I am absolutely appalled, upset, and angry at the fairy tales, fantasies, and falsehoods that are taught as Bible truth. It makes my blood boil to hear this garbage! False ideas about the Bible are widespread. Second, there is much wonderful truth in the Bible that even experienced Bible students seem to miss. A huge truth vacuum exists. I wrote *Learn What the Bible* Really *Says -- Fast!* because I want to help people replace false ideas with truth.

Three facts have enabled me to write *Learn What the Bible* Really *Says -- Fast!* (1) I have studied the Bible for 40 years. (2) Because I am a Christian (see chapter 3, "What is a Christian?") the Holy Spirit has revealed truth as I studied. (3) God has given me analytical skills to organize what I have learned.

The Holy Spirit and analytical reasoning are two gifts I have received from God. God is the source of all good gifts:
"Every good and perfect gift is from above, coming down from the Father of the heavenly lights, who does not change like shifting shadows."
(James 1:17 *NIV*)

I am not unique in being one to whom God has revealed Bible truth. I expect that God, through the Holy Spirit, has, during the last 2,000 years (and even before in the Old Testament period) revealed Bible truth to thousands and possibly even millions of men and women. Many of those individuals did not possess the tools to organize and spread this information to others. Perhaps some of those who *did* have the tools to organize and spread this information had their work cut short in a Satan-influenced world. Even today there are a number of sources of Bible truth. However, one must search diligently to find them.

I didn't *have* to write *Learn What the Bible* Really *Says -- Fast!* Even with Bible understanding, I could have simply joined a run-of-the-mill church and sat comfortably (or uncomfortably?) in the pews every Sunday morning and forgotten about giving God's truth to others. However, I have decided to do what I can in sharing Bible truth. Life is short. One must do what one can while God still gives one breath. "Make hay while the sun shines" is one of my favorite sayings.

Erasmus -- My Favorite Biblical Scholarship Role Model

Erasmus (1466-1536 AD) was an important scholar at the time of the Protestant Reformation and is my favorite Biblical scholarship role model. He was the bastard son of a Roman Catholic priest, who impregnated a washerwoman. Both his parents died when he was eighteen years old. Erasmus was not only a great scholar but also a prolific writer. In the 1530s AD, 300,000 copies of his *Greek New Testament* and over 750,000 copies of his other works were circulating -- incredible numbers for that time in history. For Erasmus the Bible was the center of Christian understanding. He wanted everyone -- regardless of his or her job or status in society -- to read the Bible in his or her own language. Erasmus believed that Bible reading was essential to salvation. He also believed that salvation was a matter between an individual and God. No institution or priesthood could interfere with that relationship.

Unlike contemporaries such as Protestant reformers Martin Luther (1483-1546 AD) and John Calvin (1509-1564 AD), and unlike the Roman Catholic Pope, Erasmus believed that theology should be kept to a minimum. Luther, Calvin, and the Pope promoted theology; Erasmus promoted learning. Erasmus essentially asked, "Why should institutions establish detailed doctrine in areas where God -- in the Bible -- has not made the subject clear?" I agree with Erasmus.

Policies Used in Writing *Learn What the Bible* Really *Says -- Fast!*

Learn What the Bible Really *Says -- Fast!* has absolutely *no* relationship to any church, denomination, or organization. When you use *Learn What the Bible* Really *Says -- Fast!* you are imbibing pure Bible *truth*, which will be truth forever.

To obtain a complete understanding of what the Bible says about a given subject, *all* Scriptures on that subject must be considered. This key principle of Bible study was enunciated by Jesus when he was discussing the Bible with Israelites:
"...the Scripture cannot be broken..." (John 10:35 *NIV*)
When all of the Scriptures are considered, a clear picture emerges. This approach has been used in creating *Learn What the Bible* Really *Says -- Fast!*

Bible Translations Used

My preference in Bible translations is modern ones. (Before judging my comment, see chapter 32, "Bible Translations.") Therefore my preference would have been to use modern translations throughout *Learn What the Bible Really Says -- Fast!* However, most Bible translations are copyrighted.

Some Bible translation copyright owners allow persons to use their works with limitations. For example, the Division of Christian Education of the National Council of Churches of Christ in the United States of America, which holds the copyright of the *New Revised Standard Version*, allows the use of 500 verses without written permission if the *NRSV* verses comprise less than 50% of the total work. The International Bible Society, which holds the copyright of the *New International Version*, allows the use of 500 verses without written permission if the *NIV* verses comprise less than 25% of the total work. The *King James Version* is not copyrighted; its use is not limited in any way.

In *Learn What the Bible Really Says -- Fast!* I have used modern translations for Scripture as much as legally possible. The remainder is quoted from the *KJV*.

Personal Pronouns for Christ

When Jesus Christ was born of Mary, eventually to become the Messiah, he was fully a human being. (See chapter 16, "Jesus Christ.") Therefore, when Jesus Christ is mentioned during his life as a human being on Earth the personal pronoun is not capitalized (he). When Jesus Christ is mentioned after his resurrection the personal pronoun is capitalized (He).

Bible Translation Abbreviations Used in *Learn What the Bible* Really *Says -- Fast!*

KJV = King James Version
Lamsa = Holy Bible from the Ancient Eastern Text by George M. Lamsa
NEB = New English Bible
NIV = New International Version

NRSV = New Revised Standard Version
REB = Revised English Bible
RSV = Revised Standard Version

How to Study the Bible

CHAPTER 1

© 2005, Robert M. Kelley

Look up all Scriptures in your own Bible. Read and/or write the Scriptures on paper. Writing Scriptures on paper slows down your mind and causes the Bible verses to be more deeply burned into your mind.

All Scripture is inspired and true. However, you cannot learn everything at once. Therefore, the most important Scripture on this subject is in **bold** type. (No Scriptures on this subject are underlined.)

---

1.   Studying the Bible is one of the most important actions a human being can perform. It is impossible to over-estimate the value of Bible study. The purpose of human life is to establish an eternal relationship with God. No relationship can exist without communication. All relationships -- husband & wife, parent & child, employer & employee, God & man -- require two-way communication. In a person's relationship with God, two-way communication is required. Listen to God by studying the Bible. Talk to God by praying. This chapter 1, "How to Study the Bible," covers listening to God. (Chapter 2, "How to Pray," covers talking to God.)

2.   The first and simplest way to study the Bible is to read the Bible. Bible reading is the first step in Bible study. Bible reading enables you to first look at the entire forest before looking at individual trees. Bible reading gives you a complete overview of the Bible. You should select a Bible translation with which you feel comfortable. (For more information on Bible translations, see chapter 32, "Bible Translations.") The best Bible translation for Bible study is not necessarily the best Bible translation for Bible reading.

3.   How much of the Bible should you read per day? This is an individual decision. If you have never read the Bible before and are starving for spiritual knowledge, then a high rate might be preferred. If you are reading the Bible for the twentieth time, then a lower rate might be preferred. Don't set an unrealistic goal -- one which is not easy to achieve.
One way to pace yourself is to read three chapters of the Bible per day. The Bible (the *King James Version*, or *KJV*) contains 1,189 chapters. If you were to read three Bible chapters per day, you could read the entire Bible in 13 months. A problem with the x-chapters-per-day approach is that Bible chapters vary greatly in size. Some days would require little reading; other days would require much reading.
Another way to pace yourself in reading the Bible is to read two, four, or six (or more) pages of the Bible per day. I am currently reading the Oxford-published *The Holy Bible, New Revised Standard Version* (*NRSV*). It is 1,280 pages in size.

At six pages per day (my current rate) I will complete reading this Bible in a little over seven months.

4.   <u>Remember that the content of the Bible varies a lot in terms of enjoyable readability</u>. Chapters in Judges and I & II Samuel where Samson is slaughtering the Philistines or David is slaying Goliath are very exciting. There is not a single boring sentence in the books Esther and Ruth. However, chapters which give detailed Old Covenant priestly procedures (in Leviticus) or genealogies and lists of names (in I Chronicles) are just plain boring. Reading procedures and lists is not exciting. Boring passages should not deter you from reading the entire Bible.

5.   <u>Be sure to read all of the Bible -- both Old Testament & New Testament</u>. (To better understand the value of the Old Testament, see chapter 4, "The Old Covenant.") Both the Old Testament & New Testament are inspired. Both are necessary for a relationship with God.

6.   <u>When reading the Bible feel free to underline, highlight, or color-code with a colored pencil, ball-point pen, roller-ball pen, gel ink pen, fountain pen, highlighter, or marker</u>. Although the words of God are sacred, the paper and ink which compose a printed Bible are not. It is OK to mark your Bible. Create your own personalized marking system: yellow for God, orange for the Holy Spirit, green for sin, blue for promises, red for Satan and his demons, etc. The possibilities are endless. Your goal should be to learn the Holy Bible. Any legal means of doing so is valid.

7.   <u>A second way to study the Bible is to study all of the Scriptures on a given subject</u>. God has inspired the Bible to be written in such a way that the Scriptures on a given subject are scattered throughout the Bible. If you want to study a particular subject, you should look at the particular Scriptures which deal with that subject. <u>How do you find out which Scriptures deal with a particular subject?</u> <u>You need to use a book called a Bible concordance</u>. A Bible concordance lists Bible verses which contain a given English word. For example, if you wanted to find Bible verses which contain the word "love," then you would look up, in a concordance, the word "love." Concordance entries are listed alphabetically. Under the entry "love" would be listed, in Biblical order, the Bible verses containing the word "love."

8.   <u>Bible concordances can be described in terms of features</u>. A Bible concordance is always based on a certain Bible translation. The words listed in a concordance are those found in that particular translation. For example, in the *King James Version* (*KJV*) of the Bible one cannot find the word "sex." (The Puritan "sex is evil" idea was very strong in 1611 when the *KJV* was created.) There is plenty of sex described in the Bible; however, the word "sex" is not used in the *KJV*. (The *New International Version* (*NIV*) uses the word "sex" 2 times, "sexual" 47 times, and "sexually" 8 times.) Another feature which distinguishes concordances is whether or not a concordance is exhaustive or non-exhaustive.

An exhaustive concordance lists every single word (even "the" and "a") and every place it appears in a translation. Non-exhaustive concordances do not list each and every word and appearance. Because I always want to be thorough in my Bible research I always use exhaustive concordances. Three popular exhaustive concordances are *The Exhaustive Concordance of the Bible* (based on the *KJV*) by James Strong, *The NIV Exhaustive Concordance* by Edward W. Goodrich & John R. Kohlenberger III, and *The NRSV Concordance Unabridged* by John R. Kohlenberger III.

9.   Using a concordance for Bible study, look up the word which represents the subject of your study. Begin at the top of the list of Bible verses given and look up each verse in the Bible. Some verses will shed no light on the subject. Other verses will reveal meaning. Write (on paper) or type (with a typewriter or computer) meaningful verses. <u>Methodically look up each verse, read it, and either write it or ignore it.</u> After having gone through all Bible verses with the desired word, you will have written or typed only the verses which reveal meaning about the word.
(To facilitate this step I usually copy the appropriate concordance pages, and check off each verse listed on the copy as I progress through the list. I copy the pages because an exhaustive concordance is a very large and heavy book with which to work.)

10.   <u>The next step in performing a concordance Bible study is to organize the meaningful Bible verses into categories.</u> Each category is a statement of fact about the subject. The Bible verses are the Bible proof that each fact is correct. <u>The end result is a list of facts about the subject.</u> <u>The list of facts reveals the Bible truth about the subject.</u>

11.   <u>A third way to study the Bible is to focus on a particular portion of the Bible.</u> For example, what should you do to learn more about the book of Psalms (or the major prophets or the minor prophets, etc.)? You should read each Psalm in order. You might choose to use several Bible translations. In addition, you might want to use one or more Bible commentaries to learn what commentators say about each Psalm. A Bible commentary is a book written by one or more authors. Commentary authors are great scholars who have usually spent lifetimes exploring the original source Bible languages (Hebrew, Chaldee, and Aramaic) and/or secondary languages (Greek). Commentators often discuss the meaning of the original words. This information gives a much greater depth of understanding of each verse. I find it useful to mark Bible commentaries as I use them. <u>Using commentaries and different translations, you can learn a great deal about a particular portion of the Bible.</u>

12.   <u>When performing a Bible study in the four Gospel books (Matthew, Mark, Luke, and John), a very useful book is a Gospel harmony.</u> A Gospel harmony is a book which presents every Gospel verse in time sequence. Most people do not realize that most of the verses in each Gospel book are *not* in time order. That is,

although each Gospel book begins with the birth of Christ and ends with his crucifixion, in most cases the verses in between are *not* in time sequence. In order to have a meaningful study in the Gospels, you should look at the Gospels in time sequence. Some expert scholars have arranged all Gospel verses into a time sequence. The result is called a Bible harmony. A Bible harmony book I use is *A Harmony of the Gospels* by A.T. Robertson, © 1922, 1950, published by Harper & Row, New York (ISBN 0-06-066890-3).

13.   A fourth way to study the Bible is what I call the "message follow-up method." The message follow-up method can be used to follow up a spoken sermon, TV sermon, booklet -- any kind of verbal or written message. When listening to a spoken message (in person, TV, radio, audio cassette, video cassette, CD, dvd), or when reading from a written or printed text, you can take notes. Notes should list the Scriptures mentioned. To perform the message follow-up method, simply write or type (with a typewriter or computer) the listed Scriptures from the Bible. By writing and studying the Bible verses given, two results can occur. You may find that the Bible verses give back-up and reinforce the main points of the presentation. You can *accept* such a message because it is in harmony with the Bible. On the other hand, you may find that the Bible verses given do *not* relate to the main points of the presentation. If the Bible verses do not relate, then there is no reason to accept the message. Such a message should be *rejected* because it is not in harmony with the Bible.

There is a Biblical basis for the message follow-up method:

> "When he takes the throne of his kingdom, he is to write for himself on a scroll a copy of this law, taken from that of the priests, who are Levites. It is to be with him, and he is to read it all the days of his life so that he may learn to revere the LORD his God and follow carefully all the words of this law and these decrees and not consider himself better than his brothers and turn from the law to the right or to the left..."
> **(Deuteronomy 17:18-20** *NIV*)

God knew that the children of Israel would eventually choose the kingdom form of government. God gave instructions specific to kings in Deuteronomy 17:14-20. "A copy of this law" is the rendering in the *KJV*, *New King James*, *NIV*, and *The Holy Scriptures According to the Masoretic Text*. "This law" refers to "this deuteronomy."

(The word "deuteronomy" literally means "second law." The book Deuteronomy ("second law") is a summary of laws previously given in the other books of the Pentateuch (Genesis, Exodus, Leviticus, and Numbers). For example, the Ten Commandments first appear in Exodus 20; they are repeated in Deuteronomy 5. Another example: Clean and unclean food laws are first given in Leviticus 11; they are repeated in Deuteronomy 14.)

The king was to write, by hand, "a copy of this law." The king had to write an entire copy of the book of Deuteronomy. Deuteronomy consists of 34 chapters (959 verses). At eight verses per page, the king had to write 120 pages; this was a virtual book. *The Soncino Books of the Bible* reports that the king actually made two copies. One copy was kept in the treasury. The other copy went with the king, at campsites or wherever the king might be.

The king had plenty of servants. He could easily have ordered his servants to copy the book of Deuteronomy for him. Why did God command the king to hand write it *himself*? Because writing forces your mind to slow down and digest the content. By analogy, eating food takes only a few minutes; however, digesting that food takes 24 hours. You can read text quickly. However, you must slow down to write text; slowing down enables you to mentally digest the content. God wanted the king to know His word *deeply*.

If you want to learn the Bible deeply, you should write Scripture.

Summary. 1. It is impossible to over-estimate the value of Bible study. 2. The first and simplest way to study the Bible is to read the Bible. 3. How much of the Bible should you read per day? This is an individual decision. 4. Remember that the content of the Bible varies a lot in terms of enjoyable readability. 5. Be sure to read *all* of the Bible -- both Old Testament & New Testament. 6. When reading the Bible, feel free to underline, highlight, or color-code with a colored pencil, ball-point pen, roller-ball pen, gel ink pen, fountain pen, highlighter, or marker. 7. A second way to study the Bible is to study all of the Scriptures on a given subject. How do you find out which Scriptures deal with a particular subject? You need to use a book called a Bible concordance. 8. Bible concordances can be described in terms of features. 9. Methodically look up each verse, read it, and either write it or ignore it. 10. The next step in performing a concordance Bible study is to organize meaningful Bible verses into categories. The end result is a list of facts about the subject. The list of facts reveals the Bible truth about the subject. 11. A third way to study the Bible is to focus on a particular portion of the Bible. Using commentaries and different translations, you can learn a great deal about a particular portion of the Bible. 12. When performing a Bible study in the four Gospel books (Matthew, Mark, Luke, and John), a very useful book is a Gospel harmony. 13. A fourth way to study the Bible is what I call the "message follow-up method." To perform the message follow-up method, simply write or type (with a typewriter or computer) the listed Scriptures from the Bible. There is a Biblical basis for the message follow-up method.

How to Pray

CHAPTER 2

© 2005, Robert M. Kelley

    Look up all Scriptures in your own Bible. Read and/or write the Scriptures on paper. Writing Scriptures on paper slows down your mind and causes the Bible verses to be more deeply burned into your mind.

    All Scripture is inspired and true. However, you cannot learn everything at once. Therefore, the three most important Scriptures on this subject are in **bold** type and the next seven most important Scriptures on this subject are underlined.

----

1.   Praying is one of the most important actions a human being can perform. It is impossible to over-estimate the value of prayer. The purpose of human life is to establish an eternal relationship with God. No relationship can exist without communication. All relationships -- husband & wife, parent & child, employer & employee, God & man -- require two-way communication. In a person's relationship with God, two-way communication is required. Listen to God by studying the Bible. Talk to God by praying. This chapter 2, "How to Pray," covers talking to God. (Chapter 1, "How to Study the Bible," covers listening to God.)

2.   How to pray is not something you learn naturally. The disciples often watched Jesus pray. They did not know how to pray and asked Jesus about it:

> "He was praying in a certain place, and after he had finished, one of his disciples said to him, 'Lord, teach us to pray, as John taught his disciples.'" (Luke 11:1 *NRSV*)

Prayer is something that must be taught. Perhaps some individuals (who I don't know) learned how to pray by themselves. However, most people must be taught. A minister taught me how to pray. In the spring of 1965 I heard a minister deliver a message on prayer. This message was both instructional and inspirational. God was working with me at the time. I had begun, for the first time in my life, daily Bible reading six months earlier. In the spring of 1965, I knew that I absolutely *had* to start talking to God. The Holy Spirit moved me to take action on this minister's message.

3.   Jesus gave all human beings an outline for prayer:

> "Pray then in this way:
>
> Our Father in heaven,
>   hallowed be your name.
>   Your kingdom come.
>   Your will be done,
>   on earth as it is in heaven.
>   Give us this day our daily bread [margin: or *our bread for tomorrow*],
>   And forgive us our debts,

> as we also have forgiven our debtors.
> And do not bring us to the time of trial [margin: Or *us into temptation*],
> but rescue us from the evil one [margin: Or *from evil*. Other ancient
> authorities add, in some form, *For the kingdom and the power and
> the glory are yours forever. Amen*]." (**Matthew 6:9-13** *NRSV*)

Some people call this passage the "Lord's Prayer." However, neither Jesus nor the Bible calls this passage the Lord's Prayer. Luke's version of the Lord's Prayer follows immediately after Luke 11:1 (quoted above), where the disciples asked Jesus to teach them *how* to pray. Matthew 6:9-13 is *instruction* on how to pray, not an actual prayer you should pray. Instead of *following* Jesus' instruction, and praying one's *own* prayer using Matthew 6:9-13 as a *model*, some people (and churches) recite Matthew 6:9-13 word-for-word as a prayer.

You should create your own prayer, using Matthew 6:9-13 as an outline or model. From the model, the first part of your prayer should be glorifying God. Second, you should ask God to bring the Kingdom of God to Earth. Third, you should ask God for daily needs. Fourth, you should ask God to forgive your sins. Fifth, you should ask God to keep you from severe trial. Last, you should end the prayer by glorifying God again.

The *real* Lord's Prayer is given in John 17 (entire chapter). John 17 is the prayer the Lord (Jesus) prayed before his crucifixion.

4. <u>You should always address your prayer to God</u>. Note carefully Jesus' instruction:

> "Pray then in this way:
> Our Father in heaven,..." (Matthew 6:9 *NRSV*)

Jesus instructed human beings to address all prayers to God. Jesus did *not* instruct human beings to address prayers to himself or the Holy Spirit.

5. <u>You should end your prayer in the name of Jesus Christ</u>. During Jesus' last night on Earth as a human being he told his disciples:

> "Very truly, I tell you, if you ask anything of the Father in my name, he will give it to you." (<u>John 16:23</u> *NRSV*)

Because of this statement (and similar statements made by Jesus that same night) it is customary to end prayer with "In the name of Jesus Christ, Amen." One may wonder why Jesus did not mention ending prayer in his name in the Lord's Prayer. The Lord's Prayer instruction was given early in Christ's ministry. At that time not all of the twelve disciples were convinced that Jesus was the Messiah. At the end of Christ's ministry his disciples *were* convinced.

6. <u>Jesus warned about improper motives in prayer</u>:

> "And whenever you pray, do not be like the hypocrites; for they love to stand and pray in the synagogues and at the street corners, so that they may be seen by others. Truly I tell you, they have received their reward. But whenever you pray, go into your room and shut the door and pray to your Father who is in secret, and your Father who sees in secret will reward you [margin: Other ancient authorities add *openly*]."
> (**Matthew 6:5-6** *NRSV*)

Prayer is between one person and God. However, the Pharisees had adopted a habit of performing personal prayers in public. The motivation of the Pharisees in performing personal prayers in public was *not* to talk to God, but to be *seen by men*! The Pharisees wanted the praise of men for appearing pious. ("Look, there is Joe Pharisee over there praying in public. Joe is so good!") Since being seen by men was their motive, I expect that many Pharisees did *not* perform personal prayers in private. Jesus was reminding people that the purpose of prayer is to *communicate with God*, not to be seen by men.

Some Christians openly pray before eating a meal in a public restaurant. A Christian can always pray silently, in a way that no one will know he or she is praying. Therefore, what is the *motive* in openly praying a personal prayer in a public place? Are others supposed to "know" by this habit that one is a Christian?

> "God is a spirit, and those who worship him must worship in spirit and truth." (John 4:24 *NRSV*)

Never forget the Bible definition of a Christian:

> "Anyone who does not have the Spirit of Christ does not belong to him." (Romans 8:9 *NRSV*)

If you are a Christian, then others will *see* the Holy Spirit working in you.

7.   <u>Jesus warned about grandiose speaking and repetition in prayer</u>:

> "When you are praying, do not heap up empty phrases as the Gentiles do; for they think that they will be heard because of their many words. Do not be like them, for your Father knows what you need before you ask him." (**Matthew 6:7-8** *NRSV*)

I have known people who have adopted a kind of *King James Version* style of prayer habit. They talk to God in "thee's" and "thou's" and other *KJV*-isms as if God can only understand 1611 AD vintage English. In speaking to humans they use modern English; in speaking to God they use *KJV* English.

God does not require an unusual speech style. Normal, natural speaking works just fine. Some people pray by endlessly repeating words or phrases. God is not deaf. The purpose of prayer is to communicate with God, not to become a hypnotized zombie.

8.   <u>For what should you pray? Jesus, in his outline of prayer (Matthew 6:9-13), explained what to pray about. In addition, Jesus said to pray for your enemies</u> (Matthew 5:44, Luke 6:28) <u>and to pray in times of trial</u> (Matthew 26:41, Mark 14:38, Luke 22:40, 46). In prayer it is easy to develop a case of the "Give-me's" ("Give me this, give me that," etc.). In prayer, if you (a) thank God for what He has already done and (b) ask God to intervene on the behalf of others' needs, then you can pray for hours about these two subjects alone.

9.   <u>Where should you pray</u>? Jesus explained that prayer is a private matter, between one person and God:

> "But whenever you pray, go into your room and shut the door and pray to your Father who is in secret; and your Father who sees in secret will reward you [margin: Other ancient authorities add *openly*]." (Matthew 6:6 *NRSV*)

The Gospels record Jesus praying alone:
> "And after he had dismissed the crowds, he went up the mountain by himself to pray..." (Matthew 14:23 *NRSV*)

> "After saying farewell to them, he went up on the mountain to pray." (Mark 6:46 *NRSV*)

Jesus taught that you should pray in a private place, alone.

My favorite places to pray are in my office and bedroom. I have used living rooms, kitchens, and closets for prayer. I have prayed outdoors. When pressed for time I have prayed while driving.

However, most examples of prayer shown in the Bible are of a person praying alone while kneeling on his or her knees in a private place.

10.   When should you pray? It depends upon your constitution.

Some people are morning people. They get up with the birds and are really roaring at 5 a.m. However, when the sun goes down morning people are almost ready for bed.

Other people are night people. When the sun goes down they turn on. By 10 p.m. these people are really moving. However, in the morning it takes some night people eight cups of coffee to open both eyes.

The question is, which are you? Schedule prayer time during your most productive hours.

11.   How long should you pray? There are no magic numbers for prayer length. However, there are some guidelines. I will never forget the first time I seriously prayed. (This experience should not be confused with childhood prayers like "Now I lay me down to sleep..." or "Now we thank you for this food.") In the spring of 1965, I began my first attempt to develop a serious prayer habit. I was using a bedroom clothes closet. I knelt with both knees on the floor, with my arms supported by a chair. I prayed about everything I could think of. When my prayer was over I looked at my watch. I had prayed for three and one-half minutes!

Presently daily prayer on my knees averages one-half hour. On many occasions I have prayed for more than one hour.

Jesus' life, as recorded in the Bible, shows that he stayed up all night praying on two occasions: before he chose the twelve apostles and before his crucifixion.

In prayer you are building a relationship with God. Prayer enables you to get to know God as a friend. Relationship building takes time. You cannot build an adequate prayer habit instantly.

12.   Be persistent in prayer:
> "Then Jesus told them a parable about their need to pray always and not to lose heart." (Luke 18:1 *NRSV*)

Jesus then told the Parable of the Persistent Widow. Jesus ended the parable:
> "And will not God grant justice to his chosen ones who cry to him day and night? Will he delay long in helping them? I tell you, he will quickly grant justice to them..." (Luke 18:7-8 *NRSV*

Summary. 1. It is impossible to over-estimate the value of prayer. 2. How to pray is not something you learn naturally. 3. Jesus gave all human beings an outline for prayer. 4. You should always address your prayer to God. 5. You should end your prayer in the name of Jesus Christ. 6. Jesus warned about improper motives in prayer. 7. Jesus warned about grandiose speaking and repetition in prayer. 8. For what should you pray? Jesus, in his outline of prayer (Matthew 6:9-13), explained what to pray about. In addition, Jesus said to pray for your enemies and to pray in times of trial. 9. Where should you pray? Jesus taught that you should pray in a private place, alone. 10. When should you pray? Schedule prayer time during your most productive hours. 11. How long should you pray? There are no magic numbers for prayer length. 12. Be persistent in prayer.

What is a Christian?

CHAPTER 3
© 2005, Robert M. Kelley

Look up all Scriptures in your own Bible. Read and/or write the Scriptures on paper. Writing Scriptures on paper slows down your mind and causes the Bible verses to be more deeply burned into your mind.

All Scripture is inspired and true. However, you cannot learn everything at once. Therefore, the three most important Scriptures on this subject are in **bold** type and the next six most important Scriptures on this subject are underlined.

----

1.   What is a Christian? To some this is a foolish question. After all, everybody knows the answer to this question, don't they? People give all kinds of answers to this question:

√   "A Christian follows Christ."
√   "A Christian says he or she is saved."
√   "A Christian has given his or her heart to the Lord."
√   "A Christian reads the Bible."
√   "A Christian prays."
√   "A Christian has love."
√   "A Christian helps other people."
√   "A Christian joins a church."
√   "A Christian donates money or even tithes to his or her church."
√   "A Christian wears a cross."
√   "A Christian has a fish symbol on his or her automobile."
√   "A Christian has a religious statue on his or her automobile dashboard."
√   "A Christian wears WWJD (What would Jesus do?) jewelry."
(Is WWJD a 50,000-watt, clear channel AM radio station in Cleveland, Ohio?)
None of the above statements defines a Christian!

2.   It is necessary to distinguish between a *behavior* and a *definition*. Gold is a good example to use to explain this difference. With the example of gold it is necessary to distinguish between a *property* and a *definition*.
People could use these statements to "define" gold: Gold is a precious metal. Gold is yellow in color. Gold is malleable. Gold is often used to establish the value of money. Gold is a good electrical conductor. Gold is a popular metal for jewelry, dental work, and electronics. Gold holds its value, over time, better than any other commodity. Gold has a melting point of 1,063 °C. Gold has a boiling point of 2,966 °C. Gold has an atomic weight of 196.967. All of the above statements about gold are true. However, none of these statements *defines* gold. Instead, the above statements describe the *properties* of gold.
Gold has one *definition*: Gold is a chemical element with an atomic number of 79.

3.   What is a Christian? The first paragraph (1. above) describes some of the *behaviors* of a Christian. It did not contain the *definition* of a Christian.
The Bible uses the word "Christian" only three times (*King James Version* and most other translations). Two of those times the word is used by non-Christians (Acts 11:26 and Acts 26:28). One time the word is used by a Christian: Peter in I Peter 4:16.
Paul gives the *definition* of a Christian:
> "...And if anyone does not have the Spirit of Christ, he does not belong to Christ." (**Romans 8:9** *NIV*)

<u>The Bible *definition* of a Christian: A Christian has the Holy Spirit.</u>
A Christian has the Holy Spirit and therefore is a New Covenant participant. In fact, "Christian" and "New Covenant participant" are totally synonymous. (For more information, see chapter 5, "The New Covenant," and chapter 17, "The Holy Spirit.")

4.   <u>Many people believe</u>: (a) <u>Some people are naturally good.</u> (b) <u>These good people perform good works.</u> (c) <u>Therefore the good works prove that these good people are Christians.</u>
<u>But what does the Bible say</u>? First, <u>there are *no* naturally good people</u>:
> "And, behold, one came and said unto him, Good Master, what good thing shall I do, that I may have eternal life?
> And he said unto him, Why callest thou me good? there is none good but one, that is, God..." (Matthew 19:16-17 *KJV*)

Jesus was a human being (see chapter 16, "Jesus Christ"). This is why he said that only God, his Father, was good. Paul corroborated Jesus' comments by showing that no human being is naturally good:
> "As it is written, There is none righteous, no, not one:
> There is none that understandeth, there is none that seeketh after God.
> They are all gone out of the way, they are together become unprofitable;
> there is none that doeth good, no, not one." (**Romans 3:10-12** *KJV*)

Consider Mahatma Gandhi (1869-1948 AD). Gandhi was considered good by many. He had good works. Gandhi used nonviolent disobedience as a tool for India to gain political independence from Great Britain. (Great Britain was guilt-ridden and wanted to rid herself of her colony. In probably no other known case in world history has independence (revolution) been achieved by nonviolent means.) Yet Gandhi utterly rejected Christianity (and Jesus Christ).
Second, it is true that a Christian does have good works. Good works are a *behavior* of a Christian. <u>Good works do not *define* a Christian</u>.

5.   <u>It is a common belief that if one believes in Jesus Christ, then one is a Christian</u>. Consider this Scripture:
> "Thou believest that there is one God; thou doest well: the devils also believe, and tremble." (James 2:19 *KJV*)

Demons believe in God. They also know that Jesus Christ is the Messiah. However, demons are not Christians. Believing in Jesus Christ is a necessary *behavior* of a Christian (see chapter 5, "The New Covenant"). <u>Believing in Jesus</u>

does not *define* a Christian.

6.   Because a Christian has the Holy Spirit, his or her life will reveal this.
Paul explains how the possession of the Holy Spirit changes the behaviors of a
person in Galatians 5:16-26. Paul describes the life of one who has the Holy Spirit:
>   "But the fruit of the Spirit is love, joy, peace, patience, kindness,
>   goodness, faithfulness, gentleness and self-control..."
>   (**Galatians 5:22-23** *NIV*)

Christians are people who exhibit these behaviors. If a person has these
behaviors, then he or she is a Christian. Paul also describes the behaviors of
people who are *not* Christians:
>   "The acts of the sinful nature are obvious: sexual immorality,
>   impurity and debauchery; idolatry and witchcraft; hatred, discord,
>   jealousy, fits of rage, selfish ambition, dissensions, factions and envy;
>   drunkenness, orgies, and the like..." (Galatians 5:19-21 *NIV*)

If a person exhibits these behaviors, then he or she is *not* a Christian.

7.   Some people are bothered by the idea that there are true Christians and
false Christians. (Actually the question is one of determining who is or is not a
Christian. The term "false Christian" is an oxymoron. The term "true Christian"
is redundant.) Some are worried, "Should one be concerned about whether a
person is or is not a Christian?" Jesus gave many warnings concerning those
who believed they were Christians but were not:
>   "Enter through the narrow gate. For wide is the gate and broad is the road
>   that leads to destruction, and many enter through it. But small is the gate
>   and narrow the road that leads to life, and only a few find it."
>   (Matthew 7:13-14 *NIV*)

Jesus said that it was the *few*, not the many, who find salvation. Jesus, in his
Parable of the Ten Virgins in Matthew 25, indicates that only 50% of Christians
will be ready for his return:
>   "Later the others also came. 'Sir! Sir!' they said. 'Open the door for
>   us!'
>   But he replied, 'I tell you the truth, I don't know you.'"
>   (Matthew 25:11-12 *NIV*)

Five of ten virgins (the ten virgins represented the church) were not successful as
Christians. Jesus, in his Parable of the Talents in Matthew 25, indicates that only
67% of Christians will be successful:
>   "His master replied, 'You wicked, lazy servant!'"...
>   "'And throw that worthless servant outside, into the darkness, where there
>   will be weeping and gnashing of teeth.'"
>   (Matthew 25:26, 30 *NIV*)

One of three servants (analogous to Christians) did not make it. Jesus, in his
Parable of the Sheep & Goats in Matthew 25, indicates that a substantial portion of
all humanity will fail at salvation:
>   "When the Son of Man comes in his glory, and all the angels with
>   him, he will sit on his throne in heavenly glory. All the nations will be
>   gathered before him, and he will separate the people one from another as a

shepherd separates the sheep from the goats. He will put the sheep on his right and the goats on his left." (<u>Matthew 25:31-33</u> *NIV*)

The sheep are given eternal life. The goats are cast into the Lake of Fire, where they suffer the Second Death.

Jesus talked a lot about who was a Christian and who was not. <u>Since Jesus was concerned about this question, anyone who wants to follow Jesus should also be concerned about this question.</u>

<u>Summary</u>. 1. What is a Christian? None of the above statements define a Christian! 2. It is necessary to distinguish between a *behavior* and a *definition*. 3. The Bible *definition* of a Christian: A Christian has the Holy Spirit. 4. Many people believe: (a) Some people are naturally good. (b) These good people perform good works. (c) Therefore the good works prove that these good people are Christians. But what does the Bible say? There are *no* naturally good people. Good works do not *define* a Christian. 5. It is a common belief that if one believes in Jesus Christ, then one is a Christian. Believing in Jesus does not *define* a Christian. 6. Because a Christian has the Holy Spirit, his or her life will reveal this. 7. Some people are bothered by the idea that there are true Christians and false Christians. Jesus gave many warnings concerning those who believed they were Christians but were not. Since Jesus was concerned about this question, anyone who wants to follow Jesus should also be concerned about this question.

The Old Covenant

CHAPTER 4

© 2005, Robert M. Kelley

Look up all Scriptures in your own Bible. Read and/or write the Scriptures on paper. Writing Scriptures on paper slows down your mind and causes the Bible verses to be more deeply burned into your mind.

All Scripture is inspired and true. However, you cannot learn everything at once. Therefore, the most important Scripture on this subject is in **bold** type and the next most important Scripture on this subject is underlined.

----

1.   Some people are biased against the Old Testament. They wonder, "Why is the Old Testament so big?" Of the 66 books in the Bible, the Old Testament consists of 39 books and the New Testament consists of 27 books. The Old Testament, then, comprises about two-thirds of the Bible. People wonder why. (Even worse, some have estimated that as much of one-fifth of the New Testament consists of direct quotations from the Old Testament.)
The New Testament is concerned with the New Covenant and the Old Testament is concerned with the Old Covenant. (In fact, the *NRSV* New Testament has this title: "The New Covenant commonly called the New Testament.")
If the Old Covenant cannot "work" as a method of salvation (it can neither forgive sins nor grant eternal life, as will be seen later), then why did God ever create it? Why did God wait about 4,000 years -- from about 4000 BC to about the year zero -- to introduce the New Covenant? Why didn't God introduce the New Covenant first? (These vital questions will be answered in this chapter 4 and in chapter 5, "The New Covenant.")
The New Covenant cannot be understood without knowledge of the Old Covenant. In fact, many people do not understand the New Covenant *because* they do not understand the Old Covenant. The Old Testament & New Testament are inextricably linked; the Old Covenant & New Covenant are inextricably linked.

2.   A covenant is an agreement or contract between two parties. The Old Covenant was an agreement between the twelve-tribe nation of Israel and God. Essentially *no* others could participate in the Old Covenant. If one was not a citizen of Israel, then one could not participate in the Old Covenant.

3.   The Old Covenant consisted of a written agreement. The Old Covenant agreement consisted of two parts: (a) the Ten Commandments, stated in Exodus 20:10-17 (repeated in Deuteronomy 5:6-21), and (b) the judgments and statutes of Exodus, chapters 21-23. The Ten Commandments told people what not to do. The judgments and statutes told the people what was to occur if anyone disobeyed the Ten Commandments. Moses wrote the Old Covenant down in a book, called the "Book of the Covenant":

"Moses then wrote down everything the LORD had said..." (Exodus 24:4 *NIV*)

4.   A formal ceremony occurred in which the Israelites agreed to the Old Covenant. This ceremony is described in Exodus, chapter 24. Blood was used as a symbol to confirm the Old Covenant. Moses describes the confirmation:
"Then he took the Book of the Covenant and read it to the people. They responded, 'We will do everything the LORD has said; we will obey.'
Moses then took the blood, sprinkled it on the people and said, 'This is the blood of the covenant that the LORD has made with you in accordance with all these words.'" (**Exodus 24:7-8** *NIV*)

5.   The essence of the Old Covenant was physical blessings and curses. If the Israelites obeyed the physical laws of God, then God would give them physical blessings. If Israel failed to obey the physical laws of God, then God would give them physical curses. The blessings and curses of the Old Covenant are carefully spelled out in the chapters of Leviticus 26 and Deuteronomy 28.

6.   There is nothing spiritual about the Old Covenant. There was no forgiveness of sin in the Old Covenant. There was no promise of eternal life in the Old Covenant. The Old Covenant dealt with this physical life only.

7.   Faith was not a requirement of the Old Covenant. One does not need faith to avoid murdering his or her neighbor (the sixth commandment). A few Old Testament examples of individual faith are given in Hebrews 11. However, overall, Paul, in the New Testament, continually used the Israelites in the Old Testament under the Old Covenant as examples of *faithlessness*. The children of Israel did not exercise faith when they followed Moses out of Egypt: They were frightened by the power demonstrated by God through Moses. They saw Pharaoh's army following them and they saw the Red Sea parted; they took a physical way of escape by walking between the sea walls. They were carnal, not faith-filled.

8.   The Old Covenant welded together government and religion. Moses headed the government portion. Aaron, via the Aaronic priesthood, headed the religion portion. The Old Covenant represented a theocracy in which God ruled the nation of Israel.

9.   Most of the Old Testament is based on the Old Covenant. When Solomon dedicated the Temple (in II Chronicles 6) he essentially repeated the Old Covenant terms: The nation would be physically blessed for obedience, and physically cursed for disobedience.
The Old Testament books of Psalms and Proverbs are, for example, loaded with Old Covenant thinking. If one obeys God, then God will send rain to make one's crops abundant, one's animal (sheep and goats) offspring will multiply, one will have a full barn, one will have abundant, healthy children, etc. However, if one disobeys God then terrible physical curses (the opposite of physical blessings) will

overcome one.

10.   <u>Many people confuse the Old Covenant with the New Covenant</u>. <u>An example of this confusion is the "Prosperity Gospel."</u> The Prosperity Gospel is the belief that if you have a proper relationship with God, then prosperity will immediately come to you. In your job you will be promoted to a higher level, higher paying position. You will move into a larger, more expensive house. You will purchase a newer, larger, and more expensive automobile. You will own better clothing and expensive jewelry. You will purchase a boat, airplane, or second home in the country or on the seashore. You will own stocks, bonds, precious metals, and other investments.
The Prosperity Gospel is based solely on Old Covenant promises (from the Old Testament). The Prosperity Gospel is nothing more than a repackaging of the Old Covenant.

<u>Summary</u>. 1. Some people are biased against the Old Testament. The New Testament is concerned with the New Covenant and the Old Testament is concerned with the Old Covenant. The New Covenant cannot be understood without knowledge of the Old Covenant. 2. The Old Covenant was an agreement between the twelve-tribe nation of Israel and God. 3. The Old Covenant consisted of a written agreement. 4. A formal ceremony occurred in which the Israelites agreed to the Old Covenant. 5. The essence of the Old Covenant was physical blessings and curses. 6. There is nothing spiritual about the Old Covenant. 7. Faith was not a requirement of the Old Covenant. 8. The Old Covenant welded together government and religion. 9. Most of the Old Testament is based on the Old Covenant. 10. Many people confuse the Old Covenant with the New Covenant. An example of this confusion is the "Prosperity Gospel."

The New Covenant

CHAPTER 5

© 2005, Robert M. Kelley

Look up all Scriptures in your own Bible. Read and/or write the Scriptures on paper. Writing Scriptures on paper slows down your mind and causes the Bible verses to be more deeply burned into your mind.

All Scripture is inspired and true. However, you cannot learn everything at once. Therefore, the three most important Scriptures on this subject are in **bold** type and the next seven most important Scriptures on this subject are underlined.

1.　　A covenant is an agreement or contract between two parties. The New Covenant is an agreement between an individual human being and God. The New Covenant has been offered, or is now being offered, or will be offered to every human being. *Every* human who has ever lived (in the past), or is living (now), or will live (in the future) will be offered the New Covenant. *No* human being will be excluded from the offer of the New Covenant.

2.　　In the Old Testament God prophesied the coming of the New Covenant:
"'The time is coming,' declares the LORD,
　'when I will make a new covenant
with the house of Israel
　and with the house of Judah.
It will not be like the covenant
　I made with their forefathers
when I took them by the hand
　to lead them out of Egypt,
because they broke my covenant,
　though I was a husband to them,'
　　declares the LORD.
'This is the covenant I will make with the house of Israel
　after that time,' declares the LORD.
'I will put my law in their minds
　and write it on their hearts.
I will be their God,
　and they will be my people.'" (**Jeremiah 31:31-33** *NIV*)
Here God discusses both the Old Covenant & New Covenant. In the New Covenant God puts His law in human beings' minds and hearts via the Holy Spirit. In the New Covenant the Holy Spirit guides the thinking of human beings.

3.　　A New Covenant participant is literally motivated and empowered by the mind of God:
"for it is God who works in you to will and to act according to his good

purpose." (Philippians 2:13 *NIV*)

The Holy Spirit gives the New Covenant participant both the will ("to will") and the power ("to act") to perform God's desires.

If one is a New Covenant participant and performs the works of God, then all honor and glory for these works go to God, since He has both motivated them and given the power to perform them.

4.   <u>Jesus said that the relationship between himself and a human being formed via his blood is the New Covenant</u>:

> "In the same way, after supper he took the cup, saying, 'This cup is the new covenant in my blood; do this, whenever you drink it, in remembrance of me.'" (**I Corinthians 11:25** *NIV*)

<u>Because a New Covenant participant has the Holy Spirit, he or she is a Christian</u>:

> "...And if anyone does not have the Spirit of Christ, he does not belong to Christ." (**Romans 8:9** *NIV*)

In fact, "New Covenant participant" and "Christian" are totally synonymous. (For more information, see chapter 3, "What is a Christian?" and chapter 17, "The Holy Spirit.")

5.   <u>Beginning the New Covenant involves two calls</u>: <u>First, God must call a person to Christ</u>:

> "No one can come to me unless the Father who sent me draws him..." (<u>John 6:44</u> *NIV*)

One can preach to a person throughout his or her entire life. However, if God is not calling that person to Christ in this life and at this time, than that person will not and *cannot* respond. God calls each and every person to the New Covenant at the time and place of His choosing (see 6. below).

<u>Second, the called person must respond by calling on God</u>:

> "And everyone who calls on the name of the Lord will be saved." (<u>Acts 2:21</u> *NIV* as quoted from Joel 2:32)

The New Covenant cannot begin in a person's life until: (a) God draws a person to Christ, and (b) that person calls on the name of Jesus. This second call is the person's acceptance of Jesus' blood sacrifice for sin and the beginning of the New Covenant for that person.

6.   *When* <u>does God call each person to the New Covenant</u>? In God's Master Plan Period One God is *not* calling *all* persons to Jesus. Consider this fact: Between about 4000 BC to about 33 AD -- about 4,033 years -- *no one* was called to Christ.

(To learn more about *when* God will call certain groups of people, see the chapters dealing with God's Master Plan:

9	"God's Master Plan: Overview"
10	"God's Master Plan: Period One"
11	"God's Master Plan: Period Two"
12	"God's Master Plan: Period Three")

Jesus talked about categories of people on Earth in reference to the New Covenant:

> "And I will ask the Father, and he will give you another Counselor to be

with you forever -- the Spirit of truth. The world cannot accept him, because it neither sees him nor knows him. But you know him, for he lives with you and will be in you." (<u>John 14:16-17</u> *NIV*)

<u>Jesus defines three categories of people on Earth during Period One of God's Master Plan: (a) the world, which neither sees nor hears the Holy Spirit, (b) those who God is calling (the Holy Spirit is *with* them), and (c) Christians (the Holy Spirit is *in* them).</u>

7. <u>In entering into the New Covenant one begins a direct relationship with God & Jesus Christ</u>:

> "Jesus replied, 'If anyone loves me, he will obey my teaching. My Father will love him, and we will come to him and make our home with him." (John 14:23 *NIV*)

<u>No human institution, priesthood, or ministry can interfere with this relationship.</u>

8. <u>The New Covenant requires faith</u>. New Covenant participants must believe: (a) in Jesus Christ, (b) in Christ's sacrifice, and (c) that God will perform His part of the New Covenant. "Believing in Christ" refers to the faith one must have to participate in the New Covenant.

> "Jesus answered, 'The work of God is this: to believe in the one he has sent.'" (John 6:29 *NIV*)

> "For my Father's will is that everyone who looks to the Son and believes in him shall have eternal life, and I will raise him up at the last day.'" (John 6:40 *NIV*)

The New Testament book of Romans (chapters 1-8) is the only place in the Bible where the New Covenant is laid out in a methodical way. <u>The entire chapter of Romans 4 describes the faith required for the New Covenant.</u>

9. When the New Covenant relationship begins, <u>Christ's blood forgives one's sins. One is forgiven and made totally clean. One is justified and made righteous before God</u>:

> "But now a righteousness from God, apart from law, has been made known, to which the Law and the Prophets testify. This righteousness from God comes through faith in Jesus Christ to all who believe. There is no difference, for all have sinned and fall short of the glory of God, and are justified freely by his grace through the redemption that came by Christ Jesus." (<u>Romans 3:21-24</u> *NIV*)

> "God made him who had no sin to be sin [margin: Or *be a sin offering*] for us, so that in him we might become the righteousness of God." (II Corinthians 5:21 *NIV*)

By oneself one can do *nothing* to be right with God. God has given all human beings the free gift of Christ's sacrifice, so one can be forgiven, made clean, and made righteous before God. By contrast, the Old Covenant *never* offered forgiveness of sins.

10.   <u>One of the rewards of successful participation in the New Covenant is eternal life</u>. A number of Scriptures in the New Testament show this. Here are three:

> "For God so loved the world that he gave his one and only Son [margin: Or *his only begotten Son*], that whoever believes in him shall not perish but have eternal life." (<u>John 3:16</u> *NIV*)
> "Whoever believes in the Son has eternal life, but whoever rejects the Son will not see life, for God's wrath remains on him." (John 3:36 *NIV*)
> "but whoever drinks the water I give him will never thirst. Indeed, the water I give him will become in him a spring of water welling up to eternal life." (John 4:14 *NIV*)

By contrast, the Old Covenant *never* offered eternal life.

11.   <u>A New Covenant participant becomes a new creation</u>. The receiving of the Holy Spirit gives a person an entirely new outlook and approach to life. Throughout the New Testament, life under the New Covenant is described as *new*:

> "Therefore, if anyone is in Christ, he is a new creation; the old has gone, the new has come!" (II Corinthians 5:17 *NIV*)

12.   <u>Entering into the New Covenant is often referred to as being "born again"</u> (or "born from above" or "born anew" in some translations):

> "In reply Jesus declared, 'I tell you the truth, no one can see the kingdom of God unless he is born again [margin: Or *born from above*].'" (John 3:3 *NIV*)

13.   <u>In contrast to the Old Covenant, the New Covenant is not written</u>.

> "But now, by dying to what once bound us, we have been released from the law so that we serve in the new way of the Spirit, and not in the old way of the written code." (<u>Romans 7:6</u> *NIV*)

The Old Covenant was written. Although the Old Covenant was given by God, men felt compelled to add many additional "rules" so that one would know "how" to keep the Old Covenant. The result was a mess which no one could keep. As Peter said:

> "Now then, why do you try to test God by putting on the necks of the disciples a yoke that neither we nor our fathers have been able to bear?" (Acts 15:10 *NIV*)

The New Covenant is not written. In the place of a written New Covenant, a Christian has the Holy Spirit in his or her mind. The Holy Spirit gives one the very mind of God. One's thoughts and actions become like God's thoughts and actions.

14.   All New Covenant participants will occasionally sin; these sins can be forgiven:

> "...the blood of Jesus Christ his Son cleanseth us from all sin.
> If we say that we have no sin, we deceive ourselves, and the truth is not in us.

If we confess our sins, he is faithful and just to forgive us our sins, and to cleanse us from all unrighteousness." (I John 1:7-9 *KJV*)

In addition, in the Lord's Prayer, which is an outline for prayer, Jesus told human beings to ask for forgiveness of sin:

"And forgive us our debts, as we forgive our debtors." (Matthew 6:12 *KJV*)

However, <u>if one is a New Covenant participant, one is not going to exhibit a pattern of prevalent sin</u>:

"No one who is born of God will continue to sin, because God's seed remains in him; he cannot go on sinning, because he has been born of God." (I John 3:9 *NIV*)

"We know that no child of God commits sin; he is kept safe by the Son of God, and the evil one cannot touch him." (I John 5:18 *REB*)

All persons are continually influenced by the world and Satan. However, those who are not seeking God have no defense for sin influences, and therefore sin frequently. New Covenant participants, however, will sin occasionally, but *not* exhibit a pervasive sin pattern.

In Romans 7 Paul talks about struggling to obey God. Many people have misunderstood what Paul says here. The struggle to obey God -- keeping the law vs. doing what is carnal -- is a struggle which occurs in Old Covenant participants. This is *not* a struggle which occurs in New Covenant participants.

15.   <u>At the time of John the Baptist the message from God changed from the Old Covenant to the New Covenant</u>. Note carefully this Scripture:

"From the days of John the Baptist until now, the kingdom of heaven has been forcefully advancing, and forceful men lay hold of it. For all the Prophets and the Law prophesied until John." (Matthew 11:12-13 *NIV*)

Here Jesus is explaining God changing His message from the Old Covenant to the New Covenant. The point in time for this transition was the beginning of John the Baptist's ministry. In the Bible the term "Law" (capitalized) refers to the first five books of the Old Testament (the Pentateuch). The term "Prophets" (capitalized) refers to the Old Testament prophetic books: the major prophets (Isaiah, Jeremiah, Ezekiel) and the twelve minor prophets (Hosea through Malachi). The Law and Prophets (portions of the Old Testament) spoke only of the Old Covenant. The "kingdom of heaven" is synonymous with "kingdom of God"; it refers to the New Covenant. Only successful New Covenant participants will be in the Kingdom of God.

One of the reasons why the Israelites could not understand Jesus' (New Covenant) message was that the New Covenant was totally new to them.

16.   <u>When the New Covenant arrived, it necessitated the end of the Old Covenant</u>:

"Christ is the end of the law..." (Romans 10:4 *NIV*)

In the New Testament the word "law" (lower-case L) usually means the Old Covenant. (In the New Testament the word "Law" (upper-case L) usually means the Pentateuch.) When New Testament writers posed the question, "Are you living under law or grace?" they might as well have said, "Are you living under the Old Covenant or New Covenant?"

"Now that faith has come, we are no longer under the supervision of the law." (Galatians 3:25 *NIV*)

"By calling this covenant 'new,' he has made the first one obsolete; and what is obsolete and aging will soon disappear." (Hebrews 8:13 *NIV*)

Some people today are still trying to live under the Old Covenant. Good luck! The Old Covenant is *all over*.

17. The New Covenant was created *before* the Old Covenant. Some people believe that God first created the Old Covenant; when the Old Covenant "failed" He created the New Covenant. No statement could be further from the truth. God always offers the best first. God announced the New Covenant 430 years before the Old Covenant was created! Paul explains:

"What I mean is this: The law, introduced 430 years later, does not set aside the covenant previously established by God and thus do away with the promise." (Galatians 3:17 *NIV*)

Read carefully Galatians 3. The "covenant previously established by God" (verse 17) was the New Covenant. Paul explained (a little earlier, in Galatians 3:8) that God announced the New Covenant to Abram in Genesis 12:3 -- the very first time God spoke to Abram.

18. Romans (chapters 1-8) is the only Bible book which methodically explains the New Covenant:

Chapter(s)	Theme
1	All mankind has chosen sin.
2	Israelites (then mostly Jews) are not saved by the Old Covenant (the law).
3	All have sinned. Only the blood of Jesus can save.
4	The New Covenant requires faith.
5-6	History and nature of the Old Covenant & New Covenant.
7	The mental struggle which occurs in those who live under the Old Covenant.
8	New Covenant participants (Christians) live by the Holy Spirit.

Summary. 1. The New Covenant is an agreement between an individual human being and God. 2. In the Old Testament God prophesied the coming of the New Covenant. In the New Covenant God puts His law in human beings' minds and hearts via the Holy Spirit. In the New Covenant the Holy Spirit guides the thinking of human beings. 3. A New Covenant participant is literally motivated and empowered by the mind of God. 4. Jesus said that the relationship between himself and a human being formed via his blood is the New Covenant. Because a New Covenant participant has the Holy Spirit, he or she is a Christian. 5. Beginning the New Covenant involves two calls. First, God must call a person to Christ. Second, the called person must respond by calling on God. 6. *When* does God call each person to the New Covenant? Jesus defines three categories of people on Earth during Period One of God's Master Plan: (a) the world, which neither sees nor hears the Holy Spirit, (b) those whom God is calling (the Holy Spirit is *with* them), and (c) Christians (the Holy Spirit is *in* them). 7. In entering into the New Covenant one begins a direct relationship with God & Jesus Christ. No human institution, priesthood, or ministry can interfere with this relationship. 8. The New Covenant requires faith. The entire chapter of Romans 4 describes the faith required for the New Covenant. 9. Christ's blood forgives one's sins. One is forgiven and made totally clean. One is justified and made righteous before God. 10. One of the rewards for successful participation in the New Covenant is eternal life. 11. A New Covenant participant becomes a new creation. 12. Entering into the New Covenant is often referred to as being "born again." 13. In contrast to the Old Covenant, the New Covenant is not written. 14. If one is a New Covenant participant, one is not going to exhibit a pattern of prevalent sin. 15. At the time of John the Baptist the message from God changed from the Old Covenant to the New Covenant. 16. When the New Covenant arrived, it necessitated the end of the Old Covenant. 17. The New Covenant was created *before* the Old Covenant. 18. Romans (chapters 1-8) is the only Bible book which methodically explains the New Covenant.

The Kingdom of God: Jesus

CHAPTER 6

© 2005, Robert M. Kelley

Look up all Scriptures in your own Bible. Read and/or write the Scriptures on paper. Writing Scriptures on paper slows down your mind and causes the Bible verses to be more deeply burned into your mind.

All Scripture is inspired and true. However, you cannot learn everything at once. Therefore, the three most important Scriptures on this subject are in **bold** type and the next seven most important Scriptures on this subject are underlined.

There are three Kingdom of God chapters:

6   "The Kingdom of God: Jesus"
7   "The Kingdom of God: Pre-Jesus"
8   "The Kingdom of God: Post-Jesus"

----

1.   Many people are confused about the message of Jesus Christ. Jesus was born, of Mary, to become the Messiah. The ministry of Jesus lasted about three and one-half years. Jesus taught and preached during this period. However, what was Jesus' message? Was Jesus' message that people should "do good": perform good works? Was Jesus' message secular humanism? A careful review of what the Bible says shows that Jesus' message was about the Kingdom of God. This chapter 6 is large because it comprehensively verifies that Jesus' message was about the Kingdom of God.

2.   This chapter 6 reviews what Jesus Christ, when he walked on Earth and qualified to become the Messiah, said about the Kingdom of God. The life of Jesus is reviewed in chronological order. The only way to do this is to use a Gospel harmony. *A Harmony of the Gospels* by A.T. Robertson (Harper & Row, New York, © 1922, 1950, ISBN 0-06-066890-3) was used. The first recorded event in Jesus' ministry was being baptized by John the Baptist in the Jordan River. The second recorded event was the temptation by Satan in the wilderness. The third recorded event was performing his first miracle: creating 120-160 gallons of wine from water.

3.   Jesus' first recorded message was the interview with Nicodemus in Jerusalem during the Passover. Note some of the things Jesus said:

"Jesus answered him, 'Very truly, I tell you, no one can see the kingdom of God without being born from above [margin: Or *born anew*].'"
(John 3:3 *NRSV*)

"Jesus answered, 'Very truly, I tell you, no one can enter the kingdom of

God without being born of water and Spirit.'" (John 3:5 *NRSV*)
Jesus characterized a Christian (one "born from above") as one who sees the Kingdom of God. <u>Jesus described the end result of the successful Christian as entering the Kingdom of God</u>. The purpose of being born from above (or born again or born anew) is to enter the Kingdom of God!

4.   Continuing chronologically in Christ's life, the Biblical record shows Christ's message being described as the Kingdom of God. Christ's preaching in Galilee is described:

> "Now after John was arrested, Jesus came to Galilee, proclaiming the good news [margin: Or *gospel*] of God, and saying, 'The time is fulfilled, and the kingdom of God has come near [margin: Or *is at hand*]; repent, and believe in the good news [margin: Or *gospel*].'"
> (<u>Mark 1:14-15</u> *NRSV*)
> "From that time Jesus began to proclaim, 'Repent, for the kingdom of heaven has come near [margin: Or *is at hand*].'" (Matthew 4:17 *NRSV*)

Christ described his Gospel as "good news." <u>Christ's Gospel -- the good news -- is about the Kingdom of God</u>.

5.   <u>Christ defined his message as the Kingdom of God</u> as he continued his mission (in this case on the first tour of Galilee):

> "But he said to them, 'I must proclaim the good news of the kingdom of God to the other cities also; for I was sent for this purpose.'"
> (Luke 4:43 *NRSV*)
> "Jesus went throughout Galilee, teaching in their synagogues and proclaiming the good news [margin: Gk *gospel*] of the kingdom and curing every disease and every sickness among the people."
> (Matthew 4:23 *NRSV*)

6.   <u>In the "Sermon on the Mount," Christ again spoke of the Kingdom of God</u>:

> "...Blessed are you who are poor,
>   for yours is the kingdom of God." (Luke 6:20 *NRSV*)
> "Blessed are the poor in spirit, for theirs is the kingdom of heaven."
> (Matthew 5:3 *NRSV*)

Jesus said that the poor or poor in spirit would receive the Kingdom of God. (Matthew uses the phrase "kingdom of heaven" while the other Gospel writers in recording the same speech use the phrase "kingdom of God." It is commonly believed that Matthew was directing his gospel to Israelites. Israelites believed that it was sacrilegious to pronounce the name of God.)
Christ continued:

> "Blessed are those who are persecuted for righteousness' sake, for theirs is the kingdom of heaven." (<u>Matthew 5:10</u> *NRSV*)

Continuing in the Sermon on the Mount, Jesus said:

> "Therefore, whoever breaks [margin: Or *annuls*] one of the least of these commandments, and teaches others to do the same, will be called least in the kingdom of heaven. For I tell you, unless your righteousness exceeds that of the scribes and Pharisees, you will never enter the kingdom of

heaven." (Matthew 5:19-20 *NRSV*)

In the so-called "Lord's Prayer" (which is actually an outline for prayer), Christ said that after acknowledging the great Name of the Father, the *first* thing humans should ask God for was:

"Your kingdom come..." (**Matthew 6:10** *NRSV*)

After telling people not to worry about physical needs, Christ said:

"But strive first for the kingdom of God and his [margin: Or *its*] righteousness, and all these things will be given to you as well." (Matthew 6:33 *NRSV*)

The Kingdom of God was the central theme of Christ's message.

7.	In healing a Centurion's servant at Capernaum, Jesus said:

"I tell you, many will come from east and west and will eat with Abraham and Isaac and Jacob in the kingdom of heaven, while the heirs of the kingdom will be thrown into the outer darkness, where there will be weeping and gnashing of teeth." (Matthew 8:11-12 *NRSV*)

Successful Christians will enter the Kingdom of God.

8.	After John the Baptist was thrown into prison by the wicked Roman King Herod, Jesus said this (among other things) about John:

"Truly I tell you, among those born of women no one has arisen greater than John the Baptist; yet the least in the kingdom of heaven is greater than he. From the days of John the Baptist until now the kingdom of heaven has suffered violence [margin: Or *has been coming violently*], and the violent take it by force. For all the prophets and the law prophesied until John came;" (Matthew 11:11-13 *NRSV*)

Two things are stated here. First, those who enter the Kingdom of God will be greater than any physical human being. (See chapter 5, "The New Covenant.") Second, until God sent John the Baptist on his mission, the main message from God was the Old Covenant as contained in the Law and Prophets sections of the Old Testament. Upon the arrival of John the Baptist the main message from God was changed from the Old Covenant to the Kingdom of God (New Covenant).

9.	On Jesus' second tour of Galilee, he preached the Kingdom of God:

"Soon afterwards he went on through cities and villages, proclaiming and bringing the good news of the kingdom of God..." (Luke 8:1 *NRSV*)

10.	The Pharisees accused Jesus of performing miracles by the power of Satan. Here is part of Jesus' reply:

"But if it is by the Spirit of God that I cast out demons, then the kingdom of God has come to you." (Matthew 12:28 *NRSV*)

The Kingdom of God is powered and sustained by the Spirit of God.

11.	Christ often delivered his message in parables. Jesus used parables to tell people about the Kingdom of God:

"And he said to them, 'To you has been given the secret [margin: Or

mystery] of the kingdom of God, but for those outside, everything comes in parables; in order that
> "they may indeed look, but not perceive,
> and may indeed listen, but not understand;
> so that they may not turn again and be forgiven.""

(Mark 4:11-12 *NRSV*)

Jesus explained the Parable of the Sower:
> "Hear then the parable of the sower. When anyone hears the word of the kingdom and does not understand it, the evil one comes and snatches away what is sown in the heart..." (Matthew 13:18-19 *NRSV*)

Jesus describes the message of the parables as that of the Kingdom of God. Jesus continued and added the Parable of the Mustard Seed:
> "...The kingdom of heaven may be compared to someone who sowed good seed in his field;" (Matthew 13:24 *NRSV*)

> "He also said, 'With what can we compare the kingdom of God, or what parable will we use for it? It is like a mustard seed...'"

(Mark 4:30-31 *NRSV*)

Jesus continued with the Parable of the Yeast:
> "He told them another parable: 'The kingdom of heaven is like yeast that a woman took and mixed in with [margin: Gk *hid in*] three measures of flour until all of it was leavened.'" (Matthew 13:33 *NRSV*)

Jesus explained the Parable of the Tares:
> "The Son of Man will send his angels, and they will collect out of his kingdom all causes of sin and all evildoers," (Matthew 13:41 *NRSV*)
> "Then the righteous will shine like the sun in the kingdom of their Father..." (Matthew 13:43 *NRSV*)

Jesus continued with the parables of Hidden Treasure, Pearl of Great Price, and Fish & Nets:
> "The kingdom of heaven is like treasure hidden in a field..."

(Matthew 13:44 *NRSV*)

> "Again, the kingdom of heaven is like a merchant in search of fine pearls;" (Matthew 13:45 *NRSV*)

> "Again, the kingdom of heaven is like a net that was thrown into the sea and caught fish of every kind;" (Matthew 13:47 *NRSV*)

12. <u>Jesus continued preaching the Kingdom of God during his third tour of Galilee</u>:
> "Then Jesus went about all the cities and villages, teaching in their synagogues, and proclaiming the good news of the kingdom, and curing every disease and every sickness." (Matthew 9:35 *NRSV*)

Jesus sent forth his twelve disciples on a training tour. He instructed them:
> "and he sent them out to proclaim the kingdom of God and to heal."
> (Luke 9:2 *NRSV*)

13. The twelve disciples returned, wanted to be debriefed by Jesus, but were interrupted by an unexpected crowd:
> "...he welcomed them, and spoke to them about the kingdom of God, and

healed those who needed to be cured." (Luke 9:11 *NRSV*)

Jesus fed the five thousand in that crowd. However, Jesus talked about the Kingdom of God so much that:

"When Jesus realized that they were about to come and take him by force to make him king, he withdrew again to the mountain by himself." (John 6:15 *NRSV*)

<u>Some people believed that the Kingdom of God would rule Earth at that time.</u>

14.   Jesus spoke with his twelve disciples near Caesarea Philippi. <u>In talking to Peter, Jesus talked about the keys to the Kingdom of God:</u>

"I will give you the keys of the kingdom of heaven, and whatever you bind on earth will be bound in heaven, and whatever you loose on earth will be loosed in heaven." (Matthew 16:19 *NRSV*)

15.   <u>Three of the disciples saw a vision of the Kingdom of God:</u>

"Truly I tell you, there are some standing here who will not taste death before they see the Son of Man coming in his kingdom."
(Matthew 16:28 *NRSV*)

The very next chapter, Matthew 17, describes the "Transfiguration," when the three disciples *did* see Christ as he will be in his return to earth (the second coming).

16.   <u>The twelve disciples argued about who would be greatest in the Kingdom of God</u>:

"At that time the disciples came to Jesus and asked, 'Who is the greatest in the kingdom of heaven?'" (Matthew 18:1 *NRSV*)

"and said, 'Truly I tell you, unless you change and become like children, you will never enter the kingdom of heaven. Whoever becomes humble like this child is the greatest in the kingdom of heaven."
(Matthew 18:3-4 *NRSV*)

The only example of kingdom leadership the disciples had seen was that of the Roman Empire. The Roman Empire example -- typical of all of man's governments -- was characterized by self-love, vanity, and arrogance. Jesus taught his disciples that Kingdom of God leadership is characterized by child-like humility.

17.   <u>Jesus urged his disciples to live to enter the Kingdom of God:</u>

"And if your eye causes you to stumble, tear it out; it is better for you to enter the kingdom of God with one eye than to have two eyes and to be thrown into hell [margin: Gk *Gehenna*]," (Mark 9:47 *NRSV*)

18.   <u>Jesus reminded his disciples of the cost of discipleship for the Kingdom of God</u>:

"Jesus said to him, 'No one who puts a hand to the plow and looks back is fit for the kingdom of God.'" (Luke 9:62 *NRSV*)

19.   Jesus sent out 70 men (in addition to the 12 sent earlier) on a training

mission:

> "cure the sick who are there, and say to them, 'The kingdom of God has come near to you [margin: Or *is at hand for you*].'" (Luke 10:9 *NRSV*)
> "...Yet know this: the kingdom of God has come near [margin: Or *is at hand*].'" (Luke 10:11 *NRSV*)

The 70 were instructed to preach the Kingdom of God.

20.   Jesus was again accused of performing miracles by the power of Satan. Jesus responded that casting out demons demonstrated the power of the Kingdom of God:

> "But if it is by the finger of God that I cast out the demons, then the kingdom of God has come to you." (Luke 11:20 *NRSV*)

21.   In his later Judean ministry, Jesus talked about the Kingdom of God:

> "Instead, strive for his kingdom, and these things will be given to you as well.
>
> Do not be afraid, little flock, for it is your Father's good pleasure to give you the kingdom." (Luke 12:31-32 *NRSV*)

22.   Jesus again described the Kingdom of God with the Parables of Mustard Seed and Yeast:

> "He said therefore, 'What is the kingdom of God like? And to what should I compare it? It is like a mustard seed that someone took and sowed in the garden..." (Luke 13:18-19 *NRSV*)
> "And again he said, 'To what should I compare the kingdom of God? It is like yeast that a woman took and mixed in with [margin: Gk *hid in*] three measures of flour until all of it was leavened.'" (Luke 13:20-21 *NRSV*)

23.   In his later Perean ministry Jesus talked about people entering the Kingdom of God:

> "There will be weeping and gnashing of teeth when you see Abraham and Isaac and Jacob and all the prophets in the kingdom of God, and you yourselves thrown out. Then people will come from east and west, from north and south, and will eat in the kingdom of God." (Luke 13:28-29 *NRSV*)

24.   During dinner in the home of a Pharisee, a guest commented on the Kingdom of God:

> "One of the dinner guests, on hearing this, said to him, 'Blessed is anyone who will eat bread in the kingdom of God!'" (Luke 14:15 *NRSV*)

25.   Jesus again explained the transition of God's message from the Old Covenant to the Kingdom of God (New Covenant):

> "The law and the prophets were in effect until John came; since then the good news of the kingdom of God is proclaimed, and everyone tries to enter it by force [margin: Or *everyone is strongly urged to enter it*]."
> (**Luke 16:16** *NRSV*)

26.	<u>In Samaria or Galilee, the Pharisees asked Jesus about the Kingdom of God</u>:

> "Once Jesus was asked by the Pharisees when the kingdom of God was coming, and he answered, 'The kingdom of God is not coming with things that can be observed; nor will they say, "Look, here it is!" or "There it is!" For, in fact, the kingdom of God is among [margin: Or *within*] you.'" (Luke 17:20-21 *NRSV*)

27.	<u>Jesus again showed his disciples the attitude required for the Kingdom of God</u>:

> "But when Jesus saw this, he was indignant and said to them, 'Let the little children come to me; do not stop them; for it is to such as these that the kingdom of God belongs. Truly I tell you, whoever does not receive the kingdom of God as a little child will never enter it.'" (Mark 10:14-15 *NRSV*)

28.	<u>Jesus discussed the difficulty of the wealthy entering the Kingdom of God</u>:
> "Then Jesus looked at his disciples and said to them, How hard it is for those who have wealth to enter into the kingdom of God!
> But the disciples were surprised at his words. And Jesus answered again, saying to them, My sons, how hard it is for those who trust in their wealth to enter into the kingdom of God!
> It is easier for a rope to pass through the eye of a needle than for a rich man to enter into the kingdom of God.
> But they were the more astonished, saying among themselves, Who then can be saved?" (Mark 10:23-26 *Lamsa*)

Jesus said that the saved enter the Kingdom of God. Being (eventually) saved and entering the Kingdom of God are synonymous. In the same chronological passage the twelve disciples asked about their reward in the Kingdom of God. <u>Jesus said the twelve disciples would rule over the twelve tribes of Israel in the Kingdom of God</u>:

> "Jesus said to them, 'Truly I tell you, at the renewal of all things, when the Son of Man is seated on the throne of his glory, you who have followed me will also sit on twelve thrones, judging the twelve tribes of Israel.'" (Matthew 19:28 *NRSV*)

Jesus continued talking about the Kingdom of God with the Parable of the Vineyard Laborers:

> "For the kingdom of heaven is like a landowner who went out early in the morning to hire laborers for his vineyard." (Matthew 20:1 *NRSV*)

29.	<u>The mother of James and John requested special Kingdom of God positions for her sons</u>:

> "Then the mother of the sons of Zebedee came to him with her sons, and kneeling before him, she asked a favor of him. And he said to her, 'What do you want?' She said to him, 'Declare that these two sons of mine will sit, one at your right hand and one at your left, in your kingdom.'" (Matthew 20:20-21 *NRSV*)

"He said to them, 'You will indeed drink my cup, but to sit at my right hand and at my left, this is not mine to grant, but it is for those for whom it has been prepared by my Father.'" (Matthew 20:23 *NRSV*)

The Kingdom of God is a real kingdom. Christ will be King. Christ will rule Earth. There will be someone on his right and left in this Kingdom.

30.   Before telling the Parable of the Pounds, Jesus said:
> "As they were listening to this, he went on to tell a parable, because he was near Jerusalem, and because they supposed that the kingdom of God was to appear immediately." (Luke 19:11 *NRSV*)

<u>Jesus spoke about the Kingdom of God so much that the people thought that this Kingdom would be established immediately</u>. The purpose of the parable was to show them that the establishment of the Kingdom on Earth was far into the future.

31.   When Jesus entered Jerusalem near the end of his earthly life (an event called "Palm Sunday" by some), note what the people said:
> "...Hosanna!
>> Blessed is the one who comes in the name of the Lord!
>> Blessed is the coming kingdom of our ancestor David!
> Hosanna in the highest heaven!" (Mark 11:9-10 *NRSV*)

<u>Many people believed that Jesus would institute his Kingdom at that time</u>.

32.   During Jesus' last public ministry in Jerusalem, the chief priests and the elders questioned his authority. After the Parable of the Two Sons:
> "...Jesus said to them, 'Truly I tell you, the tax collectors and the prostitutes are going into the kingdom of God ahead of you. For John came to you in the way of righteousness and you did not believe him, but the tax collectors and the prostitutes believed him; and even after you saw it, you did not change your minds and believe him.'" (Matthew 21:31-32 *NRSV*)

The goal of the Christian is to enter the Kingdom of God. <u>One enters the Kingdom of God by repenting and believing God's servants</u> (in this case John the Baptist). Jesus continued talking to the chief priests and the Pharisees:
> "Therefore I tell you, the kingdom of God will be taken away from you and given to a people that produces the fruits of the kingdom."
> (Matthew 21:43 *NRSV*)

Jesus continued with the Parable of the Wedding Banquet:
> "Once more Jesus spoke to them in parables, saying: 'The kingdom of heaven may be compared to a king who gave a wedding banquet for his son." (Matthew 22:1-2 *NRSV*)

33.   After routing the Sadducees, Jesus answered a Pharisaic lawyer's question. <u>This Pharisee was close to the Kingdom of God</u>:
> "When Jesus saw that he answered wisely, he said to him, 'You are not far from the kingdom of God.' After that no one dared to ask him any question." (Mark 12:34 *NRSV*)

34.   <u>Jesus criticized the Pharisees, in part, for keeping people out of the</u>

kingdom of God:

> "But woe to you, scribes and Pharisees, hypocrites! For you lock people out of the kingdom of heaven. For you do not go in yourselves, and when others are going in, you stop them." (Matthew 23:13 *NRSV*)

35.   In the famous "Olivet Prophecy" recorded in Matthew 24, Jesus prophesied that the Kingdom of God would be preached before his return:

> "And this good news [margin: Or *gospel*] of the kingdom will be proclaimed throughout the world, as a testimony to all the nations; and then the end will come." (Matthew 24:14 *NRSV*)

Jesus talked about the signs which would precede his second coming:

> "So also, when you see these things taking place, you know that the kingdom of God is near." (Luke 21:31 *NRSV*)

When the events which Jesus spoke of in these passages come to pass, the beginning of the Kingdom of God on Earth is near.

36.   Jesus followed the Matthew 24 Olivet Prophecy with the Parable of the Ten Virgins:

> "Then the kingdom of heaven will be like this. Ten bridesmaids took their lamps and went to meet the bridegroom." (Matthew 25:1 *NRSV*)

Jesus continued with the Parable of the Sheep & Goats:

> "Then the king will say to those at his right hand, 'Come, you that are blessed by my Father, inherit the kingdom prepared for you from the foundation of the world;" (Matthew 25:34 *NRSV*)

This parable explains how the righteous will enter the Kingdom of God, and the wicked will be cast into the Lake of Fire, where they suffer the Second Death.

37.   At the "Last Supper" Jesus spoke about the Kingdom of God:

> "When the hour came, he took his place at the table, and the apostles with him. He said to them, 'I have eagerly desired to eat this Passover with you before I suffer; for I tell you, I will not eat it [margin: Other ancient authorities read *never eat it again*] until it is fulfilled in the kingdom of God.'" (Luke 22:14-16 *NRSV*)

At the Last Supper, Jesus repeated information about the reward, in the Kingdom of God, which awaited the twelve disciples:

> "You are those who have stood by me in my trials; and I confer on you, just as my Father has conferred on me, a kingdom, so that you may eat and drink at my table in my kingdom, and you will sit on thrones judging the twelve tribes of Israel." (Luke 22:28-30 *NRSV*)

During the Last Supper, Jesus commented on the wine he was drinking as he introduced the New Covenant symbols:

> "Truly I tell you, I will never again drink of the fruit of the vine until that day when I drink it new in the kingdom of God." (Mark 14:25 *NRSV*)

38.   On trial for his life before the Roman governor Pilate, this exchange occurred:

> "Then Pilate entered the headquarters [margin: Gk *the praetorium*]

---

again, summoned Jesus, and asked him, 'Are you the King of the Jews?' Jesus answered, 'Do you ask this on your own, or did others tell you about me?' Pilate replied, 'I am not a Jew, am I? Your own nation and the chief priests have handed you over to me. What have you done?' Jesus answered, 'My kingdom is not from this world. If my kingdom were from this world, my followers would be fighting to keep me from being handed over to the Jews. But as it is, my kingdom is not from here.' Pilate asked him, 'So you are a king?' Jesus answered, 'You say that I am a king. For this I was born, and for this I came into the world, to testify to the truth. Everyone who belongs to the truth listens to my voice.'" **(John 18:33-37** *NRSV*)

Jesus knew that he was born to be the "King of kings" and "Lord of lords" (Revelation 19:16 *NRSV*). Yes, Jesus is the Messiah. <u>Jesus is also the King of the Kingdom of God</u>.

39. A criminal who was crucified at the same time spoke to Jesus:
"Then he said, 'Jesus, remember me when you come into [margin: Other ancient authorities read *in*] your kingdom.' He replied, 'Truly I tell you, today you will be with me in Paradise.'" (Luke 23:42-43 *NRSV*)

<u>The criminal knew that Christ would rule in the Kingdom of God</u>. When Jesus replied, Jesus acknowledged that he (Jesus) would be the Ruler in the Kingdom of God.

40. After Jesus' death, Joseph asked Pilate for Jesus' body:
"When evening had come, and since it was the day of Preparation, that is, the day before the sabbath, Joseph of Arimathea, a respected member of the council, who was also himself waiting expectantly for the kingdom of God, went boldly to Pilate and asked for the body of Jesus." (Mark 15:42-43 *NRSV*)

Joseph was a follower of Jesus. <u>Followers of Jesus are waiting for the Kingdom of God</u>.

41. After Jesus was resurrected He again spoke to the disciples about the Kingdom of God:
"After his suffering he presented himself alive to them by many convincing proofs, appearing to them during forty days and speaking about the kingdom of God." (Acts 1:3 *NRSV*)

<u>The disciples asked Jesus when the Kingdom of God was going to be instituted</u>:
"So when they had come together, they asked him, 'Lord, is this the time when you will restore the kingdom to Israel?'" (Acts 1:6 *NRSV*)

<u>Summary</u>. 1. Many people are confused about the message of Jesus Christ. Jesus' message was about the Kingdom of God. 2. This chapter 6 reviews what Jesus Christ, when he walked on Earth and qualified to become the Messiah, said about the Kingdom of God. 3. Jesus described the end result of the successful Christian as entering the Kingdom of God. 4. Christ's Gospel -- the good news -- is about the Kingdom of God. 5. Christ defined his message as the Kingdom of

God. 6. In the "Sermon on the Mount," Christ again spoke of the Kingdom of God.
7. Successful Christians will enter the Kingdom of God. 8. Upon the arrival of
John the Baptist the main message from God was changed from the Old Covenant
to the Kingdom of God (New Covenant). 9. On Jesus' second tour of Galilee, he
preached the Kingdom of God. 10. The Kingdom of God is powered and sustained
by the Spirit of God. 11. Jesus used parables to tell people about the Kingdom of
God. 12. Jesus continued preaching the Kingdom of God during his third tour of
Galilee. 13. Some people believed that the Kingdom of God would rule Earth at
that time. 14. In talking to Peter, Jesus talked about the keys to the Kingdom of
God. 15. Three of the disciples saw a vision of the Kingdom of God. 16. The twelve
disciples argued about who would be greatest in the Kingdom of God. 17. Jesus
urged his disciples to live to enter the Kingdom of God. 18. Jesus reminded his
disciples of the cost of discipleship for the Kingdom of God. 19. The 70 were
instructed to preach the Kingdom of God. 20. Jesus responded that casting out
demons demonstrated the power of the Kingdom of God. 21. Jesus talked about
the Kingdom of God. 22. Jesus again described the Kingdom of God with the
Parables of Mustard Seed and Yeast. 23. Jesus talked about people entering the
Kingdom of God. 24. During dinner in the home of a Pharisee, a guest
commented on the Kingdom of God. 25. Jesus again explained the transition of
God's message from the Old Covenant to the Kingdom of God (New Covenant). 26.
In Samaria or Galilee, the Pharisees asked Jesus about the Kingdom of God. 27.
Jesus again showed his disciples the attitude required for the Kingdom of God.
28. Jesus discussed the difficulty of the wealthy entering the Kingdom of God.
Jesus said that the saved enter the Kingdom of God. Jesus said the twelve
disciples would rule over the twelve tribes of Israel in the Kingdom of God. 29.
The mother of James and John requested special Kingdom of God positions for
her sons. 30. Jesus spoke about the Kingdom of God so much that the people
thought that this Kingdom would be established immediately. 31. Many people
believed that Jesus would institute his Kingdom at that time. 32. One enters the
Kingdom of God by repenting and believing God's servants. 33. This Pharisee was
close to the Kingdom of God. 34. Jesus criticized the Pharisees, in part, for
keeping people out of the Kingdom of God. 35. Jesus prophesied that the Kingdom
of God would be preached before his return. 36. This parable explains how the
righteous will enter the Kingdom of God. 37. At the "Last Supper" Jesus spoke
about the Kingdom of God. 38. Jesus is also the King of the Kingdom of God. 39.
The criminal knew that Christ would rule in the Kingdom of God. 40. Followers
of Jesus are waiting for the Kingdom of God. 41. The disciples asked Jesus when
the Kingdom of God was going to be instituted.

The Kingdom of God: Pre-Jesus

CHAPTER 7
© 2005, Robert M. Kelley

Look up all Scriptures in your own Bible. Read and/or write the Scriptures on paper. Writing Scriptures on paper slows down your mind and causes the Bible verses to be more deeply burned into your mind.

All Scripture is inspired and true. However, you cannot learn everything at once. Therefore, the three most important Scriptures on this subject are in **bold** type and the next five most important Scriptures on this subject are underlined.

There are three Kingdom of God chapters:

6   "The Kingdom of God: Jesus"
7   "The Kingdom of God: Pre-Jesus"
8   "The Kingdom of God: Post-Jesus"

----

1.   This chapter 7 reviews what the Bible says about the Kingdom of God, *before* Jesus Christ was born of Mary and walked on Earth as a human being. As one can see from chapter 6, "The Kingdom of God: Jesus," Jesus had a *lot* to say about the Kingdom of God. However, when Jesus spoke about the Kingdom of God he was not introducing a new idea. The Old Testament has a lot to say about the Kingdom of God. In fact, the reason why people thought that Jesus, as a physical human being, would immediately usher in the Kingdom of God was because the people had already learned about the Kingdom of God from the Old Testament. This chapter 7 looks at some of the references to the Kingdom of God in the Old Testament.

2.   God promised to establish David's throne forever. David, king of the twelve-tribe nation of Israel, was the only king to whom God promised an eternal throne. God had a special fondness for David. This is revealed in a speech which Paul gave in Antioch (in Pisidia):

"When he had removed him, he made David their king. In his testimony about him he said, 'I have found David, son of Jesse, to be a man after my heart, who will carry out all my wishes.'" (Acts 13:22 *NRSV*)

God promised that David's throne would be eternal:

"Moreover the LORD declares to you that the LORD will make you a house. When your days are fulfilled and you lie down with your ancestors, I will raise up your offspring after you, who shall come forth from your body, and I will establish his kingdom. He shall build a house for my name, and I will establish the throne of his kingdom forever." (II Samuel 7:11-13 *NRSV*)

"Your house and your kingdom shall be made sure forever before me [margin: Gk Heb Mss: MT *before you*]; your throne shall be established forever." (II Samuel 7:16 *NRSV*)

Solomon was the son of David "who shall build a house for my name." Solomon built the Temple. David was the one whose kingdom would last forever. A Psalmist repeated this promise from God:

> "Once and for all I have sworn by my holiness;
>   I will not lie to David.
> His line shall continue forever,
>   and his throne endure before me like the sun.
> It shall be established forever like the moon,
>   an enduring witness in the skies." (Psalm 89:35-37 *NRSV*)

Note carefully what the angel Gabriel said to Mary before Jesus was born:

> "The angel said to her, 'Do not be afraid, Mary, for you have found favor with God. And now, you will conceive in your womb and bear a son, and you will name him Jesus. He will be great, and will be called the Son of the Most High, and the Lord God will give to him the throne of his ancestor David. He will reign over the house of Jacob forever, and of his kingdom there will be no end.'" (**Luke 1:30-33** *NRSV*)

Readers of the Old Testament knew that the throne of David would last forever. Israelites looked forward to the time when the throne of David would be established over Earth in the Kingdom of God. Jesus is the King who will rule in the Kingdom of God. Jesus' rule will not begin until He returns to Earth as a conquering King. Jesus will rule Earth for 1,000 years. (Jesus' rule is covered in detail in chapter 23, "Christians Do Not Go to Heaven After Death," and in chapter 27, "The Millennium.")

3.   In a public prayer, David recognized God's Kingdom:
> "...yours is the kingdom, O LORD, and you are exalted as head above all."
> (I Chronicles 29:11 *NRSV*)

4.   The psalmist of Psalm 2 tells how God will one day rule the world and all of the kings in it:
> "'I have set my king on Zion, my holy hill.'" (Psalm 2:6 *NRSV*)
> "Ask of me, and I will make the nations your heritage,
>   and the ends of the earth your possession.
> You shall break them with a rod of iron,
>   and dash them in pieces like a potter's vessel." (Psalm 2:8-9 *NRSV*)

5.   David spoke about the Kingdom of God in Psalm 145:
> "They shall speak of the glory of your kingdom,
>   and tell of your power,
> to make known to all people your mighty deeds,
>   and the glorious splendor of your kingdom.
> Your kingdom is an everlasting kingdom,
>   and your dominion endures throughout all generations."
> (Psalm 145:11-13 *NRSV*)

6.   <u>Isaiah 9 contains a major prophecy about Jesus Christ. It speaks of Jesus'
rule over Earth</u>:
> "For a child has been born for us,
>   a son given to us;
> authority rests upon his shoulders;
>   and he is named
> Wonderful Counselor, Mighty God,
>   Everlasting Father, Prince of Peace.
> His authority shall grow continually,
>   and there shall be endless peace
> for the throne of David and his kingdom.
>   He will establish and uphold it
> with justice and with righteousness
>   from this time onward and forevermore.
> The zeal of the LORD of hosts will do this." (**Isaiah 9:6-7** *NRSV*)

7.   The book of Daniel contains a great deal of prophetic information. Daniel
was a House of Judah royal captive in Babylon. Nebuchadnezzar ruled the
empire of Babylon. Early in his reign Nebuchadnezzar had a dream. Daniel gave
God's interpretation to Nebuchadnezzar. This chapter 7 focuses only on what the
Old Testament says about the Kingdom of God. God, through Daniel, foretold the
establishment of the Kingdom of God on Earth in the Millennium:
> "And in the days of those kings the God of heaven will set up a kingdom
> that shall never be destroyed, nor shall this kingdom be left to another
> people. It shall crush all these kingdoms and bring them to an end, and it
> shall stand forever;" (<u>Daniel 2:44</u> *NRSV*)

The establishment of the Kingdom of God on Earth was also the subject of a dream
which Daniel later experienced:
> "As I watched in the night visions,
> I saw one like a human being [margin: Aram *one like a son of man*]
>   coming with the clouds of heaven.
> And he came to the Ancient One [margin: Aram *the Ancient of Days*]
>   and was presented before him.
> To him was given dominion
>   and glory and kingship,
> that all peoples, nations, and languages
>   should serve him.
> His dominion is an everlasting dominion
>   that shall not pass away,
> and his kingship is one
>   that shall never be destroyed." (<u>Daniel 7:13-14</u> *NRSV*)

When Daniel delivered God's interpretation, more detail was added:
> "But the holy ones of the Most High shall receive the kingdom and possess
> the kingdom forever -- forever and ever." (<u>Daniel 7:18</u> *NRSV*)
> "until the Ancient One [margin: Aram *the Ancient of Days*] came; then
> judgment was given for the holy ones of the Most High, and the time
> arrived when the holy ones gained possession of the kingdom."

(Daniel 7:22 *NRSV*)

"Then the sovereignty, power and greatness of the kingdoms under the whole heaven will be handed over to the saints, the people of the Most High. His kingdom will be an everlasting kingdom, and all rulers will worship and obey him." (**Daniel 7:27** *NIV*)

Jesus, the Son of Man, will be the ruler in the Kingdom of God. The holy ones or saints -- successful Christians, with resurrected, spirit bodies -- will rule under Christ on Earth.

8. Even Nebuchadnezzar, king of Babylon, praised God for the Kingdom of God:

"How great are his signs,
  how mighty his wonders!
His kingdom is an everlasting kingdom,
  and his sovereignty is from generation to generation." (Daniel 4:3 *NRSV*)
"I blessed the Most High,
  and praised and honored the one who lives forever.
For his sovereignty is an everlasting sovereignty,
  and his kingdom endures from generation to generation."
(Daniel 4:34 *NRSV*)

9. Darius the Mede conquered Babylon. After the Daniel-in-the-lions'-den incident, Darius recognized the Kingdom of God:

"I make a decree, that in all my royal dominion people should tremble and fear before the God of Daniel:
    For he is the living God,
      enduring forever.
    His kingdom shall never be destroyed,
      and his dominion has no end." (Daniel 6:26 *NRSV*)

Summary. 1. This chapter 7 reviews what the Bible says about the Kingdom of God, *before* Jesus Christ was born of Mary and walked on Earth as a human being. 2. Israelites looked forward to the time when the throne of David would be established over Earth in the Kingdom of God. Jesus is the King who will rule in the Kingdom of God. 3. In a public prayer, David recognized God's kingdom. 4. The psalmist of Psalm 2 tells how God will one day rule the world and all of the kings in it. 5. David spoke about the Kingdom of God in Psalm 145. 6. Isaiah 9 contains a major prophecy about Jesus Christ. It speaks of Jesus' rule over Earth. 7. Jesus, the Son of Man, will be the ruler in the Kingdom of God. The holy ones or saints -- successful Christians, with resurrected, spirit bodies -- will rule under Christ on Earth. 8. Even Nebuchadnezzar, king of Babylon, praised God for the Kingdom of God. 9. After the Daniel-in-the-lions'-den incident, Darius recognized the Kingdom of God.

The Kingdom of God: Post-Jesus

CHAPTER 8
© 2005, Robert M. Kelley

Look up all Scriptures in your own Bible. Read and/or write the Scriptures on paper. Writing Scriptures on paper slows down your mind and causes the Bible verses to be more deeply burned into your mind.

All Scripture is inspired and true. However, you cannot learn everything at once. Therefore, the three most important Scriptures on this subject are in **bold** type and the next seven most important Scriptures on this subject are underlined.

There are three Kingdom of God chapters:

6 "The Kingdom of God: Jesus"
7 "The Kingdom of God: Pre-Jesus"
8 "The Kingdom of God: Post-Jesus"

---

1. This chapter 8 reviews what the Bible says about the Kingdom of God, *after* Jesus Christ was born of Mary and walked Earth as a human being. The entire New Testament talks a lot about the Kingdom of God. This chapter 8 looks at some of the references to the Kingdom of God in the New Testament, from Acts to Revelation.

2. After Jesus' resurrection, He talked with the disciples over a period of forty days. Note what Jesus talked to them about:

"After his suffering he presented himself alive to them by many convincing proofs, appearing to them during forty days and speaking about the kingdom of God." (Acts 1:3 *NRSV*)

In chapter 6, "The Kingdom of God: Jesus," it was seen that Jesus mentioned the Kingdom of God over 80 recorded times during his ministry. Now, after His resurrection, Jesus was again talking about the same subject, the Kingdom of God.

The Kingdom of God was on the minds of the disciples, as well:

"So when they had come together, they asked him, 'Lord, is this the time when you will restore the kingdom to Israel?'" (Acts 1:6 *NRSV*)

The disciples were concerned about *when* the Kingdom of God would take over and rule Earth. They knew that when Jesus returns to rule as "King of kings and Lord of lords" (Revelation 19:16 *NRSV*) they would rule with Him (see Luke 22:28-30).

3. At the beginning of Acts 8, a persecution in Jerusalem forced many Christians out of the city. Philip went to Samaria. What did Philip preach? He

45

<u>preached the Kingdom of God</u>:

> "But when they believed Philip, who was proclaiming the good news about the kingdom of God and the name of Jesus Christ, they were baptized, both men and women." (Acts 8:12 *NRSV*)

4.   After Jesus' resurrection, Paul was the man whom God used most in the New Testament period. Paul wrote 14 -- half -- of the New Testament's 27 books. Paul knew four languages fluently: Aramaic, Greek, Latin, and Hebrew. <u>Looking at the book of Acts, what message did Paul preach</u>?

> "There they strengthened the souls of the disciples and encouraged them to continue in the faith, saying, 'It is through many persecutions that we must enter the kingdom of God.'" (<u>Acts 14:22 *NRSV*</u>)

Some believe that the subject of the Kingdom of God was of interest to Israelites only, not Gentiles. It is true that when Jesus is ruling Earth in the Millennium, the nation of Israel will play a leading role. However, the Kingdom of God refers not only to the Millennium, but also to God's rule of a person's mind in all ages. The Kingdom of God is of vital interest to all Christians: Israelites *and* Gentiles.

> "He entered the synagogue and for three months spoke out boldly, and argued persuasively about the kingdom of God." (Acts 19: 8 *NRSV*)

When Paul was saying farewell to the Ephesian elders, he reviewed his work among them:

> "And now I know that none of you, among whom I have gone about proclaiming the kingdom, will ever see my face again." (<u>Acts 20:25 *NRSV*</u>)

Near the end of his ministry, Paul preached in Rome:

> "After they had set a day to meet with him, they came to him at his lodgings in great numbers. From morning until evening he explained the matter to them, testifying to the kingdom of God and trying to convince them about Jesus both from the law of Moses and from the prophets." (<u>Acts 28:23 *NRSV*</u>)

Luke wrote the book of Acts. Luke's last two verses summarized Paul's ministry in Rome:

> "He lived there two whole years at his own expense and welcomed all who came to him, proclaiming the kingdom of God and teaching about the Lord Jesus Christ with all boldness and without hindrance." (**Acts 28:30-31** *NRSV*)

<u>Paul referred to the Gospel he preached as that of the Kingdom of God</u>.

5.   <u>Paul's preaching of the Kingdom of God is evident in other New Testament books</u>.

Paul was talking about strong members easily offending weak members in Romans 14:

> "For the kingdom of God is not food and drink but righteousness and peace and joy in the Holy Spirit." (<u>Romans 14:17 *NRSV*</u>)

Paul described the way of the Christian, the way of the church, as the way of the Kingdom of God:

> "For the kingdom of God depends not on talk but on power." (I Corinthians 4:20 *NRSV*)

Paul described the result of being a successful Christian as inheriting the Kingdom of God:

> "Do you not know that wrongdoers will not inherit the kingdom of God? Do not be deceived! Fornicators, idolaters, adulterers, male prostitutes, sodomites, thieves, the greedy, drunkards, revilers, robbers -- none of these will inherit the kingdom of God."
> **(I Corinthians 6:9-10** *NRSV*)

Paul described Jesus delivering the Kingdom of God to the Father (near the end of God's Master Plan Period Two):

> "Then comes the end [margin: Or *Then come the rest*], when he hands over the kingdom to God the Father, after he has destroyed every ruler and every authority and power." (I Corinthians 15:24 *NRSV*)

Paul said that only successful Christians, with resurrected, spirit bodies, would inherit the Kingdom of God:

> "What I am saying, brothers and sisters [margin: Gk *brothers*], is this: flesh and blood cannot inherit the kingdom of God, nor does the perishable inherit the imperishable." (I Corinthians 15:50 *NRSV*)

Paul described the evil habits which can keep one out of the Kingdom of God:

> "...I am warning you, as I warned you before: those who do such things will not inherit the kingdom of God." (Galatians 5:21 *NRSV*)

Paul again described evil habits which can keep one out of the Kingdom of God:

> "Be sure of this, that no fornicator or impure person, or one who is greedy (that is, an idolater), has any inheritance in the kingdom of Christ and of God." (Ephesians 5:5 *NRSV*)

Paul continually referred to the Kingdom of God:

> "He has rescued us from the power of darkness and transferred us into the kingdom of his beloved Son, in whom we have redemption, the forgiveness of sins." (Colossians 1:13-14 *NRSV*)

Paul referred to his companions as "co-workers for the kingdom of God":

> "...These are the only ones of the circumcision among my co-workers for the kingdom of God, and they have been a comfort to me."
> (Colossians 4:11 *NRSV*)

Paul said that Christians were called into the Kingdom of God:

> "urging and encouraging you and pleading that you lead a life worthy of God, who calls you into his own kingdom and glory."
> (I Thessalonians 2:12 *NRSV*)

Paul said that successful Christians would be worthy of the Kingdom of God:

> "This is evidence of the righteous judgment of God, and is intended to make you worthy of the kingdom of God, for which you are also suffering." (II Thessalonians 1:5 *NRSV*)

Paul continually talked about Christ's kingdom:

> "In the presence of God and of Christ Jesus, who is to judge the living and the dead, and in view of his appearing and his kingdom, I solemnly urge you:" (II Timothy 4:1 *NRSV*)

Paul's goal was to enter the Kingdom of God:

> "The Lord will rescue me from every evil attack and save me for his heavenly kingdom..." (II Timothy 4:18 *NRSV*)

Paul, author of Hebrews, quoted from the Old Testament about the Kingdom of God:

"But of the Son he says,
'Your throne, O God, is forever and ever,
and the righteous scepter is the scepter of your kingdom."
(Hebrews 1:8 *NRSV*)

Paul referred to the future reward of the Christian as the Kingdom of God:
"Therefore, since we are receiving a kingdom that cannot be shaken, let us give thanks, by which we offer to God an acceptable worship with reverence and awe; for indeed our God is a consuming fire." (Hebrews 12:28-29 *NRSV*)

6.   <u>The apostle James said that Christians would inherit the Kingdom of God</u>:
"Listen, my beloved brothers and sisters [margin: Gk *brothers*]. Has not God chosen the poor in the world to be rich in faith and to be heirs of the kingdom that he has promised to those who love him?" (James 2:5 *NRSV*)

7.   <u>The apostle John, writing in the book of Revelation, spoke a lot about the Kingdom of God</u>:
"...To him who loves us and freed [margin: Other ancient authorities read *washed*] us from our sins by his blood, and made us to be a kingdom, priests serving his God and Father..." (Revelation 1:5-6 *NRSV*)

"I, John, your brother who share with you in Jesus the persecution and the kingdom and the patient endurance, was on the island called Patmos because of the word of God and the testimony of Jesus."
(Revelation 1:9 *NRSV*)

The four living creatures and twenty-four elders said this before God:
"you have made them to be a kingdom and priests serving our God,
and they will reign on earth." (<u>Revelation 5:10</u> *NRSV*)

This next verse is one of my favorites. It depicts the moment when all power and authority over Earth is given to Jesus Christ. This moment occurs at the seventh (or last) trumpet:
"Then the seventh angel blew his trumpet, and there were loud voices in heaven, saying,
'The kingdom of the world has become the kingdom of our Lord
and of his Messiah [margin: Gk *Christ*],
and he will reign forever and ever.'" (**Revelation 11:15** *NRSV*)

Revelation 12 depicts the history of the church. This verse portrays the moment when successful Christians, now resurrected with spirit bodies, begin ruling Earth under Christ:
"Then I heard a loud voice in heaven, proclaiming,
'Now have come the salvation and the power
and the kingdom of our God
and the authority of his Messiah [margin: Gk *Christ*],
for the accuser of our comrades [margin: Gk *brothers*] has been thrown down,
who accuses them day and night before our God.'"
(Revelation 12:10 *NRSV*)

8.   Chapter 6, "The Kingdom of God: Jesus," shows that Jesus' message was about the Kingdom of God. Chapter 7, "The Kingdom of God: Pre-Jesus," shows that the Kingdom of God is mentioned throughout the Old Testament. This chapter 8, "The Kingdom of God: Post-Jesus," shows that the Kingdom of God is mentioned throughout the New Testament. <u>The Kingdom of God is the dominant theme of the Bible</u>. The Kingdom of God encompasses what God has been doing, is now doing, and will be doing. <u>Since God places great emphasis on the Kingdom of God, anyone who desires to follow God will also place great emphasis on the Kingdom of God</u>. Followers of God, just like God, will be teaching all about the Kingdom of God: what it is, when it will arrive, what it will be like, how one can enter it, etc.

<u>Summary</u>. 1. This chapter 8 reviews what the Bible says about the Kingdom of God, *after* Jesus Christ was born of Mary and walked Earth as a human being. 2. Now, after His resurrection, Jesus was again talking about the same subject, the Kingdom of God. The Kingdom of God was on the minds of the disciples, as well. 3. What did Philip preach? He preached the Kingdom of God. 4. Looking at the book of Acts, what message did Paul preach? Paul referred to the Gospel he preached as that of the Kingdom of God. 5. Paul's preaching of the Kingdom of God is evident in other New Testament books. 6. The apostle James said that Christians would inherit the Kingdom of God. 7. The apostle John, writing in the book of Revelation, spoke a lot about the Kingdom of God. 8. The Kingdom of God is the dominant theme of the Bible. Since God places great emphasis on the Kingdom of God, anyone who desires to follow God will also place great emphasis on the Kingdom of God.

God's Master Plan: Overview

CHAPTER 9
© 2005, Robert M. Kelley

Look up all Scriptures in your own Bible. Read and/or write the Scriptures on paper. Writing Scriptures on paper slows down your mind and causes the Bible verses to be more deeply burned into your mind.

All Scripture is inspired and true. However, you cannot learn everything at once. Therefore, the two most important Scriptures on this subject are in **bold** type. (No Scriptures on this subject are underlined.)

There are four God's Master Plan chapters:

9	"God's Master Plan: Overview"
10	"God's Master Plan: Period One"
11	"God's Master Plan: Period Two"
12	"God's Master Plan: Period Three"

----

1.   God has a Master Plan! People who study the Bible are often confused. So much is going on! In addition, the Bible spans an enormous amount of time. On the one hand, one can read about Adam & Eve in the Garden of Eden in the book of Genesis. Since man's recorded history goes back to about 4000 BC, Adam & Eve's living in the Garden of Eden could have occurred at about that date. On the other hand, portions of the book of Revelation deal with time thousands of years off into the future. What God is doing on Earth I call God's Master Plan.

2.   Knowledge of God's Master Plan can greatly facilitate your understanding of the Bible. An analogy is illustrative. If you are making an automobile trip across the US with only a list of highways and whether to turn left or right, then your trip will likely be filled with confusion and uncertainty. However, if you are making such a trip using a *road map*, which shows the entire route from start to finish, then your trip will be filled with vision and confidence.

The same principle applies to Bible study. If you are performing a specific Bible study with only a Scripture list, then confusion can easily ensue. However, if you have already acquired the *road map* of God's Master Plan, then your specific Bible study will be enriching and meaningful. God's Master Plan is a "road map" of the Bible, a palpable framework of overview Bible knowledge. If you *first* know God's Master Plan, specific Bible study will simply add detail to an already known Bible knowledge framework. *Without* knowledge of God's Master Plan I have seen Bible students become confused and quit. *With* knowledge of God's Master Plan I have seen Bible students progress rapidly.

51

3.   I have found that dividing God's Master Plan into time-defined periods is useful. The question arises, "What *criterion* should be used in dividing God's Master Plan into time periods?" I have decided that *government* -- who is ruling whom -- is the best criterion in dividing God's Master Plan into time periods. <u>Government is the best criterion for defining time periods in God's Master Plan</u>.

4.   <u>God's Master Plan has three time periods</u>. In terms of government, there are three time periods in God's Master Plan. God's Master Plan Period One begins with Adam & Eve in the Garden of Eden and ends with Christ's return. God's Master Plan Period Two begins with Christ's return and ends with the New Heavens & Earth. God's Master Plan Period Three begins with the New Heavens & Earth and continues forever.
Governmentally, here is what is happening in all three periods. In God's Master Plan Period One human beings (influenced by Satan) are ruling; human beings are the subjects. In God's Master Plan Period Two Jesus Christ and successful Christians, with resurrected, spirit bodies, are ruling; human beings are the subjects. In God's Master Plan Period Three God and successful Christians, with resurrected, spirit bodies, are ruling; the subjects are unknown.

5.   <u>God's Master Plan Period One begins with Adam & Eve in the Garden of Eden and ends with Christ's return</u>. The government in God's Master Plan Period One is human beings (influenced by Satan) ruling other human beings. The approximate calendar dates for God's Master Plan Period One are from about 4000 BC to about 2000 AD, a period of approximately 6,000 years. (For justification of the number 6,000 see chapter 10, "God's Master Plan: Period One.") The approximate 4,000 years from about 4000 BC to 0 AD essentially comprise the time period covered in the Old Testament (and Old Covenant) of the Bible. The approximate 2,000 years from 0 AD to about 2000 AD essentially comprise the time period covered in the New Testament (and New Covenant) of the Bible.

6.   <u>Lessons are learned in God's Master Plan Period One</u>. (a) Religions of physical requirements -- the Old Covenant and other religions -- cannot work. (b) Jesus Christ introduces the New Covenant. (c) In the New Covenant man is endued with God's thoughts and God's strength via the Holy Spirit. (d) Successful New Covenant participants receive, in a resurrection after physical death (the First Death), a spirit body and eternal life. (e) In a world influenced by Satan, God's way -- the New Covenant -- is proved superior to all other ways.

7.   <u>God's Master Plan Period Two begins with Christ's return and ends with the New Heavens & Earth</u>. The government in God's Master Plan Period Two is Jesus Christ and successful Christians, with resurrected, spirit bodies, ruling human beings. God's Master Plan Period Two begins about 2000 AD and goes for more than 1,000 years. The first part of God's Master Plan Period Two is Christ's 1,000-year reign over Earth, called the Millennium. After the Millennium, the many billions of people who lived before about 33 AD and the billions of people who lived between about 33 AD and about 2000 AD who have not been offered the New Covenant will be physically resurrected to live again on Earth. This second

physical life will give them their opportunity of salvation, the New Covenant. At the end of God's Master Plan Period Two every human being who has ever lived will have been offered the New Covenant. Physical human beings will stop being born near the end of God's Master Plan Period Two. The final resurrection of Christian human beings from flesh to immortal spirit bodies occurs near the end of God's Master Plan Period Two. The Lake of Fire (the Second Death) occurs at the end of God's Master Plan Period Two.

8.   <u>Lessons are learned in God's Master Plan Period Two</u>. (a) The Millennium -- Christ's 1,000-year rule over Earth -- will have proved that God's rule works. (b) God's way of the New Covenant will have been proved successful in every people and culture in the history of mankind. (c) Justice will have finally and totally prevailed. All of the righteous will have become spirit beings with immortal, spirit bodies. All of the wicked will have experienced total death -- the Second Death -- in the Lake of Fire. (d) The creation of spirit beings (resurrected former physical Christians) will have been completed. God will have completed His sorting process of all human beings ever born. With this completed product -- billions of spirit beings -- God will then be ready to begin the truly great projects of all eternity!

9.   <u>God's Master Plan Period Three begins with the New Heavens & Earth and continues forever</u>. The government in God's Master Plan Period Three is God and successful Christians, with resurrected, spirit bodies, ruling. It is not known *who* God and resurrected Christians will be ruling. God has not yet revealed this knowledge. God's Master Plan Period Three begins with the New Heavens & Earth and is probably endless. Time will probably be meaningless in God's Master Plan Period Three. In God's Master Plan Period Three the only beings left on Earth are God, Christ, successful Christians, with resurrected, spirit bodies, and angels. (Heaven (the Third Heaven) will, at that time, be on Earth. Satan and demons will have been confined in a place of black darkness.)

10.   <u>Lessons are learned in God's Master Plan Period Three</u>. The wonderful knowledge, truth, and lessons to be learned in God's Master Plan Period Three are not known. God is not telling present human beings much about God's Master Plan Period Three.
Some have called the arrival of the New Heavens & Earth (the beginning of God's Master Plan Period Three) the real beginning of all eternity. At the beginning of God's Master Plan Period Three, all the human beings ever born on Earth will have had their opportunity of the New Covenant. Those who were successful became resurrected, spirit beings. Those who were unsuccessful were eternally destroyed in the Lake of Fire (the Second Death). At the end of God's Master Plan Period Two God will have completed the sifting process of all human beings born on Earth.
<u>At the beginning of God's Master Plan Period Three God is now ready with His team -- billions of resurrected, spirit beings who were once humans.</u>
<u>Who knows what great plans God has for God's Master Plan Period Three?</u>
<u>However, enough of God's nature is known that, whatever those plans are, they</u>

are wonderful beyond man's imagination. As the apostle Paul says:
> "But, as it is written,
>> 'What no eye has seen, nor ear heard,
>>> nor the human heart conceived,
>> what God has prepared for those who love him' --
> these things God has revealed to us through the Spirit..."
> (I Corinthians 2:9-10 *NRSV*)

11.   When talking about God's Master Plan and the future, one major fact must always be borne in mind: One's knowledge can be, at best, partial. Anyone who claims complete and total knowledge about the future is kidding himself or herself. The history of religion is filled with stories of persons who "knew" exactly what God was going to do and exactly when He would do it. When time passed and expected events did *not* transpire as predicted, most people could see that these persons did *not* know what God was going to do and when He was going to do it. Consider these Bible verses:
> "So when they had come together, they asked him, 'Lord, is this the time when you will restore the kingdom to Israel?' He replied, 'It is not for you to know the times or periods that the Father has set by his own authority." (**Acts 1:6-7** *NRSV*)

Jesus had been resurrected for weeks before this occurrence. The twelve disciples were anxious to learn when many events, and especially those relating to the Kingdom of God, were going to occur. Jesus said that one *cannot* know.
Paul commented on man's partial knowledge of God's plans:
> "For we know only in part, and we prophesy only in part;"
> "For now we see in a mirror, dimly [margin: Gk *in a riddle*]..."
> "...Now I know only in part..." (**I Corinthians 13:9, 12** *NRSV*)

Certain Bible truths are revealed to human beings at this time. Other truths are *not* revealed to human beings at this time. Each human being should thank God for what He does reveal and also admit that there are many things which are presently unknown. God reveals sufficient truth so that human beings can be totally successful in the New Covenant. Those who base their salvation on knowledge of future events do not understand the New Covenant and may not be New Covenant participants.

12.   Time periods change quickly in the Bible. Ignorance of God's Master Plan often causes some people confusion when reading the Bible. The story flow in the Bible often jumps back and forth between one time period and another. An example is Isaiah, chapters 60-66. This passage shifts from God's Master Plan Period Two to God's Master Plan Period Three:
> "For I am about to create new heavens
>   and a new earth;
> the former things shall not be remembered
>   or come to mind." (Isaiah 65:17 *NRSV*)

God's Master Plan Period Two is described before this verse. God's Master Plan Period Three is described in this verse.

13.   <u>An overview of God's Master Plan can be summarized</u>. In God's Master Plan Period One God's way, the New Covenant, is introduced in competition with all other ways of thinking and living. God did not introduce the New Covenant until all religions of physical ways -- including the Old Covenant -- were shown to be unworkable, fruitless, null and void. In God's Master Plan Period One Satan is allowed to do his thing; he is pretty much unrestrained. In a world filled with Satan's influence, evil, and ungodly governments, God's way -- the New Covenant -- wins! God's Master Plan Period One is the *demonstration* period. In totally open and unrestrained competition, the New Covenant is shown to be the winner. In God's Master Plan Period Two the New Covenant is opened to all citizens of Earth for 1,000 years and, after that, to the remainder of all human beings who have ever lived. (In God's Master Plan Period One the New Covenant is offered to only a few people.) God's Master Plan Period Two is the *application* period. In God's Master Plan Period Two all people living for 1,000 years, plus those who have lived before, process through the New Covenant. At the end of God's Master Plan Period Two a vast sorting process will be complete. Those who have successfully embraced the New Covenant will have resurrected, spirit bodies. Those who have rejected the New Covenant are executed (not tortured forever, but killed -- the Second Death) in the Lake of Fire.

In God's Master Plan Period Three the only remaining "human" beings are those who have been successful in the New Covenant. As resurrected, spirit beings, they work with God on wonderful new projects, which cannot be imagined. No physical human beings are living in God's Master Plan Period Three.

14.   <u>Each of the three time periods can be summarized in one sentence</u>. In God's Master Plan Period One the New Covenant is proven superior to all other ways. In God's Master Plan Period Two most human beings process through the New Covenant. In God's Master Plan Period Three the ultimate destiny of mankind -- performing fantastic, yet unimaginable, projects as spirit beings under God -- finds fulfillment.

<u>Summary</u>. 1. God has a Master Plan! What God is doing on Earth I call God's Master Plan. 2. Knowledge of God's Master Plan can greatly facilitate your understanding of the Bible. God's Master Plan is a "road map" of the Bible, a palpable framework of overview Bible knowledge. If you *first* know God's Master Plan, specific Bible study will simply add detail to an already known Bible knowledge framework. 3. Government is the best criterion for defining time periods in God's Master Plan. 4. God's Master Plan has three time periods. 5. God's Master Plan Period One begins with Adam & Eve in the Garden of Eden and ends with Christ's return. 6. Lessons are learned in God's Master Plan Period One. 7. God's Master Plan Period Two begins with Christ's return and ends with the New Heavens & Earth. 8. Lessons are learned in God's Master Plan Period Two. 9. God's Master Plan Period Three begins with the New Heavens & Earth and continues forever. 10. Lessons are learned in God's Master Plan Period Three. At the beginning of God's Master Plan Period Three God is now ready with His team -- billions of resurrected, spirit beings who were once humans. Who knows what great plans God has for God's Master Plan Period

Three? However, enough of God's nature is known that, whatever those plans are, they are wonderful beyond man's imagination. 11. When talking about God's Master Plan and the future, one major fact must always be borne in mind: One's knowledge can be, at best, partial. 12. Time periods change quickly in the Bible. 13. An Overview of God's Master Plan can be summarized. 14. Each of the three time periods can be summarized in one sentence.

God's Master Plan: Period One

CHAPTER 10
© 2005, Robert M. Kelley

Look up all Scriptures in your own Bible. Read and/or write the Scriptures on paper. Writing Scriptures on paper slows down your mind and causes the Bible verses to be more deeply burned into your mind.

All Scripture is inspired and true. However, you cannot learn everything at once. Therefore, the three most important Scriptures on this subject are in **bold** type and the next five most important Scriptures on this subject are underlined.

There are four God's Master Plan chapters:

9 "God's Master Plan: Overview"
10 "God's Master Plan: Period One"
11 "God's Master Plan: Period Two"
12 "God's Master Plan: Period Three"

---

1. God's Master Plan Period One begins with Adam & Eve in the Garden of Eden and ends with Christ's return. The government in God's Master Plan Period One is human beings (influenced by Satan) ruling other human beings. How many years will God's Master Plan Period One span? No one really knows, but some people believe that God's Master Plan Period One will span 6,000 years.

2. Some people believe that God's Master Plan Period One -- the time period in which man rules himself -- will span 6,000 years. Where do they get this idea? First, when Jesus Christ returns to rule Earth, he will rule for 1,000 years. (This rule occurs in God's Master Plan Period Two.)

"Then I saw an angel coming down from heaven, holding in his hand the key to the bottomless pit and a great chain. He seized the dragon, that ancient serpent, who is the Devil and Satan, and bound him for a thousand years, and threw him into the pit, and locked and sealed it over him, so that he would deceive the nations no more, until the thousand years were ended. After that he must be let out for a little while.

Then I saw thrones, and those seated on them were given authority to judge. I also saw the souls of those who had been beheaded for their testimony to Jesus [margin: Or *for the testimony of Jesus*] and for the word of God. They had not worshiped the beast or its image and had not received its mark on their foreheads or their hands. They came to life and reigned with Christ a thousand years. (The rest of the dead did not come to life until the thousand years were ended.) This is the first resurrection. Blessed and holy are those who share in the first resurrection. Over these

the second death has no power, but they will be priests of God and of Christ, and they will reign with him a thousand years." (<u>Revelation 20:1-6</u> *NRSV*)
Second, these people look at this Scripture:

"But do not ignore this one fact, beloved, that with the Lord one day is like a thousand years, and a thousand years are like one day."
(<u>II Peter 3:8</u> *NRSV*)

Third, these people use the Sabbath principle:

"And on the seventh day God finished the work that he had done, and he rested on the seventh day from all the work that he had done. So God blessed the seventh day and hallowed it, because on it God rested from all the work that he had done in creation." (<u>Genesis 2:2-3</u> *NRSV*)

Based on the three Scripture passages above, these people reason: (a) Christ will rule for 1,000 years. (b) This 1,000 years is a "Sabbath" of man's time on Earth. (c) Since the Sabbath is the seventh day of seven days, man's rule over man will last 6,000 years. (d) Recorded human history goes back to 4000 BC. (e) Therefore the time from the Garden of Eden to Christ's return is 6,000 years, or from about 4,000 BC to about 2000 AD. Now that 2005 AD is here, is it surprising that some people are getting excited about Bible prophecy?

3.   This Scripture defines the beginning of God's Master Plan Period One:

"Then God said, 'Let us make humankind [margin: Heb *adam*] in our image, according to our likeness; and let them have dominion over the fish of the sea, and over the birds of the air, and over the cattle, and over all the wild animals of the earth, and over every creeping thing that creeps upon the earth.'

So God created humankind [margin: Heb *adam*] in his image,
    in the image of God he created them [margin: Heb *him*];
    male and female he created them." (**Genesis 1:26-27** *NRSV*)

<u>God's Master Plan Period One begins with Adam & Eve in the Garden of Eden</u>. Genesis, chapters 1-2, covers this event in detail.

4.   This Scripture begins the events which occur at the end of God's Master Plan Period One (which is the beginning of God's Master Plan Period Two):

"Then the seventh angel blew his trumpet, and there were loud
    voices in heaven, saying,
'The kingdom of the world has become the kingdom of our Lord
    and of his Messiah [margin: Gk *Christ*],
    and he will reign forever and ever.'" (**Revelation 11:15** *NRSV*)

The seven trumpets sound in the fulfillment of the seventh seal.
At the sounding of the seventh trumpet Christ begins his rule over Earth:

"On that day his feet shall stand on the Mount of Olives, which lies before
    Jerusalem on the east..."
"And the LORD will become king over all the earth..."
(<u>Zechariah 14:4, 9</u> *NRSV*)

Remember that the return of Jesus Christ to rule Earth has been prophesied since Creation. When Jesus was on Earth he continually talked about the Kingdom of God (see chapter, 6, "The Kingdom of God: Jesus"). <u>God's Master Plan Period</u>

One ends with Christ's return.

5. What has happened, is happening, and will happen in God's Master Plan Period One? <u>One major event in God's Master Plan Period One was the Genesis Flood</u>, described in Genesis, chapters 6-9. <u>Another major event in God's Master Plan Period One was the Tower of Babel</u> incident, which is described in Genesis, chapter 11.

6. <u>From Genesis, chapter 12, on to the end of the Old Testament, God essentially deals only with one man, Abraham, and Abraham's descendants.</u> Abraham, Isaac, and Jacob are the big three, as grandfather, father, and son. Jacob's name was changed to Israel. Israel fathered twelve sons by four wives. These twelve sons became twelve tribes, known as the "Twelve Tribes of Israel," the "children of Israel," or simply "Israel." Israel's large family spent 430 years living in Egypt. Then, in the Exodus, Moses (and later Joshua) led Israel to the Promised Land. After Joshua's death, Israel was ruled by a succession of judges. The last of the judges was Samuel.
At the time of Samuel, the form of government of the twelve-tribe nation of Israel was changed from a theocracy (ruled by God) administered by judges to a kingdom (ruled by a physical king). Saul was the first king. Three kings -- Saul, David, and Solomon -- ruled in succession over the twelve-tribe nation of Israel. After Solomon's death, Israel divided into two kingdoms. The House of Israel, with its capital (north) in Samaria, consisted of ten tribes. The House of Judah, with its capital (south) in Jerusalem, consisted of two tribes, Judah and Benjamin. (Later many of the members of the tribe of Levi moved from the House of Israel to the House of Judah.) The books of I & II Kings and I & II Chronicles record the two separate histories of these two kingdoms. These two kingdoms lasted for most of the Old Testament period.

7. <u>A major event in God's Master Plan Period One was the Old Covenant</u>. The Old Covenant is described thoroughly in chapter 4. However, to summarize, the Old Covenant was an agreement between God and the twelve-tribe nation of Israel. Essentially no one else could participate. The Old Covenant required physical obedience and promised physical rewards. The Old Covenant did not require faith, did not forgive sins, and did not promise eternal life. The Old Covenant was a written agreement and consisted of the Ten Commandments of Exodus 20 and the judgments given in Exodus, chapters 21-23. The Old Covenant was confirmed by Israel in Exodus, chapter 24.

8. <u>Another major event in God's Master Plan Period One is the beginning of the New Covenant</u>. The New Covenant is described thoroughly in chapter 5. However, to summarize, the New Covenant is an agreement between God and (potentially) every human being ever born. In the New Covenant one receives the Holy Spirit, which gives direction and energy to live a totally new life. In the New Covenant, one literally has the mind of God. The New Covenant requires faith. The result of successful participation in the New Covenant is eternal life. The New Covenant is not written. As God prophesied hundreds of years earlier:

"...I will put my law within them, and I will write it on their hearts..." (**Jeremiah 31:33** *NRSV*)

Jesus said that the relationship between himself and a human being formed via his blood is the New Covenant:

"...'This cup is the new covenant in my blood. Do this, as often as you drink it, in remembrance of me.'" (I Corinthians 11:25 *NRSV*)

These words were spoken by Jesus during his last night as a human on Earth.

9. A major characteristic of God's Master Plan Period One is the unrestrained influence of Satan the Devil. Since the Garden of Eden (and probably even before) Satan has been allowed to roam Earth freely with his minions (billions?) of demons. The influence of Satan the Devil in God's Master Plan Period One is covered in chapter 21, "This is Satan's World."

10. In God's Master Plan Period One there is a life-and-death competition of all religions. In addition, this competition occurs in a world where man is under the total influence of Satan. I call God's Master Plan Period One the *demonstration* period. All of the religions of the world are competing in God's Master Plan Period One. This competition is covered in chapter 21, "This is Satan's World." In this competition, God's way -- the New Covenant -- wins.

11. Lessons are learned in God's Master Plan Period One. (a) Religions of physical requirements -- the Old Covenant and other religions -- cannot work. (b) Jesus Christ introduces the New Covenant. (c) In the New Covenant man is endued with God's thoughts and God's strength via the Holy Spirit. (d) Successful New Covenant participants receive, in a resurrection after physical death (the First Death), a spirit body and eternal life. (e) In a world influenced by Satan, God's way -- the New Covenant -- is proved superior to all other ways.

Summary. 1. God's Master Plan Period One begins with Adam & Eve in the Garden of Eden and ends with Christ's return. 2. Some people believe that God's Master Plan Period One -- the time period in which man rules himself -- will span 6,000 years. 3. God's Master Plan Period One begins with Adam & Eve in the Garden of Eden. 4. God's Master Plan Period One ends with Christ's return. 5. One major event in God's Master Plan Period One was the Genesis Flood. Another major event in God's Master Plan Period One was the Tower of Babel. 6. From Genesis, chapter 12, on to the end of the Old Testament, God essentially deals only with one man, Abraham, and Abraham's descendants. 7. A major event in God's Master Plan Period One was the Old Covenant. 8. Another major event in God's Master Plan Period One is the beginning of the New Covenant. 9. A major characteristic of God's Master Plan Period One is the unrestrained influence of Satan the Devil. 10. In God's Master Plan Period One there is a life-and-death competition of all religions. In this competition, God's way -- the New Covenant -- wins. 11. Lessons are learned in God's Master Plan Period One.

God's Master Plan: Period Two

CHAPTER 11
© 2005, Robert M. Kelley

Look up all Scriptures in your own Bible. Read and/or write the Scriptures on paper. Writing Scriptures on paper slows down your mind and causes the Bible verses to be more deeply burned into your mind.

All Scripture is inspired and true. However, you cannot learn everything at once. Therefore, the three most important Scriptures on this subject are in **bold** type and the next seven most important Scriptures on this subject are underlined.

There are four God's Master Plan chapters:

9   "God's Master Plan: Overview"
10   "God's Master Plan: Period One"
11   "God's Master Plan: Period Two"
12   "God's Master Plan: Period Three"

----

1.   <u>God's Master Plan Period Two begins with Christ's return and ends with the New Heavens & Earth.</u> The government in God's Master Plan Period Two is Jesus Christ and successful Christians, with resurrected, spirit bodies, ruling human beings.

2.   Revelation 20 reveals a lot about God's Master Plan Period Two. <u>In the first part of God's Master Plan Period Two, successful Christians, with resurrected, spirit bodies, rule with Christ for 1,000 years:</u>

> "Then I saw thrones, and those seated on them were given authority to judge. I also saw the souls of those who had been beheaded for their testimony to Jesus [margin: Or *for the testimony of Jesus*] and for the word of God. They had not worshiped the beast or its image and had not received its mark on their foreheads or their hands. They came to life and reigned with Christ a thousand years. (The rest of the dead did not come to life until the thousand years were ended.) This is the first resurrection. Blessed and holy are those who share in the first resurrection. Over these the second death has no power, but they will be priests of God and of Christ, and they will reign with him a thousand years." (Revelation 20:4-6 *NRSV*)

<u>This 1,000-year period is called the Millennium.</u> (For more information, see chapter 27, "The Millennium.")

Other Scriptures give details. For example, Revelation 19 tells about Jesus' return to Earth as:

> "...King of kings and Lord of lords." (Revelation 19:16 *NRSV*)

(For more information on successful Christians ruling Earth with Christ for

1,000 years, see chapter 23, "Christians Do Not Go to Heaven After Death.")
The exact length of God's Master Plan Period Two is not known. However, God's Master Plan Period Two lasts for more than 1,000 years.
<u>Note carefully that the resurrection of the saints to rule Earth with Christ is called the *first* resurrection. Naming this resurrection the *first* resurrection implies that there are *others*.</u> It will be seen later that the Bible reveals a *number* of resurrections.

3.   <u>At the beginning of God's Master Plan Period Two, most human beings who have ever lived have never received the opportunity of salvation.</u>
At the end of God's Master Plan Period One (which is the beginning of God's Master Plan Period Two), very few human beings ever born have had the opportunity of salvation. God did not cause Jesus to be born until mankind had been on Earth for about 4,000 years (from about 4000 BC to about year zero). Since Jesus' sacrifice did not occur until about 33 AD, *all* the people living on Earth for about 4,033 years *never* had the opportunity of salvation! In addition, consider the many people who have lived since Christ's sacrifice in about 33 AD (about 33 AD to about 2000 AD). Have *all* of these many billions of people had the opportunity of salvation? How effective have Christians been in preaching the Gospel to the entire world during the last 2,000 years? If one is honest, the answer is "not very effective." Consider countries like China, India, and Japan. Very few citizens of these countries have ever heard the Gospel.
In summary, very few people who have lived in God's Master Plan Period One have ever had the opportunity of salvation.
What about these many billions of people who have lived in God's Master Plan Period One and have *not* had the opportunity of salvation? Will many billions of people all "burn in hell" because they just *happened* to be born before Christ came to Earth? Will additional billions of people who were born after Christ came to Earth all "burn in hell" because Christian missionaries were not very effective?

4.   I have met people who believe that all the many people who have never had the opportunity of salvation *will* "burn in hell." Does the Bible confirm people's worst fears? What is God's nature?
Consider this verse:
> "The Lord is not slow about his promise, as some think of slowness, but is patient with you, not wanting any to perish, but all to come to repentance." (II Peter 3:9 *NRSV*)

The Bible clearly shows that God wants *everyone* to have the opportunity of salvation and be successful in salvation. Again, God says:
> "For God shows no partiality." (Romans 2:11 *NRSV*)

<u>God's will is that *all* human beings ever born will have the opportunity of salvation.</u>

5.   Some people believe that only during this present age (essentially God's Master Plan Period One) will people have the opportunity of salvation. These people cite this verse as proof:
> "For he says,

> 'In the time of my favor I heard you,
> and in the day of salvation I helped you.'
> I tell you, now is the time of God's favor, now is the day of salvation."
> (II Corinthians 6:2 NIV)

The idea that human beings have only *one* day of salvation, and that day is *now* -- at this time -- is a popular idea. This idea is based *solely* on II Corinthians 6:2. However, look carefully at II Corinthians 6:2. If one checks the margin of one's Bible, one can see that II Corinthians 6:2 is a direct quote from Isaiah 49:8. Therefore, the rendering of II Corinthians 6:2 *must* be totally aligned with the rendering of Isaiah 49:8. The question is, "What is the correct rendering of Isaiah 49:8?" Isaiah 49:8 was God-inspired in the Hebrew language. (For additional information on exactly what Bible is God-inspired, see chapter 32, "Bible Translations.") This is a Hebrew scholar's translation of Isaiah 49:8:

> "Thus saith the LORD:
> In an acceptable time have I answered thee,
> And in a day of salvation have I helped thee..."
> (**Isaiah 49:8** *The Holy Scriptures According to the Masoretic Text*, © 1917, Jewish Publication Society)

I have checked the translation of the original Hebrew in *The Soncino Books of the Bible*. The "a day of salvation" rendering in Isaiah 49:8 is the *correct* rendering. Therefore, for alignment with the original, God-inspired Hebrew, Isaiah 49:8 and II Corinthians 6:2 *must* both read "a day of salvation" and *not* "the day of salvation." (If one checks the *KJV*, *NIV*, and *NRSV* translations, one will discover: Isaiah 49:8 is translated correctly in the *NRSV* and *KJV*, but incorrectly in the *NIV*. II Corinthians 6:2 is translated correctly in the *NRSV*, but incorrectly in the *NIV* and *KJV*.)
There is not *one* day of salvation. There are *multiple* days of salvation -- multiple times when the opportunity of salvation will be given. (Each individual human being, however, has only *one* opportunity.)

6.   The Bible shows people who have previously lived a physical life on Earth being physically resurrected to again live a physical life on Earth. Look carefully at Ezekiel 37. This chapter has puzzled many since it talks about the physical resurrection of an entire nation:

> "...and the bones came together, bone to its bone. I looked, and there were sinews on them, and flesh had come upon them, and skin had covered them..." (Ezekiel 37:7-8 NRSV)
> "...breath came into them, and they lived, and stood on their feet, a vast multitude.
> Then he said to me, 'Mortal, these bones are the whole house of Israel..." (Ezekiel 37:10-11 NRSV)
> "Therefore prophesy, and say to them, Thus says the Lord GOD: I am going to open your graves, and bring you up from your graves, O my people; and I will bring you back to the land of Israel." (Ezekiel 37:12 NRSV)

I Corinthians 15 shows successful Christians being *spiritually* resurrected (with spirit bodies) upon Christ's return. However, note that Ezekiel 37 talks about the *physical* resurrection of an entire nation. The *physical* aspects of this mass resurrection are clearly revealed: "bones" (verse 7), "sinews" (ligaments or muscle?, verse 8), "skin" (verse 8), and "breath" (verse 10).

7. <u>People who are physically resurrected to again live a physical life on Earth are given the offer of the New Covenant</u>. After being *physically* resurrected people are given the Holy Spirit:
> "I will put my spirit within you, and you shall live, and I will place you on your own soil; then you shall know that I, the LORD, have spoken and will act, says the LORD." (**Ezekiel 37:14** *NRSV*)

Note carefully that these people have already been given breath to physically breathe (verse 10). In addition, God gives them "my spirit" (verse 14) -- the Holy Spirit. These people become New Covenant participants. They experience their one (and only) opportunity at salvation!
<u>Salvation is available only through the New Covenant</u>.

8. <u>Physical resurrections with New Covenant opportunities will occur in God's Master Plan Period Two, *after* Christ's 1,000-year rule</u>:
> "But the rest of the dead lived not again until the thousand years were finished..." (Revelation 20:5 *KJV*)

(Other events occur in God's Master Plan Period Two. In Ezekiel 37:15-22 the two separate nations of the House of Israel (ten tribes) and the House of Judah (two tribes, Judah and Benjamin) are reunited into a single nation of all twelve tribes. In addition, in Ezekiel 37:24-25 King David will be resurrected (spiritually since he will be king forever) to rule over the reunited nation of Israel.)

9. <u>Jesus prophesied the physical resurrection of different peoples</u>. In reading the Gospels many people have failed to notice that Jesus himself spoke of the *physical* resurrection of different peoples.
> "The people of Nineveh will rise up at the judgment with this generation and condemn it, because they repented at the proclamation of Jonah, and see, something greater than Jonah is here! The queen of the South will rise up at the judgment with this generation and condemn it, because she came from the ends of the earth to listen to the wisdom of Solomon, and see, something greater than Solomon is here!" (Matthew 12:41-42 *NRSV*)

When will the people of Nineveh and the Queen of the South rise up *with* the people who were living with Jesus in 30-33 AD? The people of Nineveh and the Queen of the South lived hundreds of years before 33 AD and thus had *no* previous opportunity of salvation. Most of the generation living with Jesus were *not* called to be Christians after 33 AD. When will this judgment occur? This judgment occurs in God's Master Plan Period Two.

10. <u>Revelation 20 shows when physical resurrections will occur</u>. The story in Revelation 20 picks up at the end of the 1,000-year rule of Christ (the Millennium). At the end of the thousand years Satan is again allowed to deceive humans. Satan's deception and ensuing war is described in Revelation 20:7-10. Revelation 20 continues to describe events which lead to the end of God's Master Plan Period Two. <u>Note carefully that *two* physical resurrections are mentioned</u>.

The *first* physical resurrection is mentioned in Revelation 20:11-12:

> "Then I saw a great white throne and the one who sat on it; the earth and the heaven fled from his presence, and no place was found for them. And I saw the dead, great and small, standing before the throne, and the books were opened. Also another book was opened, the book of life. And the dead were judged according to their works, as recorded in the books." (Revelation 20:11-12 *NRSV*)

The *second* physical resurrection is mentioned in Revelation 20:13:

> "And the sea gave up the dead that were in it, Death and Hades gave up the dead that were in them, and all were judged according to what they had done." (Revelation 20:13 *NRSV*)

Note that in both of these resurrections physical people are "judged according to their works, as recorded in the books" (verse 12) and "judged according to what they had done" (verse 13). People are being physically resurrected to be given their one (and only) opportunity of salvation, the New Covenant. Sentencing takes only a moment; however, judgment takes *time*. It takes *time* for God to see "their works," "what they had done."

11.   If one follows Paul's teaching throughout the New Testament one can see that he talked a lot about the resurrection. In Hebrews 6:1-2 (*NRSV*), Paul says that "the resurrection of the dead" is one of the six components of the "basic teaching about Christ." I Corinthians 15 is known as the Resurrection Chapter. In I Corinthians 15 Paul explains more about the resurrection than in any other place in the New Testament. Paul describes the *order* of the resurrections:

> "But in fact Christ has been raised from the dead, the first fruits of those who have died [margin: Gk *fallen asleep*]. For since death came through a human being, the resurrection of the dead has also come through a human being; for as all die in Adam, so all will be made alive in Christ. But each in his own order: Christ the first fruits, then at his coming those who belong to Christ. Then comes the end [margin: Or, *Then come the rest*], when he hands over the kingdom to God the Father, after he has destroyed every ruler and every authority and power."
> **(I Corinthians 15:20-24 *NRSV*)**

Note how Paul explains the order of the resurrections: (1) "Christ the first fruits," (2) "then at his coming those who belong to Christ," and (3) "Then comes the end." Note exactly when these resurrections occurred or will occur: (a) Christ was resurrected about 33 AD. (b) Christians will be resurrected "at his coming" (sometime after 2000 AD). Christ's coming is at the seventh trumpet. This resurrection is called the "first resurrection" in Revelation 20:5-6. Paul explains this resurrection:

> "For the Lord himself, with a cry of command, with the archangel's call and with the sound of God's trumpet, will descend from heaven, and the dead in Christ will rise first. Then we who are alive, who are left, will be caught up in the clouds together with them to meet the Lord in the air; and so we will be with the Lord forever." (I Thessalonians 4:16-17 *NRSV*)

(c) The next resurrection occurs at "the end," which is after Christ's 1,000-year rule, and is described in Revelation 20:11-13. At "the end" is when the physical resurrections of Ezekiel 37 and Matthew 12:41-42 will occur.

12.   <u>God does not reveal *all* knowledge at this time</u>. God does not tell when each and every nation in all past time periods will be physically resurrected and given its offer of the New Covenant. However, God does reveal sufficient information so that it can be seen that *all* humans *will* have the opportunity of salvation and that God *is* totally fair.

13.   <u>Note carefully that Paul's account of multiple resurrections in I Corinthians 15 concurs exactly with John's account of multiple resurrections in Revelation 20</u>. <u>Daniel agrees with both Paul and John</u>, but summarizes all resurrections in one verse:
> "Many of those who sleep in the dust of the earth shall awake, some to everlasting life, and some to shame and everlasting contempt."
> (Daniel 12:2 *NRSV*)

14.   <u>After all physical resurrections have occurred, after every single human being has received the offer of the New Covenant, those who chose to be unsuccessful will be cast into the Lake of Fire, where they suffer the Second Death</u>:
> "Then Death and Hades were thrown into the lake of fire. This is the second death, the lake of fire; and anyone whose name was not found written in the book of life was thrown into the lake of fire."
> (<u>Revelation 20:14-15</u> *NRSV*)

15.   <u>The apostle Peter also described the Lake of Fire in II Peter 3</u>. Peter begins the chapter talking about scoffers who believe that God does not intervene in earthly events. Peter reminds them in verse 6 that God brought about the great Genesis Flood. Then Peter tells them that God will destroy Earth with fire:
> "But by the same word the present heavens and earth have been reserved for fire, being kept until the day of judgment and destruction of the godless."
> (II Peter 3:7 *NRSV*)

Here Peter makes the statement (quoted above) that God wants all saved:
> "...but is patient with you, not wanting any to perish, but all to come to repentance." (II Peter 3:9 *NRSV*)

Peter returns to the Lake of Fire theme:
> "But the day of the Lord will come like a thief, and then the heavens will pass away with a loud noise, and the elements will be dissolved with fire, and the earth and everything that is done on it will be disclosed [margin: Other ancient authorities read *will be burned up*]." (<u>II Peter 3:10</u> *NRSV*)

Peter urges his readers to righteous living, then returns to the Lake of Fire:
> "waiting for and hastening [margin: Or *earnestly desiring*] the coming of the day of God, because of which the heavens will be set ablaze and dissolved, and the elements will melt with fire?" (II Peter 3:12 *NRSV*)

Peter then looks beyond God's Master Plan Period Two to God's Master Plan Period Three:

"But, in accordance with his promise, we wait for new heavens and a new earth, where righteousness is at home." (II Peter 3:13 *NRSV*)

16.   At the end of God's Master Plan Period Two only one category of humans is left alive: those who were successful in the New Covenant. These successful Christians have eternal, spirit bodies (as described by Paul in I Corinthians 15). Those who rejected the New Covenant or were unsuccessful in it are executed (the Second Death) in the Lake of Fire.

17.   Lessons are learned in God's Master Plan Period Two. (a) The Millennium -- Christ's 1,000-year rule over Earth -- will have proved that God's rule works. (b) God's way of the New Covenant will have been proved successful in every people and culture in the history of mankind. (c) Justice will have finally and totally prevailed. All of the righteous will have become spirit beings with immortal, spirit bodies. All of the wicked will have experienced total death -- the Second Death -- in the Lake of Fire. (d) The creation of resurrected spirit beings (former physical Christians) will have been completed. God will have completed His sorting process of all human beings ever born. With this completed product -- billions of spirit beings -- God will then be ready to begin the truly great projects of all eternity!

Summary. 1. God's Master Plan Period Two begins with Christ's return and ends with the New Heavens & Earth. 2. In the first part of God's Master Plan Period Two successful Christians, with resurrected, spirit bodies, rule with Christ for 1,000 years. This 1,000-year period is called the Millennium. Note carefully that the resurrection of the saints to rule Earth with Christ is called the *first* resurrection. Naming this resurrection the *first* resurrection implies that there are *others*. 3. At the beginning of God's Master Plan Period Two, most human beings who have ever lived have never received the opportunity of salvation. 4. God's will is that *all* human beings ever born will have the opportunity of salvation. 5. There is not *one* day of salvation. There are *multiple* days of salvation -- multiple times when the opportunity of salvation will be given. (Each individual human being, however, has only *one* opportunity.) 6. The Bible shows people who have previously lived a physical life on Earth being physically resurrected to again live a physical life on earth. 7. People who are physically resurrected to again live a physical life on Earth are given the offer of the New Covenant. Salvation is available only through the New Covenant. 8. Physical resurrections with New Covenant opportunities will occur in God's Master Plan Period Two, *after* Christ's 1,000-year rule. 9. Jesus prophesied the physical resurrection of different peoples. 10. Revelation 20 shows when physical resurrections will occur. Note carefully that *two* physical resurrections are mentioned. The *first* physical resurrection is mentioned in Revelation 20:11-12. The *second* physical resurrection is mentioned in Revelation 20:13. 11. Paul explains the order of the resurrections: (1) "Christ the first fruits," (2) "then at his coming those who belong to Christ," and (3) "Then comes the end." At "the end" is when the physical resurrections of Ezekiel 37 and Matthew 12:41-42 will occur. 12. God does not reveal *all* knowledge at this time. However, God does reveal sufficient information so that it can be seen that *all* humans *will* have the opportunity of salvation and that God *is* totally fair. 13. Note carefully that Paul's account of multiple resurrections in I Corinthians 15 concurs exactly with John's account of multiple resurrections in Revelation 20. Daniel agrees with both Paul and John. 14. After all physical resurrections have occurred, after every single human being has received the offer of the New Covenant, those who chose to be unsuccessful will be cast into the Lake of Fire, where they suffer the Second Death. 15. The apostle Peter also described the Lake of Fire in II Peter 3. 16. At the end of God's Master Plan Period Two only one category of humans is left alive: those who were successful in the New Covenant. 17. Lessons are learned in God's Master Plan Period Two.

God's Master Plan: Period Three

CHAPTER 12
© 2005, Robert M. Kelley

Look up all Scriptures in your own Bible. Read and/or write the Scriptures on paper. Writing Scriptures on paper slows down your mind and causes the Bible verses to be more deeply burned into your mind.

All Scripture is inspired and true. However, you cannot learn everything at once. Therefore, the three most important Scriptures on this subject are in **bold** type and the next six most important Scriptures on this subject are underlined.

There are four God's Master Plan chapters:

9   "God's Master Plan: Overview"
10   "God's Master Plan: Period One"
11   "God's Master Plan: Period Two"
12   "God's Master Plan: Period Three"

----

1.   God's Master Plan Period Three begins with the New Heavens & Earth and continues forever. The government in God's Master Plan Period Three is God and successful Christians, with resurrected, spirit bodies, ruling. It is not known who God and resurrected Christians will be ruling. God has not yet revealed this knowledge. In God's Master Plan Period Three all beings are spirit: God, Christ, angels, other heavenly spirit beings, and successful Christians, with resurrected, spirit bodies.

The New Heavens & Earth are descried by three Bible writers: the apostle John, the Old Testament prophet Isaiah, and the apostle Peter. The apostle John gives the most expansive description.

2.   The beginning of God's Master Plan Period Three is described in Revelation 21:

> "Then I saw a new heaven and a new earth; for the first heaven and the first earth had passed away, and the sea was no more. And I saw the holy city, the new Jerusalem, coming down out of heaven from God, prepared as a bride adorned for her husband. And I heard a loud voice from the throne saying,
> 'See, the home [margin: Gk *the tabernacle*] of God is among mortals. He will dwell with them;
> they will be his peoples [margin: Other ancient authorities read *people*],
> and God himself will be with them [margin: Other ancient authorities add *and be their God*];

he will wipe every tear from their eyes.
Death will be no more;
mourning and crying and pain will be no more,
for the first things have passed away.'
And the one who was seated on the throne said, 'See, I am making all things new.' Also he said, 'Write this, for these words are trustworthy and true.' Then he said to me, 'It is done! I am the Alpha and the Omega, the beginning and the end. To the thirsty I will give water as a gift from the spring of the water of life. Those who conquer will inherit these things, and I will be their God and they will be my children. But as for the cowardly, the faithless [margin: Or *the unbelieving*], the polluted, the murderers, the fornicators, the sorcerers, the idolaters, and all liars, their place will be in the lake that burns with fire and sulfur, which is the second death.'" (**Revelation 21:1-8** *NRSV*)

The apostle John, who wrote the book of Revelation (under inspiration of the Holy Spirit), regresses in time in his description of God's Master Plan Period Three, to detail what happened at the end of God's Master Plan Period Two. This detail clearly shows who will be cast into the Lake of Fire to suffer the Second Death.

3.   <u>An angel gave John a description of the New Heavens & Earth</u>:

"Then one of the seven angels who had the seven bowls full of the seven last plagues came and said to me, 'Come, I will show you the bride, the wife of the Lamb.' And in the spirit [margin: Or *in the Spirit*] he carried me away to a great, high mountain and showed me the holy city Jerusalem coming down out of heaven from God. It has the glory of God and a radiance like a very rare jewel, like jasper, clear as crystal. It has a great, high wall with twelve gates, and at the gates twelve angels, and on the gates are inscribed the names of the twelve tribes of the Israelites; on the east three gates, on the north three gates, on the south three gates, and on the west three gates. And the wall of the city has twelve foundations, and on them are the twelve names of the twelve apostles of the Lamb." (Revelation 21:9-14 *NRSV*)

4.   <u>The angel told John about the dimensions, walls, and gates of the Holy City, Jerusalem</u>:

"The angel who talked to me had a measuring rod of gold to measure the city and its gates and walls. The city lies foursquare, its length the same as its width; and he measured the city with his rod, fifteen hundred miles; its length and width and height are equal. He also measured its wall, one hundred forty-four cubits [margin: That is, almost seventy-five yards] by human measurement, which the angel was using. The wall is built of jasper, while the city is pure gold, clear as glass. The foundations of the wall of the city are adorned with every jewel; the first was jasper, the second sapphire, the third agate, the fourth emerald, the fifth onyx, the sixth carnelian, the seventh chrysolite, the eighth beryl, the ninth topaz, the tenth chrysoprase, the eleventh jacinth, the twelfth amethyst. And the twelve gates are twelve pearls, each of the gates is a single pearl, and the

street of the city is pure gold, transparent as glass."
(Revelation 21:15-21 NRSV)

5. John gives further details about the Holy City Jerusalem:
    "I saw no temple in the city, for its temple is the Lord God the
    Almighty and the Lamb. And the city has no need of sun or moon to shine
    on it, for the glory of God is its light, and its lamp is the Lamb. The nations
    will walk by its light, and the kings of the earth will bring their glory into
    it. Its gates will never by shut by day -- and there will be no night there.
    People will bring into it the glory and the honor of the nations. But nothing
    unclean will enter it, nor anyone who practices abomination or falsehood,
    but only those who are written in the Lamb's book of life."
    (Revelation 21:22-27 NRSV)

6. John concludes his description of the Holy City, Jerusalem:
    "Then the angel showed me the river of the water of life, bright as
    crystal, flowing from the throne of God and of the Lamb through the
    middle of the street of the city. On either side of the river is the tree of life
    with its twelve kinds of fruit, producing its fruit each month; and the
    leaves of the tree are for the healing of the nations. Nothing accursed will
    be found there any more. But the throne of God and of the Lamb will be in
    it, and his servants [margin: Gk *slaves*] will worship him; they will see
    his face, and his name will be on their foreheads. And there will be no
    more night; they need no light of lamp or sun, for the Lord God will be their
    light, and they will reign forever and ever." (Revelation 22:1-5 NRSV)

7. Isaiah describes the New Heavens & Earth:
    "For I am about to create new heavens
      and a new earth;
    the former things shall not be remembered
      or come to mind.
    But be glad and rejoice forever
      in what I am creating;
    for I am about to create Jerusalem as a joy,
      and its people as a delight.
    I will rejoice in Jerusalem,
      and delight in my people;
    no more shall the sound of weeping be heard in it,
      or the cry of distress.
    No more shall there be in it
      an infant that lives but a few days,
      or an old person who does not live out a lifetime;
    for one who dies at a hundred years will be considered a youth,
      and one who falls short of a hundred will be considered accursed."
    (Isaiah 65:17-20 NRSV)
Isaiah has one more comment about the New Heavens & Earth:
    "For as the new heavens and the new earth,

which I will make,
shall remain before me, says the LORD;
so shall your descendants and your name remain." (<u>Isaiah 66:22</u> *NRSV*)

8. <u>The apostle Peter looked forward to the New Heavens & Earth</u>:
"But, in accordance with his promise, we wait for new heavens and a new earth, where righteousness is at home." (**II Peter 3:13** *NRSV*)

9. <u>The Bible, in story flow, often jumps back and forth between God's Master Plan Period Two and God's Master Plan Period Three</u>. How can you tell which period is being described? There is a key you can use. In God's Master Plan Period Two, although there are spirit beings around (angels, demons, and successful Christians, with resurrected, spirit bodies), there are very many human beings living on Earth. At the end of God's Master Plan Period Two there are no more human beings. Human beings have either been resurrected with spirit bodies as successful Christians or executed in the Lake of Fire (the Second Death). In God's Master Plan Period Three there are no more (flesh-and-blood) human beings. Therefore if you read of wars, fighting, death, animal sacrifices, crying, and tears, etc., then God's Master Plan Period Two is being described. If you read of no tears, no crying, no death, constant light from God and the Lamb (no one needs sleep because there are no more flesh-and-blood human beings on Earth), etc., then God's Master Plan Period Three is being described.

10. <u>Lessons are learned in God's Master Plan Period Three</u>. The wonderful knowledge, truth, and lessons to be learned in God's Master Plan Period Three are not known. God is not telling present human beings much about God's Master Plan Period Three.
Some have called the arrival of the New Heavens & Earth (the beginning of God's Master Plan Period Three) the real beginning of all eternity. At the beginning of God's Master Plan Period Three all the human beings ever born on Earth will have received the opportunity of the New Covenant. Those who were successful became resurrected, spirit beings. Those who were unsuccessful were eternally destroyed in the Lake of Fire (the Second Death). At the end of God's Master Plan Period Two God will have completed the sifting process of all human beings born on Earth.
<u>At the beginning of God's Master Plan Period Three God is now ready with His team -- billions of resurrected, spirit beings who were once humans.</u>
<u>Who knows what great plans God has for God's Master Plan Period Three?</u>
<u>However, enough of God's nature is known that, whatever those plans are, they are wonderful beyond man's imagination.</u> As the apostle Paul says:
"But, as it is written,
'What no eye has seen, nor ear heard,
nor the human heart conceived,
what God has prepared for those who love him' --
these things God has revealed to us through the Spirit..."
(<u>I Corinthians 2:9-10</u> *NRSV*)

<u>Summary</u>. 1. God's Master Plan Period Three begins with the New Heavens & Earth and continues forever. 2. The beginning of God's Master Plan Period Three is described in Revelation 21. 3. An angel gave John a description of the New Heavens & Earth. 4. The angel told John about the dimensions, walls, and gates of the Holy City, Jerusalem. 5. John gives further details about the Holy City, Jerusalem. 6. John concludes his description of the Holy City, Jerusalem. 7. Isaiah describes the New Heavens & Earth. 8. The apostle Peter looked forward to the New Heavens & Earth. 9. The Bible, in story flow, often jumps back and forth between God's Master Plan Period Two and God's Master Plan Period Three. 10. Lessons are learned in God's Master Plan Period Three. At the beginning of God's Master Plan Period Three God is now ready with His team -- billions of resurrected, spirit beings who were once humans. Who knows what great plans God has for God's Master Plan Period Three? However, enough of God's nature is known that, whatever those plans are, they are wonderful beyond man's imagination.

Truth

CHAPTER 13

© 2005, Robert M. Kelley

Look up all Scriptures in your own Bible. Read and/or write the Scriptures on paper. Writing Scriptures on paper slows down your mind and causes the Bible verses to be more deeply burned into your mind.

All Scripture is inspired and true. However, you cannot learn everything at once. Therefore, the three most important Scriptures on this subject are in **bold** type and the next seven most important Scriptures on this subject are underlined.

----

1. Truth is God's Word. Jesus was talking to the Father in prayer:
    "...your word is truth." (**John 17:17** *NIV*)
    In talking to Timothy, Paul referred to the Bible:
    "...the word of truth." (II Timothy 2:15 *NIV*)
    James referred to the Bible:
    "...the word of truth..." (James 1:18 *NIV*)
    God, speaking of Himself, says:
    "...I, the LORD, speak the truth;
    I declare what is right." (Isaiah 45:19 *NIV*)
    David called the LORD:
    "...the God of truth." (Psalm 31:5 *NIV*)
    A Psalm writer made a request (to God):
    "Send forth your light and your truth..." (Psalm 43:3 *NIV*)

2. God promotes truth. David told God:
    "Surely you desire truth in the inner parts..." (Psalm 51:6 *NIV*)
    Jeremiah said:
    "O LORD, do not your eyes look for truth?..." (Jeremiah 5:3 *NIV*)
    Human beings are urged:
    "Buy the truth and do not sell it..." (Proverbs 23:23 *NIV*)
    God, through Zechariah, spoke:
    "...Therefore love truth and peace." (Zechariah 8:19 *NIV*)
    Paul said:
    "...God our Savior, who wants all men to be saved and to come to a knowledge of the truth." (I Timothy 2:3-4 *NIV*)

3. The Holy Spirit reveals truth:
    "But when he, the Spirit of truth, comes, he will guide you into all truth. He will not speak on his own; he will speak only what he hears, and he will tell you what is yet to come." (**John 16:13** *NIV*)
    In three places (all *NIV*) it is revealed that the Holy Spirit is:
    "...the Spirit of truth..." (John 14:17, John 15:26, I John 4:6)

4. <u>Jesus Christ embodies truth</u>. Jesus said:
> "...I am the way and the truth and the life..." (<u>John 14:6</u> *NIV*)

John says that:
> "...grace and truth came through Jesus Christ." (John 1:17 *NIV*)

5. <u>Truth describes the true Gospel</u>. Jesus said:
> "God is spirit, and his worshippers must worship in spirit and in truth."
> (<u>John 4:24</u> *NIV*)

Jesus said:
> "But whoever lives by the truth comes into the light, so that it may be seen
> plainly that what he has done has been done through God." (John 3:21 *NIV*)

Living by the truth means having the Holy Spirit, being a New Covenant
participant.

A Psalm writer said:
> "I have chosen the way of truth..." (Psalm 119:30 *NIV*)

Paul said:
> "For we cannot do anything against the truth, but only for the truth."
> (II Corinthians 13:8 *NIV*)

The apostle John wrote the books of II & III John near the end of the New
Testament period. This was a time when the true Gospel was under attack by
anti-God forces. John was urging Christians to be faithful to the true Gospel.
John used the word "truth" to describe the true Gospel eleven times in II John 1-4
NIV and in III John 1, 3-4, 8, 12 *NIV*.

6. <u>Degenerate societies lose truth</u>. The prophets used poetic language to
describe the societies of their times:
> "So justice is driven back,
>   and righteousness stands at a distance;
> truth has stumbled in the streets,
>   honesty cannot enter.
> Truth is nowhere to be found,
>   and whoever shuns evil becomes a prey..." (Isaiah 59:14-15 *NIV*)

> "Therefore say to them, 'This is the nation that has not obeyed the LORD its
> God or responded to correction. Truth has perished; it is vanished from
> their lips." (Jeremiah 7:28 *NIV*)

> "Friend deceives friend,
>   and no one speaks the truth.
> They have taught their tongues to lie;
>   they weary themselves with sinning." (Jeremiah 9:5 *NIV*)

> "...It prospered in everything it did, and truth was thrown to the ground."
> (Daniel 8:12 *NIV*)

7. <u>Individuals and groups which are spiritually dead have either rejected or</u>
<u>lost truth</u>. Paul, in Romans 1, talks about societies which have rejected God-
revealed truth:
> "The wrath of God is being revealed from heaven against all the
> godlessness and wickedness of men who suppress the truth by their

wickedness, since what may be known about God is plain to them, because God has made it plain to them." (Romans 1:18-19 *NIV*)

Continuing, Paul shows how idolatry and nature worship began:

"They exchanged the truth of God for a lie, and worshipped and served created things rather than the Creator -- who is forever praised. Amen." (Romans 1:25 *NIV*)

Some people flatly reject truth:

"But for those who are self-seeking and who reject the truth and follow evil, there will be wrath and anger." (Romans 2:8 *NIV*)

"...They perish because they refused to love the truth and so be saved."

"and so that all will be condemned who have not believed the truth but have delighted in wickedness." (II Thessalonians 2:10, 12 *NIV*)

"always learning but never able to acknowledge the truth. Just as Jannes and Jambres opposed Moses, so also these men oppose the truth -- men of depraved minds, who, as far as the faith is concerned, are rejected." (II Timothy 3:7-8 *NIV*)

"and will pay no attention to Jewish myths or to the commands of those who reject the truth." (Titus 1:14 *NIV*)

Paul warned about people who once knew the truth but would turn from it:

"Even from your own number men will arise and distort the truth in order to draw away disciples after them." (Acts 20:30 *NIV*)

"They will turn their ears away from the truth and turn aside to myths." (II Timothy 4:4 *NIV*)

8.   The Bible reveals miscellaneous facts about truth. <u>Truth frees</u>:

"Then you will know the truth, and the truth will set your free." (**John 8:32** *NIV*)

<u>Truth protects</u>:

"...may your love and your truth always protect me." (Psalm 40:11 *NIV*)

Paul talks about the armor of God which protects Christians:

"Stand firm then, with the belt of truth buckled around your waist..." (Ephesians 6:14 *NIV*)

<u>Truth is related to love</u>:

"Love does not delight in evil but rejoices with the truth." (I Corinthians 13:6 *NIV*)

<u>The Christian church is the foundation of truth</u>:

"...the church of the living God, the pillar and foundation of the truth." (I Timothy 3:15 *NIV*)

<u>Satan has no truth</u>:

"...He was a murderer from the beginning, not holding to the truth, for there is no truth in him..." (John 8:44 *NIV*)

Summary. 1. Truth is God's word. 2. God promotes truth. 3. The Holy Spirit reveals truth. 4. Jesus Christ embodies truth. 5. Truth describes the true Gospel. 6. Degenerate societies lose truth. 7. Individuals or groups which are spiritually dead have either rejected or lost truth. 8. Truth frees. Truth protects. Truth is related to love. The Christian church is the foundation of truth. Satan has no truth.

Lies

CHAPTER 14
© 2005, Robert M. Kelley

Look up all Scriptures in your own Bible. Read and/or write the Scriptures on paper. Writing Scriptures on paper slows down your mind and causes the Bible verses to be more deeply burned into your mind.

All Scripture is inspired and true. However, you cannot learn everything at once. Therefore, the three most important Scriptures on this subject are in **bold** type and the next seven most important Scriptures on this subject are underlined.

----

1.   Satan is the father of lies. When Jesus was talking to Israelites (mainly Jews), he made this statement:
    "You belong to your father, the devil, and you want to carry out your father's desire. He was a murderer from the beginning, not holding to the truth, for there is no truth in him. When he lies, he speaks his native language, for he is a liar and the father of lies." (**John 8:44** *NIV*)
Jesus Christ reveals the source of all lies. Those who lie follow Satan.

2.   Liars will be punished, ultimately with eternal death, the Second Death:
    "Let their lying lips be silenced..." (Psalm 31:18 *NIV*)
    "...he who pours out lies will perish." (Proverbs 19:9 *NIV*)
    "You destroy those who tell lies..." (Psalm 5:6 *NIV*)
    "But the cowardly, the unbelieving, the vile, the murderers, the sexually immoral, those who practice magic arts, the idolaters and all liars -- their place will be in the fiery lake of burning sulfur. This is the second death." (**Revelation 21:8** *NIV*)

3.   God never lies:
    "...Let God be true, and every man a liar..." (Romans 3:4 *NIV*)
    "God is not a man, that he should lie..." (Numbers 23:19 *NIV*)
    "He who is the Glory of Israel does not lie..." (I Samuel 15:29 *NIV*)
    "...God, who does not lie..." (Titus 1:2 *NIV*)
    "...it is impossible for God to lie..." (Hebrews 6:18 *NIV*)

4.   God hates lies and liars:
    "There are six things the LORD hates..."
    "...a lying tongue..." (Proverbs 6:16, 17 *NIV*)
    "The LORD detests lying lips,
      but he delights in men who are truthful." (Proverbs 12:22 *NIV*)

5.   Lying is related to other sins:
    "...a liar pays attention to a malicious tongue." (Proverbs 17:4 *NIV*)

"A lying tongue hates those it hurts..." (Proverbs 26:28 *NIV*)
"...They commit adultery and live a lie..." (Jeremiah 23:14 *NIV*)
"There is only cursing, lying and murder,
   stealing and adultery..." (Hosea 4:2 *NIV*)
"Woe to the city of blood,
   full of lies,
full of plunder,
   never without victims!" (Nahum 3:1 *NIV*)

6. <u>Degenerate societies are characterized by lies, lying, and liars</u>:
"Everyone lies to his neighbor..." (Psalm 12:2 *NIV*)
"And in my dismay I said,
   'All men are liars.'" (Psalm 116:11 *NIV*)
"...whose mouths are full of lies..."
(Psalm 144:8 *NIV*, repeated in verse 11)
"...Are you not a brood of rebels,
   the offspring of liars?" (Isaiah 57:4 *NIV*)
"...Your lips have spoken lies..." (Isaiah 59:3 *NIV*)
"...They rely on empty arguments and speak lies..." (Isaiah 59:4 *NIV*)
"...By lying to my people, who listen to lies, you have killed those who
should not have died and have spared those who should not live."
(Ezekiel 13:19 *NIV*)
"...her people are liars..." (Micah 6:12 *NIV*)

7. <u>Liars deny the truth about God, the Gospel, etc</u>. In speaking of all societies
Paul explains:
"They exchanged the truth of God for a lie, and worshipped and served
created things rather than the Creator -- who is forever praised. Amen."
(**Romans 1:25** *NIV*)
The apostle John, writing at the end of the New Testament period, identifies
hypocrites, liars, and those who deny the truth:
"The man who says, 'I know him,' but does not do what he commands is a
liar, and the truth is not in him." (I John 2:4 *NIV*)
"Who is the liar? It is the man who denies that Jesus is the Christ..."
(<u>I John 2:22</u> *NIV*)
"If anyone says, 'I love God,' yet hates his brother, he is a liar..."
(I John 4:20 *NIV*)

8. The Bible reveals miscellaneous facts about lies: <u>It is better to be poor than</u>
<u>to lie</u>:
"...better to be poor than a liar." (Proverbs 19:22 *NIV*)
<u>Sometimes those who tell the truth are called liars</u>:
"Azariah son of Hoshaiah and Johanan son of Kareah and all the arrogant
men said to Jeremiah, 'You are lying!...'" (<u>Jeremiah 43:2</u> *NIV*)
<u>Bad government is founded on lies</u>:
"If a ruler listens to lies,
   all his officials become wicked." (<u>Proverbs 29:12</u> *NIV*)

<u>Evil people destroy others with lies</u>:
> "The scoundrel's methods are wicked,
>   he makes up evil schemes
> to destroy the poor with lies,
>   even when the plea of the needy is just." (Isaiah 32:7 *NIV*)

<u>Righteous people can be disheartened with lies</u>:
> "Because you disheartened the righteous with your lies..."
> (Ezekiel 13:22 *NIV*)

<u>Hypocritical liars can lead Christians from the faith</u>:
> "The Spirit clearly says that in later times some will abandon the faith and follow deceiving spirits and things taught by demons. Such teachings come through hypocritical liars, whose consciences have been seared as with a hot iron." (<u>I Timothy 4:1-2</u> *NIV*)

<u>Summary</u>. 1. Satan is the father of lies. 2. Liars will be punished, ultimately with eternal death, the Second Death. 3. God never lies. 4. God hates lies and liars. 5. Lying is related to other sins. 6. Degenerate societies are characterized by lies, lying, and liars. 7. Liars deny the truth about God, the Gospel, etc. 8. It is better to be poor than to lie. Sometimes those who tell the truth are called liars. Bad government is founded on lies. Evil people destroy others with lies. Righteous people can be disheartened with lies. Hypocritical liars can lead Christians from the faith.

God

CHAPTER 15

© 2005, Robert M. Kelley

Look up all Scriptures in your own Bible. Read and/or write the Scriptures on paper. Writing Scriptures on paper slows down your mind and causes the Bible verses to be more deeply burned into your mind.

All Scripture is inspired and true. However, you cannot learn everything at once. Therefore, the three most important Scriptures on this subject are in **bold** type and the next seven most important Scriptures on this subject are underlined.

Note that these chapters are related:

15　"God"
16　"Jesus Christ"
17　"The Holy Spirit"
18　"The Trinity"

If you study one, be sure to study the others.

1.　The Old Testament is totally consistent in the statement that there is *one* God:

"I am the LORD thy God, which have brought thee out of the land of Egypt...
Thou shalt have no other gods before me." (Exodus 20:2-3 *KJV*)
"Unto thee it was shewed, that thou mightest know that the LORD he is God; there is none else beside him." (Deuteronomy 4:35 *KJV*)
"Know therefore this day, and consider it in thine heart, that the LORD he is God in heaven above, and upon the earth beneath: there is none else." (Deuteronomy 4:39 *KJV*)
"Hear, O Israel: The LORD our God is one LORD:"
(Deuteronomy 6:4 *KJV*)
"See now that I, even I, am he, and there is no god with me..." (Deuteronomy 32:39 *KJV*)
"...understand that I am he: before me there was no God formed, neither shall there be after me." (Isaiah 43:10 *KJV*)
"Thus saith the LORD the King of Israel, and his redeemer the LORD of hosts; I am the first, and I am the last; and beside me there is no God." (Isaiah 44:6 *KJV*)
"...I am the LORD that maketh all things; that stretcheth forth the heavens alone; that spreadeth abroad the earth by myself;" (Isaiah 44:24 *KJV*)
"And the LORD shall be king over all the earth: in that day shall there be one LORD, and his name one." (**Zechariah 14:9 *KJV***)

2.　The original twelve apostles constantly stated that there is *one* God. Peter knew that Jesus was *not* God:

"And Simon Peter answered and said, Thou art the Christ, the Son of the living God." (Matthew 16:16 *KJV*)

In the next verse (verse 17) Jesus said that the Father had revealed this truth to Peter. We know, therefore, that Peter's statement is correct.

Even after Jesus' resurrection, Peter regarded Jesus as a *man* who was resurrected:

"Ye men of Israel, hear these words; Jesus of Nazareth, a man approved of God among you by miracles and wonders and signs..." (Acts 2:22 *KJV*)

James knew there was one God and that Jesus was *not* God:

"James, a servant of God and of the Lord Jesus Christ..." (James 1:1 *KJV*)

3.   <u>The apostle Paul constantly affirmed that there is *one* God, and that Jesus was a *man*.</u>

"...and the gift by grace, which is by one man, Jesus Christ..." (Romans 5:15 *KJV*)

Paul said that Jesus was a *man*.

"But to us there is but one God, the Father..." (I Corinthians 8:6 *KJV*)

It is hard to get plainer than this simple statement.

"...but God is one." (Galatians 3:20 *KJV*)

Note that Paul did *not* say "God is three."

"There is one body, and one Spirit, even as ye are called in one hope of your calling;
One Lord, one faith, one baptism,
One God and Father of all, who is above all, and through all, and in you all." (Ephesians 4:4-6 *KJV*)

Again, Paul says that there is *one* God.

"For there is one God, and one mediator between God and men, the man Christ Jesus;" (**I Timothy 2:5** *KJV*)

Note carefully that Paul again said Jesus was a *man*.

4.   <u>God is greater than Jesus</u>:

Jesus said that God was greater than himself:

"...the Father is greater than I." (John 14:28 *NRSV*)

Of course God is greater than Jesus. God is God. Jesus is the Messiah.

When Jesus said that he and God are one, he meant one in purpose and unity:

"The Father and I are one.'" (John 10:30 *NRSV*)

5.   <u>In the Bible God is referred to in different ways</u>. In the Old Testament the most common term for God is "LORD." "LORD" is translated from the Hebrew YHVH. Some have translated YHVH into "Jehovah." Most Bible translators have translated YHVH into "LORD." Ferrar Fenton, a Bible translator, translated YHVH into "EVER-LIVING." James Moffatt, a Bible translator, translated YHVH into "Eternal."

6.   <u>God's word stands forever</u>:

"The grass withers, the flower fades;
but the word of our God will stand forever." (Isaiah 40:8 *NRSV*)

Whatever God says will stand forever. This fact explains why the Bible is important to every human being. The Bible contains God's words.

7.   <u>No one can know the mind of God</u>:
        "Who has directed the spirit of the LORD,
          or as his counselor has instructed him?
        Whom did he consult for his enlightenment,
          and who taught him the path of justice?
        Who taught him knowledge,
          and showed him the way of understanding?" (Isaiah 40:13-14 *NRSV*)

8.   <u>God rules over Earth and sometimes intervenes in human events</u>:
        "Have you not known? Have you not heard?
          Has it not been told you from the beginning?
          Have you not understood from the foundations of the earth?
        It is he who sits above the circle of the earth,
          and its inhabitants are like grasshoppers;
        who stretches out the heavens like a curtain,
          and spreads them like a tent to live in;
        who brings princes to naught,
          and makes the rulers of the earth as nothing.
        Scarcely are they planted, scarcely sown,
          scarcely has their stem taken root in the earth,
        when he blows upon them, and they wither,
          and the tempest carries them off like stubble." (Isaiah 40:21-24 *NRSV*)

9.   <u>God created the heavens</u>:
        "To whom then will you compare me,
          or who is my equal? says the Holy One.
        Lift up your eyes on high and see:
          Who created these?
        He who brings out their host and numbers them,
          calling them all by name;
        because he is great in strength,
          mighty in power,
          not one is missing." (<u>Isaiah 40:25-26</u> *NRSV*)

10.   <u>Only God can predict the future</u>:
        "Set forth your case, says the LORD;
          bring your proofs, says the King of Jacob.
        Let them bring them, and tell us
          what is to happen.
        Tell us the former things, what they are,
          so that we may consider them.
        and that we may know their outcome;
          or declare to us the things to come.
        Tell us what is to come hereafter,

that we may know that you are gods;
    do good, or do harm,
       that we may be afraid and terrified." (<u>Isaiah 41:21-23</u> *NRSV*)
Predictions of the future are called prophecies. Many of God's prophecies are in the Bible. Fulfilled Bible prophecy is a strong proof of God's existence. Fulfilled Bible prophecy is the proof that Jesus is the Messiah. (For more information on Bible prophecy, see chapter 26, "Bible Prophecy Basics.")

11.   <u>God is the Master Planner, the Master Decision Maker.</u>
When the mother of James and John came to Jesus to ask for high positions in the Kingdom of God for her two sons, Jesus replied:
> "He said to them, 'You will indeed drink my cup, but to sit at my right hand and and at my left, this is not mine to grant, but it is for those for whom it has been prepared by my Father.'" (Matthew 20:23 *NRSV*)

<u>God will appoint all positions in the Kingdom of God.</u>
Before Jesus ascended to heaven (the Third Heaven, about 40 days after His resurrection), His disciples asked about dates for God's Master Plan:
> "So when they had come together, they asked him, 'Lord, is this the time when you will restore the kingdom to Israel?' He replied, 'It is not for you to know the times or periods that the Father has set by his own authority." (<u>Acts 1:6-7</u> *NRSV*)

Jesus said that <u>God sets the dates for important events in God's Master Plan.</u>

12.   <u>God is the One to whom all human beings should pray.</u> (See chapter 2, "How to Pray.")

<u>Summary</u>. 1. The Old Testament is totally consistent in the statement that there is *one* God. 2. The original twelve apostles constantly stated that there is *one* God. Peter knew that Jesus was *not* God. James knew there was one God and that Jesus was *not* God. 3. The apostle Paul constantly affirmed that there is *one* God, and that Jesus was a *man*. 4. God is greater than Jesus. 5. In the Bible God is referred to in different ways. 6. God's word stands forever. 7. No one can know the mind of God. 8. God rules over Earth and sometimes intervenes in human events. 9. God created the heavens. 10. Only God can predict the future. 11. God is the Master Planner, the Master Decision Maker. God will appoint all positions in the Kingdom of God. God sets the dates for important events in God's Master Plan. 12. God is the One to whom all human beings should pray.

Jesus Christ

CHAPTER 16
© 2005, Robert M. Kelley

Look up all Scriptures in your own Bible. Read and/or write the Scriptures on paper. Writing Scriptures on paper slows down your mind and causes the Bible verses to be more deeply burned into your mind.

All Scripture is inspired and true. However, you cannot learn everything at once. Therefore, the three most important Scriptures on this subject are in **bold** type and the next seven most important Scriptures on this subject are underlined.

Note that these chapters are related:

15 "God"
16 "Jesus Christ"
17 "The Holy Spirit"
18 "The Trinity"

If you study one, be sure to study the others.

---

1. Jesus Christ constantly said that there is *one* God and that he was *not* God.
Jesus said there is one God:
"And Jesus answered him, The first of all the commandments is, Hear, O Israel; The Lord our God is one Lord:"
(Mark 12:29 *KJV*: a direct quote from Deuteronomy 6:4)
"How can ye believe, which receive honour one of another, and seek not the honour that cometh from God only?" (John 5:44 *KJV*)
Jesus said he was *not* God:
"And Jesus said unto him, Why callest thou me good? there is none good but one, that is, God." (Mark 10:18 *KJV*)
"And this is life eternal, that they might know thee the only true God, and Jesus Christ, whom thou hast sent." (John 17:3 *KJV*)
Jesus said that God was the Creator:
"But from the beginning of the creation God made them male and female." (Mark 10:6 *KJV*)

2. Jesus was *not* God. Jesus was 0% God.
God cannot be tempted:
"...God cannot be tempted with evil..." (James 1:13 *KJV*)
However, Jesus was tempted by Satan the Devil:
"And Jesus being full of the Holy Ghost returned from Jordan, and was led by the Spirit into the wilderness,
Being forty days tempted of the devil..." (Luke 4:1-2 *KJV*)
God cannot die. However, all men die:
"And as it is appointed unto men once to die..." (Hebrews 9:27 *KJV*)

<u>Jesus died</u> on a cross:

> "Jesus, when he had cried again with a loud voice, yielded up the ghost." (Matthew 27:50 *KJV*)

<u>God never gets tired.</u> <u>Jesus was tired</u>:

> "...Jesus therefore, being wearied with his journey, sat..." (John 4:6 *KJV*)

<u>God knows all things.</u> <u>Jesus did not know the day of his return</u>:

> "But of that day and that hour knoweth no man, no, not the angels which are in heaven, neither the Son, but the Father." (Mark 13:32 *KJV*)

<u>Jesus did not know who touched him</u>:

> "And Jesus...said, Who touched my clothes?" (Mark 5:30 *KJV*)

3.   <u>Jesus was a human being.</u> <u>Jesus was 100% human.</u>

> "Therefore he had to become like his brothers and sisters [margin: Gk *brothers*] in every respect, so that he might be a merciful and faithful high priest in the service of God, to make a sacrifice of atonement for the sins of the people. Because he himself was tested by what he suffered, he is able to help those who are being tested." (**Hebrews 2:17-18** *NRSV*)

<u>Jesus was like other humans "in every respect</u>." Jesus "was tested" and "suffered."

Another Bible verse clearly shows that Jesus was a human being:

> "For we do not have a high priest who is unable to sympathize with our weaknesses, but we have one who in every respect has been tested [margin: Or *tempted*] as we are, yet without sin." (**Hebrews 4:15** *NRSV*)

Jesus "in every respect has been tempted as we are."

Other Bible verses show that Jesus was human:

> "Who in the days of his flesh, when he had offered up prayers and supplications with strong crying and tears unto him that was able to save him from death, and was heard in that he feared;
>
> Though he were a Son, yet learned he obedience by the things which he suffered;" (<u>Hebrews 5:7-8</u> *KJV*)

Note that Jesus prayed, "feared" and "suffered." Note that "him that was able to save him from death" was God. Jesus was totally *human*; like all other humans he constantly needed *help* from God. If Jesus were God he would *not* need help from another God.

<u>In fact, anyone who claims that Jesus did *not* come in the flesh is anti-Christ</u>:

> "Hereby know ye the Spirit of God: Every spirit that confesseth that Jesus Christ is come in the flesh is of God:
>
> And every spirit that confesseth not that Jesus Christ is come in the flesh is not of God: and this is that spirit of antichrist, whereof ye have heard that it should come; and even now already is it in the world." (<u>I John 4:2-3</u> *KJV*)

4.   <u>Some believe that Jesus performed miracles because he was God.</u> <u>Nothing could be further from the truth!</u> <u>Jesus was *not* God.</u> Jesus was a human being. <u>Jesus performed miracles because the Holy Spirit flowed through him.</u>
Consider the miracle of Jesus casting out demons. Jesus said that he cast out demons by the Holy Spirit:

"But if I cast out devils by the Spirit of God, then the kingdom of God is come unto you." (Matthew 12:28 *KJV*)

Jesus performed miracles and lived without sin (Hebrews 4:15) because the Holy Spirit was given to him without limit:

"For he whom God hath sent speaketh the words of God: for God giveth not the Spirit by measure unto him." (John 3:34 *KJV*)

5.   When Jesus performed a miracle the Holy Spirit flowed through him. Look at the miracle of Jesus healing a woman with a hemorrhage affliction in Luke 8:43-48. Note carefully Jesus' description of how this miracle was performed:

"But Jesus said, 'Someone touched me; for I noticed that power had gone out from me.'" (Luke 8:46 *NRSV*)

The woman believed that she could be healed by simply touching Jesus' garment. She touched the garment; immediately power (from the Holy Spirit) flowed through Jesus to the woman.

6.   Jesus Christ is the model for all humanity:

"Jesus said to him, 'I am the way, and the truth, and the life...'" (**John 14:6** *NRSV*)

Jesus Christ came to show the *way* -- the way of life, the way of the New Covenant. Jesus Christ was a human being. Jesus went to God, his Father, in prayer to request power from the Father. God sent the Holy Spirit to flow through Jesus. Human beings can go to God in prayer to request power from God. God can send the Holy Spirit to flow through human beings. The Holy Spirit can flow through human beings exactly as it flowed through Jesus Christ.

7.   Since Jesus' resurrection, He has become the High Priest Who intercedes for all who seek access to God:

"Since, then, we have a great high priest who has passed through the heavens, Jesus, the Son of God, let us hold fast to our confession. For we do not have a high priest who is unable to sympathize with our weaknesses, but we have one who in every respect has been tested [margin: Or *tempted*] as we are, yet without sin. Let us therefore approach the throne of grace with boldness, so that we may receive mercy and find grace to help in time of need." (Hebrews 4:14-16 *NRSV*)

Because Jesus is the High Priest for every human being, you should end a prayer to God with "In the Name of Jesus, Amen." (See chapter 2, "How to Pray.")

Summary. 1. Jesus Christ constantly said that there is *one* God and that he was *not* God. Jesus said there is one God. Jesus said he was *not* God. Jesus said that God was the Creator. 2. Jesus was *not* God. Jesus was 0% God. God cannot be tempted. Jesus was tempted. God cannot die. Jesus died. God never gets tired. Jesus was tired. God knows all things. Jesus did not know the day of his return. Jesus did not know who touched him. 3. Jesus was a human being. Jesus was 100% human. Jesus was like other humans "in every respect." In fact, anyone who claims that Jesus did *not* come in the flesh is anti-Christ. 4. Some believe that Jesus performed miracles because he was God. Nothing could be further from the truth! Jesus was *not* God. Jesus performed miracles because the Holy Spirit flowed through him. 5. When Jesus performed a miracle the Holy Spirit flowed through him. 6. Jesus Christ is the model for all humanity. The Holy Spirit can flow through human beings exactly as it flowed through Jesus Christ. 7. Since Jesus' resurrection, He has become the High Priest Who intercedes for all who seek access to God.

The Holy Spirit

CHAPTER 17

© 2005, Robert M. Kelley

Look up all Scriptures in your own Bible. Read and/or write the Scriptures on paper. Writing Scriptures on paper slows down your mind and causes the Bible verses to be more deeply burned into your mind.

All Scripture is inspired and true. However, you cannot learn everything at once. Therefore, the three most important Scriptures on this subject are in **bold** type and the next seven most important Scriptures on this subject are underlined.

Note that these chapters are related:

If you study one, be sure to study the others.

----

1.   It is easy to prove that the Holy Spirit is *not* a person and is *not* God:

Mary, the mother of Jesus, was impregnated by the Holy Spirit:

> "And the angel answered and said unto her, The Holy Ghost shall come upon thee, and the power of the Highest shall overshadow thee: therefore also that holy thing which shall be born of thee shall be called the Son of God." (Luke 1:35 *KJV*)

The Holy Spirit made Mary pregnant. The Holy Spirit came from God. If the Holy Spirit was a person, a God, then the Holy Spirit would have been the father of Jesus, and Jesus would have been called "Son of the Holy Spirit." Jesus called God his Father because the Holy Spirit is the power of God.

Note carefully this verse from the apostle John:

> "And John bare record, saying, I saw the Spirit descending from heaven like a dove, and it abode upon him." (John 1:32 *KJV*)

The one time, in the Bible, in which the Holy Spirit is represented as an entity is as a dove. Therefore if the Holy Spirit was an entity and a God it would be a bird God.

Jesus said that the Holy Spirit would be in every Christian. A person cannot be in millions of Christians simultaneously.

The Holy Spirit is the power of God.

2.   The Holy Spirit recreated Earth:

> "the earth was a formless void and darkness covered the face of the deep, while a wind from God [margin: Or *while the spirit of God* or *while a mighty wind*] swept over the face of the waters." (Genesis 1:2 *NRSV*)

In Genesis 1:1 the heavens and earth were created. In Genesis 1:2 Earth became formless and dark. The implication is that some type of worldwide cataclysm occurred between these two verses. Regardless of what happened, God performed the Genesis 1 creation via the Holy Spirit.

3. <u>Throughout the Old Testament the Holy Spirit was given to certain men (and women) for short time periods in order to perform special acts for God</u>:
> "Then the spirit of the LORD rushed on him, and he went down to Ashkelton. He killed thirty men of the town, took their spoil, and gave the festal garments to those who had explained the riddle..."
> (Judges 14:19 *NRSV*)
> "...the spirit of the LORD rushed on him, and the ropes that were on his arms became like flax that has caught fire, and his bonds melted off his hands. Then he found a fresh jawbone of a donkey, reached down and took it, and with it he killed a thousand men." (Judges 15:14-15 *NRSV*)

Samson killed 30 Philistine male citizens in the first instance and 1,000 Philistine soldiers in the second instance. There are many examples of God giving the Holy Spirit to men (and women) for brief time periods in order to perform miracles.

4. God allowed the Israelites to adopt a kingdom form of government. Saul was the first king. <u>The Holy Spirit was given to Saul at different moments</u>:
> "Then the spirit of the LORD will possess you, and you will be in a prophetic frenzy along with them and be turned into a different person." (I Samuel 10:6 *NRSV*)
> "When they were going from there to Gibeah, a band of prophets met him; and the spirit of God possessed him, and he fell into a prophetic frenzy along with them." (I Samuel 10:10 *NRSV*)
> "And the spirit of God came upon Saul in power when he heard these words, and his anger was greatly kindled." (I Samuel 11:6 *NRSV*)

5. David became the next king:
> "Then Samuel took the horn of oil, and anointed him in the presence of his brothers; and the spirit of the LORD came mightily upon David from that day forward..." (I Samuel 16:13 *NRSV*)

<u>David's receiving the Holy Spirit is the first clear instance in the Bible in which the Holy Spirit was given to a human being on a continuing basis.</u>
> "Now the spirit of the LORD departed from Saul, and an evil spirit from the LORD tormented him." (I Samuel 16:14 *NRSV*)

This verse implies that perhaps Saul also possessed the Holy Spirit on a continuing basis. However, it is not totally clear that this was so.
Psalm 51 reflects David's repentance of adultery with Bathsheba. In it David implies that he possessed the Holy Spirit on a continuing basis:
> "Do not cast me away from your presence,
>   and do not take your holy spirit from me." (Psalm 51:11 *NRSV*)

In the Old Testament only a very few people ever received the Holy Spirit either momentarily or on a continuing basis.

6. <u>Jeremiah spoke of a New Covenant coming to all (twelve tribes of) Israel</u>:

"The days are surely coming, says the LORD, when I will make a new covenant with the house of Israel and the house of Judah." (Jeremiah 31:31 *NRSV*)

Jeremiah went on to explain how this New Covenant would work:

"But this is the covenant that I will make with the house of Israel after those days, says the LORD: I will put my law within them, and I will write it on their hearts..." (Jeremiah 31:33 *NRSV*)

Jeremiah showed that this New Covenant would result in people receiving the Holy Spirit.

7.   Joel prophesied that the Holy Spirit would come at the time of the "day of the LORD":

"Then afterward
  I will pour out my spirit on all flesh..." (Joel 2:28 *NRSV*)

8.   On the day of Pentecost recorded in Acts 2, the apostle Peter quoted from Joel 2:28-32, showing that the receiving of the Holy Spirit that day was a fulfillment of Joel 2:28:

"No, this is what was spoken through the prophet Joel:
       'In the last days it will be, God declares,
       that I will pour out my Spirit upon all flesh..." (Acts 2:16-17 *NRSV*)

On the day of Pentecost recorded in Acts 2, the Holy Spirit was first given to human beings as New Covenant participants.

9.   Possessing the Holy Spirit is the Bible definition of a Christian:

"...Anyone who does not have the Spirit of Christ does not belong to him." (**Romans 8:9** *NRSV*)

One who has the Holy Spirit is therefore a Christian and a New Covenant participant. In fact, "Christian" and "New Covenant participant" are synonymous. (For more information, see chapter 3, "What is a Christian?" and chapter 5, "The New Covenant.")

10.   Jesus warned that blasphemy against the Holy Spirit is unforgivable:

"Wherefore I say unto you, All manner of sin and blasphemy shall be forgiven unto men: but the blasphemy against the Holy Ghost shall not be forgiven unto men.
And whosoever speaketh a word against the Son of man, it shall be forgiven him: but whosoever speaketh against the Holy Ghost, it shall not be forgiven him, neither in this world, neither in the world to come." (Matthew 12:31-32 *KJV*)

The Holy Spirit is from God. To ascribe the work of the Holy Spirit to Satan is blasphemy, a blasphemy which Jesus says is *unforgivable*.

11.   Jesus prepared his disciples for the coming of the Holy Spirit. During his last twenty-four hours on Earth Jesus told his disciples some very important things. Jesus knew that he was leaving Earth. He gave his twelve disciples information they would need to continue after he left:

"And I will ask the Father, and he will give you another Advocate [margin: Or *Helper*], to be with you forever. This is the Spirit of truth, whom the world cannot receive, because it neither sees him nor knows him. You know him, because he abides with you, and he will be in you."
(**John 14:16-17** *NRSV*)

The "Advocate," the "Helper," the "Spirit of truth" is the Holy Spirit. Jesus promised the disciples that God would send the Holy Spirit. Jesus told the disciples that their main contact was going to change from himself to the Holy Spirit.

The Holy Spirit abided *with* these twelve disciples; it enabled them to cast out demons and heal the sick. However, at this time the disciples were still carnal. After Jesus' departure from Earth the Holy Spirit would be *in* them. The Holy Spirit was *in* them on the Day of Pentecost recorded in Acts 2.

The Holy Spirit which would come would be with them *forever*.

The Holy Spirit could not come until Jesus' sacrifice:

"Nevertheless I tell you the truth: it is to your advantage that I go away, for if I do not go away, the Advocate [margin: Or *Helper*] will not come to you; but if I go, I will send him to you." (John 16:7 *NRSV*)

12. Jesus explained the functions of the Holy Spirit. The Holy Spirit teaches human beings truth:

"But the Advocate [margin: Or *Helper*], the Holy Spirit, whom the Father will send in my name, will teach you everything, and remind you of all that I have said to you." (John 14:26 *NRSV*)

If a person can understand Bible truth, then the Holy Spirit is dealing with that person.

The Holy Spirit testifies on Jesus' behalf:

"When the Advocate [margin: Or *Helper*] comes, whom I will send to you from the Father, the Spirit of truth who comes from the Father, he will testify on my behalf." (John 15:26 *NRSV*)

The Holy Spirit reveals prophecy:

"When the Spirit of truth comes, he will guide you into all the truth; for he will not speak on his own, but will speak whatever he hears, and he will declare to you the things that are to come." (John 16:13 *NRSV*)

13. The Holy Spirit can flow through a human being's heart like rivers of water:

"On the last day of the festival, the great day, while Jesus was standing there, he cried out, 'Let anyone who is thirsty come to me, and let the one who believes in me drink. As the scripture has said, "Out of the believer's heart [margin: Gk *out of his belly*] shall flow rivers of living water."' Now he said this about the Spirit, which believers in him were to receive; for as yet there was no Spirit [margin: Other ancient authorities read *for as yet the Spirit* (others, *Holy Spirit*) *had not been given*], because Jesus was not yet glorified." (John 7:37-39 *NRSV*)

Amazing! Jesus said that through him "rivers of living water" -- the Holy Spirit

-- can flow through all human beings!

14.   The Holy Spirit not only *powers* Christians to do good, but also *motivates*
Christians to do good:
>   "for it is God who is at work in you, enabling you both to will and to work for
>   his good pleasure." (Philippians 2:13 *NRSV*)

The Holy Spirit gives Christians the motivation ("to will") to do good *and* the power
("to work") to do good. Therefore if any Christian does good, then all honor and
glory goes to God for this because God gives Christians both the motivation and
power to do good by the Holy Spirit. No Christian can take personal credit for any
good performed by him or her. All glory properly goes to God.

15.   Christians live by the Holy Spirit, as is explained in Romans 8:
>   "...those who live in accordance with the Spirit have their minds set on
>   what the Spirit desires." (Romans 8:5 *NIV*)

>   "...the mind controlled by the Spirit is life and peace;" (Romans 8:6 *NIV*)

>   "If the Spirit of him who raised Jesus from the dead dwells in you, he who
>   raised Christ from the dead will give life to your mortal bodies also through
>   his Spirit that dwells in you." (Romans 8:11 *NRSV*)

16.   Paul explains that a non-Christian -- a person *without* the Holy Spirit -- has
a life characterized by "acts of the sinful nature":
>   "The acts of the sinful nature are obvious: sexual immorality,
>   impurity and debauchery; idolatry and witchcraft; hatred, discord,
>   jealousy, fits of rage, selfish ambition, dissensions, factions and envy;
>   drunkenness, orgies, and the like..." (Galatians 5:19-21 *NIV*)

However, if a person is a Christian (*has* the Holy Spirit), then the fruits of the Holy
Spirit will be visible in his or her life:
>   "By contrast, the fruit of the Spirit is love, joy, peace, patience,
>   kindness, generosity, faithfulness, gentleness, and self-control..."
>   (**Galatians 5:22-23** *NRSV*)

The fruits or behaviors of a person demonstrate whether or not that person has
the Holy Spirit.

Summary. 1. It is easy to prove that the Holy Spirit is *not* a person and is *not* God.
If the Holy Spirit was a person, a God, then the Holy Spirit would have been the
father of Jesus, and Jesus would have been called "Son of the Holy Spirit."
Therefore if the Holy Spirit was an entity and a God it would be a bird God. A
person cannot be in millions of Christians simultaneously. The Holy Spirit is the
power of God. 2. The Holy Spirit recreated Earth. 3. Throughout the Old
Testament the Holy Spirit was given to certain men (and women) for short time
periods in order to perform special acts for God. 4. The Holy Spirit was given to
Saul at different moments. 5. David's receiving the Holy Spirit is the first clear
instance in the Bible in which the Holy Spirit was given to a human being on a
continuing basis. 6. Jeremiah spoke of a New Covenant coming to all (twelve
tribes of) Israel. Jeremiah showed that this New Covenant would result in people
receiving the Holy Spirit. 7. Joel prophesied that the Holy Spirit would come at

the time of the "day of the LORD." 8. On the day of Pentecost recorded in Acts 2, the Holy Spirit was first given to human beings as New Covenant participants. 9. Possessing the Holy Spirit is the Bible definition of a Christian. 10. Blasphemy against the Holy Spirit is unforgivable. 11. Jesus prepared his disciples for the coming of the Holy Spirit. Jesus told the disciples that their main contact was going to change from himself to the Holy Spirit. 12. Jesus explained the functions of the Holy Spirit. The Holy Spirit teaches human beings truth. The Holy Spirit testifies on Jesus' behalf. The Holy Spirit reveals prophecy. 13. The Holy Spirit can flow through a human being's heart like rivers of water. 14. The Holy Spirit not only *powers* Christians to do good, but also *motivates* Christians to do good. 15. Christians live by the Holy Spirit, as is explained in Romans 8. 16. A non-Christian -- a person *without* the Holy Spirit -- has a life characterized by "acts of the sinful nature." If a person is a Christian (*has* the Holy Spirit), then the fruits of the Holy Spirit will be visible in his or her life. The fruits or behaviors of a person demonstrate whether or not that person has the Holy Spirit.

The Trinity

CHAPTER 18
© 2005, Robert M. Kelley

Look up all Scriptures in your own Bible. Read and/or write the Scriptures on paper. Writing Scriptures on paper slows down your mind and causes the Bible verses to be more deeply burned into your mind.

All Scripture is inspired and true. However, you cannot learn everything at once. Therefore, the two most important Scriptures on this subject are in **bold** type and the next four most important Scriptures on this subject are underlined.

Note that these chapters are related:
- 15   "God"
- 16   "Jesus Christ"
- 17   "The Holy Spirit"
- 18   "The Trinity"

If you study one, be sure to study the others.

----

1.   Many people believe in what is called "the Trinity." The Trinity is the belief that God is comprised of three persons: God the Father, God the Son (Jesus), and God the Holy Spirit. Belief in the Trinity is widespread. In fact, among all groups which call themselves Christian, the Trinity is probably the most widely held belief. However, this chapter 18 will show that the Trinity *cannot* be found in the Bible. In fact, the Trinity is probably the greatest fairy tale, fantasy, and falsehood ever perpetuated upon organized Christianity. How did this incredible situation come about? The history of the Trinity is fascinating.

2.   The Trinity originally began with Constantine, emperor of the Roman Empire. Constantine was an interesting person.
At the beginning of his reign he claimed to be a Christian. However, his claiming Christian status didn't seem to affect his lifestyle. Constantine was a life-long worshiper of Sol Invictus, the sun god. He built temples to the sun god during his life, and left resources to have a Sol Invictus temple built after his death. He ordered hundreds of Frankish rebel prisoners to be slaughtered in an arena. He murdered his wife by having her boiled alive in a bathtub. He murdered an innocent son. Constantine claimed to be the thirteenth original apostle.
However, Constantine was a shrewd politician. He saw the political value of combining government and religion. By combining both he would become an even more powerful ruler.
So Constantine and the Roman Empire officially embraced Christianity.
However, Constantine saw a conflict among his Christian subjects. Antioch Christians believed that there was one God and that Jesus was born of Mary to become the Messiah. Alexandria Christians believed that Jesus was always God, and came to Earth as a god-human. Thus Alexandria Christians believed in two

97

Gods. The majority of Christians held the Antioch view; the minority of Christians held the Alexandria view. Constantine wanted no theological conflict in his now "Christian" Roman Empire.

3.   <u>Constantine convened the Council of Nicea in 325 AD</u>. Constantine was determined to settle this conflict by convening this council. The Council of Nicea was to become the most influential ecumenical council ever convened in the history of the Christian Church.

Constantine was essentially a Bible illiterate. However, he and the bishops listened to both sides of the question. It is important to consider the cultural background of each side. Antioch Christians came from an Israelite background. The Israelites always believed in one God. Alexandria Christians came from a Greek background. The Greeks always believed in many gods (polytheism); they also believed that a god can become a man and that a man can become a god. The majority of bishops chose the minority view, that of the Alexandria Christians. <u>Constantine forced attendees to sign a document which said that they believed in two Gods (God the Father and God the Son)</u>. He had all documents supporting the losing side destroyed.

Using the muscle of the Roman Empire, Constantine forced all Christians to accept the two-God view. Those who clung to the one-God view were banished from the Roman Empire.

4.   <u>The Trinity became complete about a hundred years later when a third god was added</u>. As Greek thinking continued to dominate the organized Christian Church, a third god was added. It was claimed that the Holy Spirit was a person and God. The Trinity -- three persons and three Gods -- was complete.

Compliance with belief in the Trinity was demanded by the Roman Empire and organized Christianity. Non-believers in the Trinity were persecuted. Over the years hundreds of thousands and perhaps even millions of Christians who believed in one God were executed (often by slow torture methods).

5.   <u>The Trinity is confusing</u>. <u>A large part of the confusion is caused by two underlying falsehoods</u>: (a) <u>One is three, and three is one</u>. (b) <u>A being can be both man and God</u>.

Little children are taught to count: one, two, three. Even little children learn that one is one, two is two, and three is three. However, in the Trinity this simple arithmetic logic is *wrong*. In the Trinity one is three, and three is one. However, in arithmetic, life, and the Bible one is *not* three, and three is *not* one. Imagine a man explaining that the three women who live in his home as wives, with whom he regularly has sexual intercourse, are actually "one wife"! When exposed to logic, the claim of the Trinity that "one is three, and three is one" is exposed for what it is: illogical, impossible, and *false*!

A being is either human or God. No being can be both. It's just that simple and profound. A human being feels pain, is constantly tempted, and can and will die. God knows no pain, cannot be tempted, and has and always has had eternal life. God has always existed. Jesus Christ did not exist until conceived in and born of the virgin Mary. Jesus knew pain, was tempted, and did die. Jesus was resurrected by God as an eternal, spiritual being. Jesus is the long prophesied Messiah.

The Trinity is confusing. One must "park his or her brain at the door" to believe it. <u>When confronted by logic, many believers in the Trinity cop-out with a comment such as: "The Trinity is just too mysterious to understand!" Truth from God is *never* confusing; it is always clear, pure, and sweet.</u> As Jesus said:

> "And ye shall know the truth, and the truth shall make you free."
> (<u>John 8:32</u> *KJV*)

6. <u>The Trinity is like a cancer which has infected the organized Christian church</u>. This cancer entered the Christian body early (325 AD). This cancer has metastasized and spread throughout most of the Christian body. Many Christians have been infected with this cancer. <u>Identifying this cancer and rooting it out takes much time and effort.</u>

7. <u>Most supporters of the Trinity claim that one verse in particular is the foundation verse proving the Trinity: I John 5:7.</u>

> "For there are three that bear record in heaven, the Father, the Word, and the Holy Ghost: and these three are one." (**I John 5:7** *KJV*)

Sound good? There's just one problem: <u>I John 5:7 is totally *bogus*. This verse is *not* part of the Bible.</u>

This verse does not appear in any Greek manuscript earlier than the fourteenth century. It does not appear in Jerome's original *Vulgate* translation.

How did this bogus verse get into the *King James Version*? When Erasmus published his first *Greek New Testament* in 1516 AD, he wisely left out this verse. However, since the Trinity began in 325 AD, many people already believed in the Trinity and wanted to see it in the Bible. Erasmus was criticized for leaving it out. Erasmus replied that he would put I John 5:7 in his next *Greek New Testament* edition if anyone could show him even *one* Greek manuscript which contained it. Someone *did* show him a late, poor quality Greek text which contained it. Erasmus kept his word and did include I John 5:7 in his 1522 AD edition. When Stephanus printed his *Received Text* in 1550 AD he included this verse. The *King James Version* translators worked from the *Received Text*.

The *English Revised Version* (British, 1885) and essentially all modern translations *omit* this bogus verse.

8. As can be seen from studying chapters 15-17, <u>there is abundant Bible proof that the Old Testament, Jesus himself, the original twelve apostles, and the apostle Paul all consistently state that there is *one* God. The Bible verses quoted in chapters 15-17 are *totally sufficient* to show that the Trinity is a total fraud.</u>

9. <u>However, some people believe in the "Loose Brick Theory."</u> This is the Loose Brick Theory: (a) The many verses substantiating a Bible truth can be represented as bricks in a wall. (b) There are many bricks; each brick is a verse. (c) If a person can find just *one* fuzzy verse (one loose brick) which *appears* to go against the many plain verses, then the entire brick wall (the Bible truth) will fall.

However, the Loose Brick Theory is false: One fuzzy verse can *never* stand against even one plain, clear verse. However, since many people *believe* in the Loose Brick Theory, this chapter 18 will continue. Some "gray" (fuzzy) verses will be examined.

10.   There are some Bible verses which *appear* to imply that Jesus was pre-existent. (Pre-existent means that Jesus existed *before* he was born of Mary. The term "pre-existent" is another way of saying that Jesus was God.)

There are two causes behind such verses: (a) God states that something exists before it does. (b) Since the Trinity has been around since 325 AD and most Bible translators have believed in the Trinity, this belief has caused them to translate in a way which implies that the Trinity is true.

11.   God states that something exists before it does. God does this because that is His nature. Once God has decided to do something He speaks as though it is already done. This practice is God's nature.

Paul mentioned this practice of God:

> "(As it is written, I have made thee a father of many nations,) before him whom he believed, even God, who quickeneth the dead, and calleth those things which be not as though they were." (**Romans 4:17** *KJV*)

God called Abraham "a father of many nations" when in fact he was not yet. Paul explains that God "calleth those things which be not as though they were."

Note carefully this Bible verse:

> "And all that dwell upon the earth shall worship him, whose names are not written in the book of life of the Lamb slain from the foundation of the world." (Revelation 13:8 *KJV*)

Jesus Christ is the "Lamb" mentioned in this verse. Was Jesus slain "from the foundation of the world"? Jesus was slain about 33 AD. He was *not* slain when the foundation of the world was made. So, what is the meaning of this part of this verse?

This is the meaning. God (the one and only God) decided from the foundation of the world that the Lamb would be slain. Thousands of years later Jesus was born, who then fulfilled the role of the Lamb. When God makes a decision, in His mind the act is *already* carried out, whether or not the act has been carried out in this physical world.

Note this Bible verse from Jesus:

> "And no man hath ascended up to heaven, but he that came down from heaven, even the Son of man which is in heaven." (John 3:13 *KJV*)

Had Jesus "ascended up to heaven" early in his earthly ministry? Jesus did *not* ascend up to heaven until after his crucifixion. Jesus spoke of a future event as if it had already occurred.

There are many verses in the Bible which reflect this aspect of God's thinking. This chapter 18 is intentionally brief. Many examples of this aspect of God's thinking are included in Buzzard & Hunting's book, mentioned below.

12.   Since the Trinity has been around since 325 AD and most Bible

translators have believed in the Trinity, this belief has caused them to translate in a way which implies that the Trinity is true.

Note these popular Bible verses:

"In the beginning was the Word, and the Word was with God, and the Word was God.

And the Word was made flesh, and dwelt among us, (and we beheld his glory, the glory as of the only begotten of the Father,) full of grace and truth." (John 1:1, 14 *KJV*)

Boy, if there were ever two verses which "proved" Jesus' pre-existence, these are them! Sounds good, doesn't it?

However, the translators have *not* been faithful to the original Bible text. In the original in Aramaic (and probably in most Greek translations), the word from which "Word" is translated is *not* capitalized. The Greek word from which "Word" is translated is *logos.*

This is the correct explanation of John 1:1, 14. In the beginning was the logos. The logos was a concept, an idea invented by God (the one God). Logos was not a person. The logos concept was fulfilled in the conception and birth of Jesus. The person, Jesus, fulfilled the concept of logos. Jesus, the human being, became the logos or spokesman for God. Jesus revealed God (the one God) to mankind.

William Tyndale, the famous translator of the English Bible, clearly understood the correct explanation of John 1:1, 14. Tyndale translated:

"In the beginning was the word..." (John 1:1 *Tyndale*)

Note that Tyndale did *not* capitalize "word." In describing the "word" Tyndale uses the pronoun "it" in his translation. Unlike most Bible translators, Tyndale was *faithful* to the original.

Because most Bible translators believe in the Trinity they translate John 1:1, 14 to make the translation conform to their pre-existent belief. The only pre-existence which exists is the pre-existent belief in the Trinity in the minds of most Bible translators!

There are many examples of where Bible translators have used their pre-existent belief in the Trinity to deviate from the inspired original Bible languages. This chapter 18 is intentionally brief. Many examples of pre-existent belief in the Trinity affecting Bible translation are included in Buzzard & Hunting's book, mentioned below.

13.   An excellent book which goes into a lot of detail on the Trinity is *The Doctrine of the Trinity: Christianity's Self-Inflicted Wound*, by Anthony F. Buzzard and Charles F. Hunting, © 1998, published by International Scholars Publications, 4720 Boston Way, Lanham, Maryland 20706, ISBN 1-57309-309-2 (paperback). This chapter 18 is only a brief exposure of the Trinity. Buzzard & Hunting's book is 365 pages in size. It goes into great detail on this exciting subject. This book can be ordered from Atlanta Bible College, 800-347-4261.

Summary. 1. Many people believe in what is called the Trinity. The Trinity is probably the greatest fairy tale, fantasy, and falsehood ever perpetuated upon organized Christianity. 2. The Trinity originally began with Constantine, emperor of the Roman Empire. 3. Constantine convened the Council of Nicea in

325 AD. Constantine forced attendees to sign a document which said that they believed in two Gods (God the Father and God the Son). 4. The Trinity became complete about a hundred years later when a third god was added. 5. The Trinity is confusing. A large part of the confusion is caused by two underlying falsehoods: (a) One is three, and three is one. (b) A being can be both man and God. When confronted by logic, many believers in the Trinity cop-out with a comment such as: "The Trinity is just too mysterious to understand!" Truth from God is *never* confusing; it is always clear, pure, and sweet. 6. The Trinity is like a cancer which has infected the organized Christian church. Identifying this cancer and rooting it out takes much time and effort. 7. Most supporters of the Trinity claim that one verse in particular is the foundation verse proving the Trinity: I John 5:7. I John 5:7 is totally *bogus*. This verse is *not* part of the Bible. 8. There is abundant Bible proof that the Old Testament, Jesus himself, the original twelve apostles, and the apostle Paul all consistently state that there is *one* God. The Bible verses quoted in chapters 15-17 are *totally sufficient* to show that the Trinity is a total fraud. 9. However, some people believe in the "Loose Brick Theory." The Loose Brick Theory is false: One fuzzy verse can *never* stand against even one plain, clear verse. However, since many people *believe* in the Loose Brick Theory, this chapter 18 will continue. Some "gray" (fuzzy) verses will be examined. 10. There are some Bible verses which *appear* to imply that Jesus was pre-existent. (Pre-existent means that Jesus existed *before* he was born of Mary. The term "pre-existent" is another way of saying that Jesus was God.) 11. God states that something exists before it does. 12. Since the Trinity has been around since 325 AD and most Bible translators have believed in the Trinity, this belief has caused them to translate in a way which implies that the Trinity is true. The only pre-existence which exists is the pre-existent belief in the Trinity in the minds of most Bible translators! 13. An excellent book which goes into a lot of detail on the Trinity is *The Doctrine of the Trinity: Christianity's Self-Inflicted Wound*.

Angels

CHAPTER 19

© 2005, Robert M. Kelley

Look up all Scriptures in your own Bible. Read and/or write the Scriptures on paper. Writing Scriptures on paper slows down your mind and causes the Bible verses to be more deeply burned into your mind.

All Scripture is inspired and true. However, you cannot learn everything at once. Therefore, the three most important Scriptures on this subject are in **bold** type and the next seven most important Scriptures on this subject are underlined.

----

1.   People are fascinated by angels. It seems that in these last days, shortly before the return of Jesus Christ in power and glory, there is a great interest in non-human beings. Major entertainment media -- TV and movies -- are filled with stories of angels, demons, ghosts, poltergeists, and space aliens.

2.   The Bible reveals the existence of four categories of beings and creatures: (a) God, (b) angels, (c) humans, and (d) animals. (To learn more about God, see chapter 15, "God.") Angels are spirit beings. Angels are both good (called angels and have allegiance to God) and bad (called demons and do not have allegiance to God). This chapter 19 covers angels. (To learn more about demons, see chapter 20, "Satan and Demons.") Humans are made of flesh and are temporary beings. All humans end up either as resurrected, spirit beings or as ashes after being burned to death in the Lake of Fire (the Second Death). Animals are made of flesh and are temporary creatures. There is no future life or eternal life for animals.

3.   Successful Christians, with resurrected, spirit bodies, will judge angels:
"Do you not know that we are to judge angels -- to say nothing of ordinary matters?" (**I Corinthians 6:3** *NRSV*)
Successful Christians will be resurrected with eternal, spirit bodies. One of the jobs of eternal, spirit-body Christians will be to judge angels.

4.   Angels are servants of God:
"Of the angels he says,
    'He makes his angels winds,
      and his servants flames of fire.'"
(**Hebrews 1:7** *NRSV*: Paul quotes from Psalm 104:4)
Angels perform work for God. Angels serve in the Kingdom of God and help carry out God's Master Plan.

5.   The Bible gives glimpses of the Third Heaven, where God lives. In these descriptions are angelic beings and creatures. The book of Revelation gives several of these glimpses. Here is one:

"After this I looked, and there in heaven a door stood open! And the first voice, which I had heard speaking to me like a trumpet, said, 'Come up here, and I will show you what must take place after this.' At once I was in the spirit [margin: Or *in the Spirit*], and there in heaven stood a throne, with one seated on the throne! And the one seated there looks like jasper and carnelian, and around the throne is a rainbow that looks like an emerald. Around the throne are twenty-four thrones, and seated on the thrones are twenty-four elders, dressed in white robes, with golden crowns on their heads. Coming from the throne are flashes of lightning, and rumblings and peals of thunder, and in front of the throne burn seven flaming torches, which are the seven spirits of God; and in front of the throne there is something like a sea of glass, like crystal.

Around the throne, and on each side of the throne, are four living creatures, full of eyes in front and behind: the first living creature like a lion, the second living creature like an ox, the third living creature with a face like a human face, and the fourth living creature like a flying eagle. And the four living creatures, each of them with six wings, are full of eyes all around and inside. Day and night without ceasing they sing,
'Holy, holy, holy,
the Lord God the Almighty,
 who was and is and is to come,'
And whenever the living creatures give glory and honor and thanks to the one who is seated on the throne, who lives forever and ever, the twenty-four elders fall before the one who is seated on the throne and worship the one who lives forever and ever; they cast their crowns before the throne, singing,
'You are worthy, our Lord and God,
 to receive glory and honor and power,
for you created all things,
 and by your will they existed and were created.'"
(Revelation 4:1-11 (entire chapter) *NRSV*)

The Third Heaven glimpse in Revelation 4 describes special angelic beings and creatures: twenty-four elders and four living creatures. Other angelic beings described in Revelation include cherubim and seraphim. (Cherub is singular; cherubim is plural. Seraph is singular; seraphim is plural.) These beings and creatures are all angelic. These angelic creatures are different from any physical life forms found on Earth. However, from the physical creation on Earth it is known that anything God creates is complete and beautiful. Therefore, even though humans (except for John and a few others) have not seen these angelic creatures, it is known by physical proof and faith that they must be beautiful.

6.   In chapter 1 of the book of Ezekiel a kind of spiritual "space vehicle" is described. This space vehicle is apparently used to transport God. This vehicle is composed of spiritual creatures (called "living creatures") which are apparently angelic in nature. Ezekiel 1 and the book of Revelation show that there is great variety in angelic beings.

7.   <u>Angels are spirit beings</u>. <u>There are no examples in the Bible of spirit beings dying</u>. <u>Therefore angels, being spirit beings, cannot die and are essentially eternal</u>. (See chapter 20, "Satan and Demons," where the fate of Satan and demons is described.)

8.   <u>God often sends angels to give messages about God's Master Plan</u>:
>   "The LORD appeared to Abraham by the oaks [margin: Or *terebinths*] of Mamre, as he sat at the entrance of his tent in the heat of the day. He looked up and saw three men standing near him..."
>   (<u>Genesis 18:1-2</u> *NRSV*)

Chapter 18 of Genesis records the visit to Abraham of "the LORD" and two angels. The LORD and the two angels had a mission -- investigating conditions in Sodom and Gomorrah -- which was unrelated to Abraham. Yet the LORD decided to tell Abraham about the situation.
>   "Now the angel of the LORD went up from Gilgal to Bochim, and said..." (Judges 2:1 *NRSV*)

In this situation God sent an angel to deliver a message to the twelve tribes of Israel.
>   "while I was speaking in prayer, the man Gabriel, whom I had seen before in a vision, came to me in swift flight at the time of the evening sacrifice."
>   (<u>Daniel 9:21</u> *NRSV*)

Chapter 9 of Daniel records God sending the great angel Gabriel to deliver a message of prophetic understanding to Daniel.

9.   <u>God often sends angels to speak to parents of offspring who are to have important missions in God's Master Plan</u>:
>   "And the angel of the LORD appeared to the woman and said to her..."
>   (Judges 13:3 *NRSV*)

Chapter 13 of Judges records God sending an angel to tell the future parents of Samson about the son they would have and his mission in God's Master Plan.
>   "Then there appeared to him an angel of the Lord, standing at the right side of the altar of incense." (Luke 1:11 *NRSV*)

An angel came to Zechariah to tell him that his wife, Elizabeth, would give birth to a baby who would become John the Baptist.
>   "The angel replied, 'I am Gabriel. I stand in the presence of God, and I have been sent to speak to you and to bring you this good news."
>   (<u>Luke 1:19</u> *NRSV*)

Gabriel is a powerful angel.
>   "In the sixth month the angel Gabriel was sent by God to a town in Galilee called Nazareth, to a virgin engaged to a man whose name was Joseph, of the house of David. The virgin's name was Mary."
>   (<u>Luke 1:26-27</u> *NRSV*)

God sent the angel Gabriel to Mary.

10.   <u>God sometimes sends angels to save people's lives</u>:
>   "The two angels came to Sodom in the evening, and Lot was sitting in the gateway of Sodom..." (Genesis 19:1 *NRSV*)

Most of chapter 19 of Genesis records the two angels' mission to remove Lot and his family out of Sodom before God destroyed it.

> "But during the night an angel of the Lord opened the prison doors, brought them out, and said," (<u>Acts 5:19</u> *NRSV*)

God sent an angel to let the twelve apostles out of prison.

> "Suddenly an angel of the Lord appeared and a light shone in the cell..." (<u>Acts 12:7</u> *NRSV*)

Chapter 12 of Acts records how God sent an angel to lead Peter out of prison.

11. <u>Humans are warned never to worship angels</u>:

> "Then I fell down at his feet to worship him, but he said to me, 'You must not do that! I am a fellow servant [margin: Gk *slave*] with you and your comrades [margin: Gk *brothers*] who hold the testimony of Jesus. Worship God!...'" (**Revelation 19:10** *NRSV*)

<u>Summary</u>. 1. People are fascinated by angels. 2. The Bible reveals the existence of four categories of beings and creatures: (a) God, (b) angels, (c) humans, and (d) animals. 3. Successful Christians, with resurrected, spirit bodies, will judge angels. 4. Angels are servants of God. 5. The Third Heaven glimpse in Revelation 4 describes special angelic beings and creatures: twenty-four elders and four living creatures. Other angelic beings described in Revelation include cherubim and seraphim. 6. Ezekiel 1 and the book of Revelation show that there is great variety in angelic beings. 7. Angels are spirit beings. There are no examples in the Bible of spirit beings dying. Therefore angels, being spirit beings, cannot die and are essentially eternal. 8. God often sends angels to give messages about God's Master Plan. 9. God often sends angels to speak to parents of offspring who are to have important missions in God's Master Plan. 10. God sometimes sends angels to save people's lives. 11. Humans are warned never to worship angels.

Satan and Demons

CHAPTER 20

© 2005, Robert M. Kelley

Look up all Scriptures in your own Bible. Read and/or write the Scriptures on paper. Writing Scriptures on paper slows down your mind and causes the Bible verses to be more deeply burned into your mind.

All Scripture is inspired and true. However, you cannot learn everything at once. Therefore, the three most important Scriptures on this subject are in **bold** type and the next seven most important Scriptures on this subject are underlined.

---

1.   There is a Devil. His name is Satan or Satan the Devil. Satan was an angel (actually a cherub, which is a high-ranking angel). Satan convinced other, lower-ranking angels to join him in a rebellion against God. These other rebellious angels were called, after the rebellion, demons. Satan and his demons have been and are very active in this world of God's Master Plan Period One.

2.   Satan and his demons are real. However, some people do not believe that Satan and demons exist. These people have succumbed to Satan's greatest deception of all: convincing humans that he does not exist. (It will be seen later that Satan is a master of deception.) The existence of Satan and demons is known because God, in the Bible, clearly shows that he and they do exist! This chapter 20 shows what the Bible says about Satan and demons.

3.   Two Bible passages give a lot of information about Satan. These two passages appear inserted in prophecies directed to two kings. The first passage is addressed to the king of Babylon. In the middle of this passage these verses, specific to Satan, appear:
> "How you are fallen from heaven,
>   O Day Star, son of Dawn!
> How you are cut down to the ground,
>   you who laid the nations low!
> You said in your heart,
>   'I will ascend to heaven;
> I will raise my throne
>   above the stars of God;
> I will sit on the mount of assembly
>   on the heights of Zaphon [margin: Or *assembly in the far north*];
> I will ascend to the tops of the clouds,
>   I will make myself like the Most High.'
> But you are brought down to Sheol,
>   to the depths of the Pit." (Isaiah 14:12-15 *NRSV*)

4.   <u>The second passage is addressed to the king of Tyre</u>. In the middle of this passage these verses, specific to Satan, appear:

> "...'You were the model of perfection,
>   full of wisdom and perfect in beauty.
> You were in Eden,
>   the garden of God;
> every precious stone adorned you:
>   ruby, topaz and emerald, chrysolite, onyx and jasper, sapphire [margin:
>   Or *lapis lazuli*], turquoise and beryl [margin: The precise identification of
>   some of these precious stones is uncertain.].
> Your settings and mountings were made of gold;
>   on the day you were created they were prepared.
> You were anointed as a guardian cherub,
>   for so I ordained you.
> You were on the holy mount of God;
>   you walked among the fiery stones.
> You were blameless in your ways
>   from the day you were created
>   till wickedness was found in you.
> Through your widespread trade
>   you were filled with violence,
>   and you sinned.
> So I drove you in disgrace from the mount of God,
>   and I expelled you, O guardian cherub,
>   from among the fiery stones.
> Your heart became proud
>   on account of your beauty,
> and you corrupted your wisdom
>   because of your splendor.
> So I threw you to the earth;
>   I made a spectacle of you before kings." (**Ezekiel 28:12-17** *NIV*)

5.   How does one know that the above two Bible passages describe Satan the Devil and not two earthly kings? Consider the facts revealed:
(a) The being concerned is called (in Isaiah 14:12 *NRSV*) "O Day Star, son of Dawn." The Bible shows that the word "star" is often used for an angel:

> "...the seven stars are the angels of the seven churches..."
> (Revelation 1:20 *NRSV*)

In the Bible the word "star" is *never* used for a human being.
(b) The being concerned fell from heaven ("you are fallen from heaven," Isaiah 14:12 *NRSV*) and was thrown to Earth ("I threw you to the earth," Ezekiel 28:17 *NIV*). (Note: Additional Scriptures below show Satan and his demons being thrown out of the Third Heaven to Earth.)
(c) The being concerned was in the Garden of Eden ("You were in Eden, the garden of God," Ezekiel 28:13 *NIV*). If one examines the story of the Garden of Eden in the early chapters of Genesis, one can see that only three personages on Earth are mentioned: Adam, Eve, and Satan (the serpent).

(d) The being concerned is called a "guardian cherub" (Ezekiel 28:14, 16 *NIV*). There are very few cherubim. There are only two guardian cherubim. The Holy of Holies was the center of the tabernacle which Moses constructed in the wilderness. In the Holy of Holies two covering cherubim spread their (gold) wings over the Mercy Seat. Moses described the gold cherubim:

> "You shall make two cherubim of gold; you shall make them of hammered work, at the two ends of the mercy seat. Make one cherub at the one end, and one cherub at the other; of one piece with the mercy seat you shall make the cherubim at its two ends. The cherubim shall spread out their wings above, overshadowing the mercy seat with their wings. They shall face one to another; the faces of the cherubim shall be turned toward the mercy seat." (Exodus 25:18-20 *NRSV*)

The Holy of Holies portion of the Tabernacle represented the throne of God in the Third Heaven. The being described in Ezekiel 28 was one of the two cherubim which hovered over the very throne of God in the Third Heaven!

(e) The being concerned was a "model of perfection" and "full of wisdom and perfect in beauty" (Ezekiel 28:12 *NIV*). No human being who ever lived can be described with these phrases.

Note carefully the five facts which have been established. The being concerned: (a) is called a star, (b) fell from the Third Heaven, (c) was in the Garden of Eden, (d) is called a "guardian cherub," and (e) was a perfection model with perfect beauty. These five facts clearly show that the being discussed in Isaiah 14:12-15 and Ezekiel 28:12-17 is Satan the Devil. Additional facts, which will be given, confirm this conclusion.

6.   Satan is a created being. Ezekiel 28:13 shows that Satan was created. God created Satan. Satan's name, in Isaiah 14:12 (*NRSV*), is given as "O Day Star." This same verse in the *King James Version* (*KJV*) gives Satan's name as "O Lucifer," with the marginal reference of "*O day star.*" Lucifer was Satan's original name. Lucifer (from the Hebrew) means "day star" or "morning star."

7.   Satan or Lucifer (as he was originally named), as created, was a fabulous being. Lucifer was a "model of perfection" and "full of wisdom and perfect in beauty" (Ezekiel 28:12 *NIV*). Lucifer was "anointed as a guardian cherub" (Ezekiel 28:14 *NIV*). Lucifer was (same verse) "on the holy mount of God" (the headquarters of the Kingdom of God or the Third Heaven). Lucifer was in the Garden of Eden (Ezekiel 28:13 *NIV*). Lucifer was created as a very high-level spirit being in the Kingdom of God. He dwelt with God in the Third Heaven. Lucifer was a honcho!

8.   However, one day Lucifer rebelled against God. This rebellion is described in several places in the Bible.

> "Then another portent appeared in heaven: a great red dragon, with seven heads and ten horns, and seven diadems on his heads. His tail swept down a third of the stars of heaven and threw them to the earth..." (Revelation 12:3-4 *NRSV*)

> "And war broke out in heaven; Michael and his angels fought

against the dragon. The dragon and his angels fought back, but they were defeated, and there was no longer any place for them in heaven. The great dragon was thrown down, that ancient serpent, who is called the Devil and Satan, the deceiver of the whole world -- he was thrown down to the earth, and his angels were thrown down with him." (Revelation 12:7-9 NRSV)

Lucifer decided to attack God. Note that "His tail swept down a third of the stars." As was seen earlier, the word "stars" often refers to angels. Lucifer convinced one-third of the angels to rebel with him. God let the angels fight for Him. Michael, a great archangel, led God's angelic forces. In this huge battle Lucifer's side, with one-third of the angels, lost. Michael, with two-thirds of the angels, won. Satan was cast to Earth with his angels.

The two main Bible passages above tell a lot about Lucifer's rebellion. Isaiah 14:12-15 explains how Lucifer plotted the rebellion. Ezekiel 28:12-17 explains how Lucifer was blameless until wickedness was found in him.

9.   God explains the reason for Lucifer's rebellion:
       "Your heart became proud
         on account of your beauty,
       and you corrupted your wisdom
         because of your splendor..." (Ezekiel 28:17 NIV)

God shows here the most common reason for pride, which can cause angels or humans to rebel against God. It is easy to attribute God's gifts to ourselves instead of thanking God for His gifts. Everything good comes from God. Lucifer received his beauty, wisdom, and splendor from God. Yet Lucifer attributed these qualities to himself. Lucifer perverted his thinking. Perverted thinking led Lucifer to entertain thoughts of rebellion against God and the Kingdom of God. (For more information on this kind of perverted thinking, see chapter 30, "The Greatest Sin.")

10.   Before the rebellion, Lucifer had a name which reflected the beauty with which God created him: "day star" or "morning star." After the rebellion God changed Lucifer's name to Satan. If one checks a dictionary one can see that "Satan" comes from the Hebrew and means "devil, adversary, or accuser." The angels who sided with Lucifer were, after the rebellion, called demons.

11.   Satan is nasty. Jesus Christ, when he was on Earth, described Satan's character:
       "Ye are of your father the devil, and the lusts of your father ye will do. He was a murderer from the beginning, and abode not in the truth, because there is no truth in him. When he speaketh a lie, he speaketh of his own: for he is a liar, and the father of it." (**John 8:44** KJV)

Jesus said that Satan is a murderer and a liar. Satan is evil. Satan follows no rules. Satan fights dirty.

12.   Satan's nature is to counterfeit things of God:
       "For such are false apostles, deceitful workers, transforming themselves into the apostles of Christ.

And no marvel; for Satan himself is transformed into an angel of light. Therefore it is no great thing if his ministers also be transformed as the ministers of righteousness; whose end shall be according to their works." (II Corinthians 11:13-15 *KJV*)

Here Paul says that Satan has ministers and that these ministers "are false apostles" who transform themselves "as the ministers of righteousness." There are many organizations, movies, books, etc., which *appear* to be of God. However, when one examines them carefully and compares them to the Word of God -- the Bible -- one discovers that some are actually of *Satan*! In this Period One of God's Master plan Satan has many *counterfeits* in this world.

13.   <u>Satan and his demons rule this world</u>. The details are contained in chapter 21, "This is Satan's World." God allows Satan's rule over Earth in God's Master Plan Period One.

14.   <u>When Jesus walked Earth as a human being (his first coming) he encountered both Satan and demons</u>. Jesus fought battles with Satan before he began his ministry. (For more information on these battles, see chapter 21, "This is Satan's World.") During his ministry Jesus and others cast out demons from people's minds. Demon possession is a common cause of some mental illness. Demon possession was common in Jesus' day; it is common today. The power of God is greater than that of Satan. Mark tells about Jesus casting demons out of people:

> "They came to the other side of the sea, to the country of the Gerasenes. And when he had stepped out of the boat, immediately a man out of the tombs with an unclean spirit met him. He lived among the tombs; and no one could restrain him any more, even with a chain; for he had often been restrained with shackles and chains, but the chains he wrenched apart, and the shackles he broke in pieces; and no one had the strength to subdue him. Night and day among the tombs and on the mountains he was always howling and bruising himself with stones. When he saw Jesus from a distance, he ran and bowed down before him; and he shouted at the top of his voice, 'What have you to do with me, Jesus, Son of the Most High God? I adjure you by God, do not torment me.' For he had said to him, 'Come out of the man, you unclean spirit!' Then Jesus asked him, 'What is your name?' He replied, 'My name is Legion; for we are many.' He begged him earnestly not to send them out of the country. Now there on the hillside a great herd of swine was feeding; and the unclean spirits begged him, 'Send us into the swine; let us enter them.' So he gave them permission. And the unclean spirits came out and entered the swine; and the herd, numbering about two thousand, rushed down the steep bank into the sea, and were drowned in the sea." (Mark 5:1-13 *NRSV*)

Luke adds this additional comment:

> "...For a long time he had worn no clothes, and he did not live in a house but in the tombs." (Luke 8:27 *NRSV*)

<u>From this single experience one can learn a lot about demons:</u>

(a) <u>Demons are powerful</u>. Not even chains and leg irons could restrain this naked man.

(b) <u>Demons are fascinated with death-related environments</u>. This demon-possessed man did not hang around malls (markets), used car lots (used camel lots), or horse race tracks (camel race tracks). These demons hung around tombs; dead people are buried in tombs. Ever wonder why many "horror" films, in which demonic activity is portrayed, are centered around death-related environments?

(c) <u>Demons which possess human beings cause them to exhibit strange behaviors</u>. Demons had this man running around naked, howling, and bruising himself.

(d) <u>Demons know the identity and status of anyone with the Holy Spirit</u>. Demons are spirits and know the identity of other spirits. The demons knew exactly who Jesus was. Demons know the identity of every Christian. (Only Christians have the Holy Spirit.)

(e) <u>Demons are afraid of anyone with the Holy Spirit</u>. Demons know where the power is. This demon-possessed man bowed in homage and recognized Jesus' possession of an unlimited amount of the Holy Spirit.

(f) <u>The eventual end of demons is to be tortured forever</u>. (This will be covered later.) Demons know this. However, they do not know *when* this time will come. In this instance they were essentially asking, "Is *this* the time?"

(g) <u>More than one demon can possess a human being</u>. Mary Magdalene had seven demons cast out of her (Luke 8:2). In this case, there must have been many demons to result in the demon-control of 2,000 head of swine.

15. <u>Satan is out to get people who seek God, but God has given people who seek Him power and protection from Satan and demons</u>. Jesus warned Peter:

> "And the Lord said, Simon, Simon, behold, Satan hath desired to have you, that he may sift you as wheat:
> But I have prayed for thee, that thy faith fail not: and when thou art converted, strengthen thy brethren." (Luke 22:31-32 *KJV*)

When Jesus was training his disciples he gave them power over demons, even though the twelve did *not*, at that time, have the Holy Spirit:

> "Then Jesus called the twelve together and gave them power and authority over all demons and to cure diseases," (Luke 9:1 *NRSV*)

Later the disciples *did* receive the Holy Spirit and thus became Christians on the day of Pentecost after Jesus' resurrection.

God protects people who seek Him from demons. The book of Job, chapters 1-2, records two different conversations between God and Satan. In the first conversation Satan is pointing out to God how God has protected Job:

> "Have you not put a fence around him and his house and all that he has, on every side?..." (Job 1:10 *NRSV*)

Satan described the protection which God gave to Job. People who seek God have no reason to fear demons. Demons have many reasons to fear people who seek God. Paul describes one of those possible reasons:

> "Do you not know that we are to judge angels -- to say nothing of ordinary matters?" (I Corinthians 6:3 *NRSV*)

Yes, some day successful Christians will judge angels. Whether these angels are good angels or fallen angels (demons) is not revealed.

In Ephesians 6 Paul explains how Christians war against Satan and his demons:
> "For we wrestle not against flesh and blood, but against principalities, against powers, against the rulers of the darkness of this world, against spiritual wickedness [margin: Or, *wicked spirits*] in high [margin: Or, *heavenly*] places." (Ephesians 6:12 *KJV*)

Paul explains how to put on the "whole armor of God" (Ephesians 6:11 *NRSV*) in order to fight Satan and demons.

For people who seek God and are bothered by demons, God has provided the ultimate defense:
> "...Resist the devil, and he will flee from you." (**James 4:7** *NRSV*)

16.   <u>The ultimate fate of Satan and demons is to be confined in a place of total blackness forever</u>. Jude tells about where demons will be cast:
> "...wandering stars, for whom the deepest darkness has been reserved forever." (<u>Jude 13</u> *NRSV*)

Peter discusses the hell where Satan and demons will be cast (which is different from the hell (Lake of Fire) where humans will be cast):
> "For if God did not spare the angels when they sinned, but cast them into hell [margin: Gk *Tartaros*] and committed them to chains [margin: Other ancient authorities read *pits*] of deepest darkness to be kept until the judgment;" (<u>II Peter 2:4</u> *NRSV*)

This verse has confused many:
> "And the devil who had deceived them was thrown into the lake of fire and sulfur, where the beast and the false prophet were, and they will be tormented day and night forever and ever." (Revelation 20:10 *NRSV*)

(The *KJV* rendering of Revelation 20:10 leaves out the word "they." Revelation 20:10 says that "the devil" is the one who "will be tormented day and night forever and ever.")

Note carefully that it is Satan and demons who are tormented forever. Satan and demons are *not* destroyed in the Lake of Fire. Human beings are immediately destroyed in the Lake of Fire (Second Death). Human beings will burn quickly. The Beast and the False Prophet "were" in the Lake of Fire because, being physical human beings, they burned quickly. The Bible nowhere says that human beings are tormented (by fire or any other means) forever. Satan and demons are made of spirit. They are *not* destroyed in the Lake of Fire. Satan and demons are confined in a totally black place where *they* are tormented forever. People are often confused because the Bible talks about *two* hells where punishment occurs. The Greek word *gehenna* refers to the Lake of Fire where human beings who are unsuccessful in the New Covenant are burned to death quickly, suffering the Second Death. The Greek word *tartaros* refers to the deep black place where Satan and his demons are tortured forever. (See chapter 24, "Hell.")

17.   <u>Satan has deceived man into believing that what happens to him happens to man</u>. Satan told Eve in the Garden of Eden that she would not die if she ate the forbidden fruit. However, Eve *did* die. *Satan* is the one who will not die. Satan has convinced man that men go to the Third Heaven after death. However,

human beings do *not* go to the Third Heaven after death. (See chapter 23, "Christians Do Not Go to Heaven After Death.") *Satan* is the one who went to the Third Heaven (and tried -- unsuccessfully -- to dethrone God). Satan has convinced man that Adam (and therefore mankind) "fell." *Satan* is the one who fell (from the Third Heaven). Satan has convinced man that those who are unsuccessful in the New Covenant burn forever in hell. However, human beings do *not* burn forever in hell. Human beings burn to death immediately in the Lake of Fire in the Second Death. (See chapter 11, "God's Master Plan: Period Two," and chapter 24, "Hell.") *Satan* is the one who will suffer forever (in his special hell).

Summary. 1. Satan and his demons have been and are very active in this world of God's Master Plan Period One. 2. This chapter 20 shows what the Bible says about Satan and demons. 3. Two Bible passages give a lot of information about Satan. The first passage is addressed to the king of Babylon. 4. The second passage is addressed to the king of Tyre. 5. Note carefully the five facts which have been established. The being concerned: (a) is called a star, (b) fell from heaven, (c) was in the Garden of Eden, (d) is called a "guardian cherub," and (e) was a perfection model with perfect beauty. These five facts clearly show that the being discussed in Isaiah 14:12-15 and Ezekiel 28:12-17 is Satan the Devil. 6. Satan is a created being. 7. Lucifer was created as a very high-level spirit being in the Kingdom of God. 8. However, one day Lucifer rebelled against God. 9. Perverted thinking led Lucifer to entertain thoughts of rebellion against God and the Kingdom of God. 10. After the rebellion God changed Lucifer's name to Satan. 11. Satan is nasty. 12. Satan's nature is to counterfeit things of God. 13. Satan and his demons rule this world. 14. When Jesus walked Earth as a human being (his first coming) he encountered both Satan and demons. From this single experience one can learn a lot about demons: (a) Demons are powerful. (b) Demons are fascinated with death-related environments. (c) Demons which possess human beings cause them to exhibit strange behaviors. (d) Demons know the identity and status of anyone with the Holy Spirit. (e) Demons are afraid of anyone with the Holy Spirit. (f) The eventual end of demons is to be tortured forever. (g) More than one demon can possess a human being. 15. Satan is out to get people who seek God, but God has given people who seek Him power and protection from Satan and demons. 16. The ultimate fate of Satan and demons is to be confined in a place of total blackness forever. 17. Satan has deceived man into believing that what happens to him happens to man.

This is Satan's World

CHAPTER 21
© 2005, Robert M. Kelley

Look up all Scriptures in your own Bible. Read and/or write the Scriptures on paper. Writing Scriptures on paper slows down your mind and causes the Bible verses to be more deeply burned into your mind.

All Scripture is inspired and true. However, you cannot learn everything at once. Therefore, the three most important Scriptures on this subject are in **bold** type and the next seven most important Scriptures on this subject are underlined.

----

1.   Many people believe that this world -- the world in which all human beings presently live -- is God's world. Consider the ramifications of the belief that this is God's world: God is in charge of what occurs on Earth. If something happens, it is because God *wanted* it to happen. All of the countless, mindless, spineless, tasteless, horrific, bizarre, unequal, unfair, unjust, rude and crude acts which have occurred on Earth were *willed* by God! The "this is God's world" belief blames everything bad on God. The purpose of this chapter 21 is to show what the Bible says. The Bible shows that this is Satan's world, not God's world.

2.   One of the great confrontations in the history of Earth was the temptation of Jesus Christ by Satan the Devil. This historic battle is described in Scripture:
> "Jesus, full of the Holy Spirit, returned from the Jordan and was led by the Spirit in the wilderness, where for forty days he was tempted by the devil..." (Luke 4:1-2 *NRSV*)

(For more information on Jesus being tempted, see chapter 16, "Jesus Christ.")
Consider this part of the temptation:
> "Then the devil led him up and showed him in an instant all of the kingdoms of the world. And the devil said to him, 'To you I will give their glory and all this authority; for it has been given over to me, and I give it to anyone I please. If you, then, will worship me, it will all be yours.'"
> **(Luke 4:5-7** *NRSV*)

Note that in other parts of the temptation when Satan said something which was not true, Jesus immediately corrected him. However, Jesus did *not* contradict what Satan said in Luke 4:5-7. Jesus completely *accepted* Satan's statement and did not contradict it. Satan's statement is true. All of the kingdoms of the world have been given to Satan. Satan has been and is free to give those kingdoms to anyone he pleases.

3.   Look at Satan's record in appointing this world's rulers: Evil rulers characterize this world.
Consider Herod the Great (73-1 BC), the Roman king ruling Palestine when Jesus was born. Herod murdered many babies two years old and younger in Bethlehem

when Jesus was two years old. Herod also murdered members of his own family: his wife, Mariamne, his wife's mother, Alexandra, his eldest son, Antipater, and two other sons, Alexander and Aristobulus. Augustus (63 BC - 14 AD), the Roman Emperor, once said that it was safer to be Herod's pig than Herod's son. Consider Nero (37-68 AD), another Roman Emperor. Nero, in a fit of rage, kicked his beautiful pregnant girlfriend, Poppaea Sabina, so hard that both the baby and the woman died. Nero had his own mother, Agrippina, put to death. Nero used tar-covered live Christians as burning torches in his palace gardens. Consider other famous rulers in world history. Attila the Hun (406-453 AD), Genghis Kahn (1162-1227 AD), Adolph Hitler (1889-1945 AD), Joseph Stalin (1879-1953 AD), Saddam Hussein (1937- AD), etc.: murderers, liars, deceivers, etc. -- responsible for the deaths of hundreds of millions of people.

The rulers of this world have been chosen by Satan the Devil. <u>Is it a coincidence that Satan has selected for the rulers of this world people like himself?</u>

4. <u>Satan has deceived the whole world.</u> This is one of the most startling statements in the Bible:

> "The great dragon was thrown down, that ancient serpent, who is called the Devil and Satan, the deceiver of the whole world -- he was thrown down to the earth, and his angels were thrown down with him."
> **(Revelation 12:9** *NRSV*)

The Bible does not say that Satan has deceived 50%, 75%, 90%, or even 95% of the world: Satan has deceived the *whole* world. The implications of this Bible verse are staggering. The whole world includes history, education, science & technology, commerce & industry, governments, the arts, and the social order. Did Satan give religion a pass? The fact that many people believe this is God's world is *proof* that Satan has deceived the whole world. How can this be God's world if Satan has deceived the whole world?

5. <u>Satan is "the prince of the power of the air."</u> <u>He constantly influences people to sin:</u>

> "Wherein in time past ye walked according to the course of this world, according to the prince of the power of the air, the spirit that now worketh in the children of disobedience:" (Ephesians 2:2 *KJV*)

A major cause of all the problems on Earth is people willing to listen to Satan's filthy lies. Listening to Satan started with Eve in the Garden of Eden and has continued unabated to this day.

<u>Satan is "the god of this world."</u> <u>He blinds the minds of human beings:</u>

> "In their case the god of this world has blinded the minds of the unbelievers, to keep them from seeing the light of the gospel..."
> (II Corinthians 4:4 *NRSV*)

How can this be God's world if Satan is "the god of this world"?

6. <u>Some people rally and march for peace.</u> These people -- individuals and organizations -- believe that they will bring peace to Earth. Some of these people get their "inspiration" from the "Christmas story" recorded in Luke:

> "Glory to God in the highest, and on earth peace, good will toward men."

(Luke 2:14 *KJV*)

However, the *KJV* rendering of Luke 2:14 is in *error*; the *NRSV* rendering is correct:

"'Glory to God in the highest heaven,
   and on earth peace among those whom he favors!'" (Luke 2:14 *NRSV*)

There was *no* peace on Earth when Herod the Great ruled Palestine. Peace belongs only to "those whom he favors."

Regarding peace, consider what Isaiah said:

"The way of peace they do not know..." (Isaiah 59:8 *NRSV*)

There are two kinds of peace: personal peace and international peace. Personal peace is the peace which a person experiences in his or her mind. International peace is peace between nations.

Neither kind of peace comes from rallying and marching.

Personal peace is a fruit of the Holy Spirit:

"By contrast, the fruit of the Spirit is love, joy, peace, patience, kindness, generosity, faithfulness, gentleness, and self-control..."
(Galatians 5:22-23 *NRSV*)

Very few people on Earth today have the Holy Spirit. This is why there is very little personal peace on Earth. Earth is a personal hell for most people because most people listen to Satan.

There is very little international peace on Earth because the leaders of the nations have received their jobs from Satan and are constantly influenced by Satan.

In Satan's world there is very little peace.

People who believe that *they* will bring peace to Earth are totally ignorant of God's Master Plan.

7.   This world, although now under Satan's control, will not remain this way. The very first thing Jesus instructed human beings to pray for is:

"Your kingdom come.
Your will be done,
   on earth as it is in heaven." (Matthew 6:10 *NRSV*)

Jesus instructed human beings to pray that the Kingdom of God would come (soon). At the end of God's Master Plan Period One, which is the beginning of God's Master Plan Period Two, control of Earth will be transferred from Satan the Devil to Jesus Christ. (The exact moment of this transfer marks the boundary between God's Master Plan Periods One and Two.) This moment will mark the end of Satan's world and the beginning of God's world. This moment, one of the most pivotal events of all time, is described:

"Then the seventh angel blew his trumpet, and there were loud voices in heaven, saying,
'The kingdom of the world has become the kingdom of our Lord
   and of his Messiah [margin: Gk *Christ*],
and he will reign forever and ever.'" (**Revelation 11:15** *NRSV*)

When this event occurs, Satan's rule (for the most part) will be over.

8.   In Satan's world -- God's Master Plan Period One -- there is a life-and-

death competition of all religions. This competition occurs in a world where man is under the total influence of Satan. I call God's Master Plan Period One the *demonstration* period. All of the religions of the world are competing in God's Master Plan Period One.

Remember, there is only one true religion: God's. All of the rest are creations of Satan the Devil. Satan has been very active in the competition of religions in God's Master Plan Period One. Consider the categories of the world's religions: "Christianity" counts 2,069,833,000 members. Islam counts 1,254,222,000 adherents. Huge numbers of people are adherents to Hinduism, Buddhism, and Confucianism. Animism draws huge numbers. Satan and demon worship are also big.

Don't forget the religions which were historically large. Many star constellations are named after the Greek and Roman "families" of gods.

In addition to traditional religions are cults. The *Index of Cults*, published annually by the Watchman Fellowship, lists over 1,000 cults operating in the US alone.

Countless numbers of religions have been competing with each other for man's allegiance for almost 6,000 years.

9. <u>In this religious competition in Satan's world God's New Covenant has totally trashed all the others</u>. Only the New Covenant can solve every problem which this physical life and Satan can produce. Only the New Covenant can give eternal life. Without eternal life, life ceases at the Second Death. Only the New Covenant can give one God's mind. Having God's mind is the ultimate life, whether one's body is physical or composed of spirit. Demons are made of spirit, yet have a life of hell; without God's mind all life -- spiritual or physical -- is torment.

10. <u>Some people believe that the main goal of Christians is to "make the world a better place." Such a goal for Christians betrays a colossal ignorance of the Bible</u>. No human beings are going to make this world a better place. This is Satan's world. Under Satan's invisible influence this world (this time period in Earth's history, God's Master Plan Period One) will *always* be a bad place. This world will become better only when Jesus Christ takes control of Earth at the beginning of God's Master Plan Period Two. At that time the Kingdom of God will be ruling Earth. The main goal for Christians should be to seek the Kingdom of God:
> "But strive first for the kingdom of God and his righteousness..."
> (Matthew 6:33 *NRSV*)

Consider the thinking of God-fearing humans who have already lived and died:
> "All of these died in faith without having received the promises, but from a distance they saw and greeted them. They confessed that they were strangers and foreigners on the earth, for people who speak in this way make it clear that they are seeking a homeland." (Hebrews 11:13-14 *NRSV*)
> "But as it is, they desire a better country, that is, a heavenly one. Therefore God is not ashamed to be called their God; indeed, he has prepared a city for them." (Hebrews 11:16 *NRSV*)

The city God has prepared is "the holy city, the new Jerusalem" (Revelation 21:2

NRSV). (See chapter 12, "God's Master Plan: Period Three.")

11.   Why has God allowed this world to be Satan's world? God is in full control of all things. He *could* have made this world His world.
God has allowed this world to be Satan's world so that God's Master Plan can be fulfilled. Successful New Covenant participants are given eternal life. God must know that a person will be loyal to Him for eternity. The only way God can know this is if New Covenant participants are continually tried and tested by Satan and still continue to choose God's way.
Satan is unwittingly helping God in God's Master Plan. By tempting and testing human beings Satan is helping them qualify for the Kingdom of God and eternal life! Satan's frustration must know no bounds: By performing his filth he is an essential part of God's Master Plan!

Summary. 1. The Bible shows that this is Satan's world, not God's world. 2. All of the kingdoms of the world have been given to Satan. Satan has been and is free to give those kingdoms to anyone he pleases. 3. Evil rulers characterize this world. Is it a coincidence that Satan has selected for the rulers of this world people like himself? 4. Satan has deceived the whole world. 5. Satan is "the prince of the power of the air." He constantly influences people to sin. Satan is "the god of this world." He blinds the minds of human beings. 6. Some people rally and march for peace. There are two kinds of peace: personal peace and international peace. Neither kind of peace comes from rallying and marching. People who believe that *they* will bring peace to Earth are totally ignorant of God's Master Plan. 7. At the end of God's Master Plan Period One, which is the beginning of God's Master Plan Period Two, control of Earth will be transferred from Satan the Devil to Jesus Christ. This moment will mark the end of Satan's world and the beginning of God's world. 8. In Satan's world -- God's Master Plan Period One -- there is a life-and-death competition of all religions. 9. In this religious competition in Satan's world God's New Covenant has totally trashed all the others. 10. Some people believe that the main goal of Christians is to "make the world a better place." Such a goal for Christians betrays a colossal ignorance of the Bible. 11. Why has God allowed this world to be Satan's world? God has allowed this world to be Satan's world so that God's Master Plan can be fulfilled.

Christians Go to Heaven After Death

CHAPTER 22
© 2005, Robert M. Kelley

This chapter 22 has been written by Preacher Paul and is used with Preacher Paul's permission. (There is no relationship between Preacher Paul and the apostle Paul of the New Testament.)

Look up all Scriptures in your own Bible. Read and/or write the Scriptures on paper. Writing Scriptures on paper slows down your mind and causes the Bible verses to be more deeply burned into your mind.

All Scripture is inspired and true. However, you cannot learn everything at once. Therefore, the three most important Scriptures on this subject are in **bold** type and the next four most important Scriptures on this subject are underlined.

----

1.   Ladies and gentlemen, my name is Preacher Paul, and tonight I have a most exciting subject, "Christians Go to Heaven After Death." What subject could be more basic to a Christian? I am going to show you that successful Christians go to heaven immediately after death. Now I know that you are not ordinary Christians. I believe that you are Bible-based Christians, Christians who read and study your Bibles. God says in I Thessalonians 5:21 *NIV*, "Test everything. Hold on to the good." Also in John 17:17 *NIV* Jesus told the Father, "...your word is truth." Yes, God's word -- the Bible -- is truth. <u>Tonight I am going to give you, directly from the Bible, five separate proofs that successful Christians go to heaven immediately after death.</u>

2.   <u>Proof #1: Enoch went to heaven</u>. Friends and neighbors, I want you to turn in your Bibles to Genesis 5:24, and read with me:

> "Enoch walked with God; then he was no more, because God took him away." (<u>Genesis 5:24</u> *NIV*)

Looking at the context here one can see that Enoch was a good guy. Enoch walked with God. From the previous verse one can see that Enoch lived to age 365, and in his life walked with God for 300 years. God took him away. And where did God take him? Of course, God took him to heaven!

3.   <u>Proof #2: Elijah went to heaven</u>. Turn in your Bibles to II Kings 2:1, 11:

> "When the LORD was about to take Elijah up to heaven in a whirlwind..."

> "As they were walking along and talking together, suddenly a chariot of fire and horses of fire appeared and separated the two of them, and Elijah went up to heaven in a whirlwind." (**II Kings 2:1, 11** *NIV*)

This is one of the most dramatic passages in the Bible. Scripture says very clearly, "Elijah went up to heaven." Who could possibly deny the plain words of Scripture?

4.   Proof #3: Jesus Christ himself said that heaven is the destination of the successful Christian:
> "Rejoice and be glad, because great is your reward in heaven..." (**Matthew 5:12** *NIV*)
>> "Rejoice in that day and leap for joy, because great is your reward in heaven..." (Luke 6:23 *NIV*)

In the Sermon on the Mount Jesus clearly shows that the reward of the Christian is to go to heaven!
> "In my Father's house are many rooms; if it were not so, I would have told you. I am going there to prepare a place for you. And if I go and prepare a place for you, I will come back and take you to be with me that you also may be where I am. You know the way to the place where I am going." (John 14:2-4 *NIV*)

Where did Jesus go? He went to heaven! Jesus went to heaven to prepare a place for all Christians in heaven. What could be clearer? Remember, this information comes straight from Jesus Christ himself!

5.   Proof #4: Paul said that heaven is the destination of the successful Christian:
> "But our citizenship is in heaven..." (**Philippians 3:20** *NIV*)

Paul said Christians are citizens of heaven! If you are a citizen of Cleveland, Ohio, then you live in Cleveland, Ohio. If you are a citizen of heaven, then you live in heaven. Paul shows that successful Christians go to heaven immediately after death.

6.   Proof #5: Peter said that heaven is the destination of the successful Christian:
> "Praise be to the God and Father of our Lord Jesus Christ! In his great mercy he has given us new birth into a living hope through the resurrection of Jesus Christ from the dead, and into an inheritance that can never perish, spoil or fade -- kept in heaven for you," (I Peter 1:3-4 *NIV*)

Peter says that Christians' inheritance is in heaven! Christians go to heaven immediately after death.

7.   I have given you five separate proofs that successful Christians go to heaven immediately after death. Enoch went to heaven. Elijah went to heaven. At two different times (three places in Scripture) Jesus Christ said that Christians go immediately to heaven. Paul said Christians go to heaven. Peter said Christians go to heaven. Directly from the word of God -- the Bible -- I have shown you that, unquestionably, successful Christians go to heaven immediately after death.

<u>Preacher Paul's Summary</u>. (It is expected that you will listen to Bible Bob's message (chapter 23) after listening to Preacher Paul's message (this chapter 22).) 1. Tonight, I am going to give you, directly from the Bible, five separate proofs that successful Christians to to heaven immediately after death. 2. Proof #1: Enoch went to heaven. 3. Proof #2: Elijah went to heaven. 4. Proof #3: Jesus Christ himself said that heaven is the destination of the successful Christian. 5. Proof #4: Paul said that heaven is the destination of the successful Christian. 6. Proof #5: Peter said that heaven is the destination of the successful Christian. 7. I have given you five separate proofs that successful Christians go to heaven immediately after death.

Christians Do Not Go to Heaven After Death

CHAPTER 23
© 2005, Robert M. Kelley

This chapter 23 has been written by Bible Bob and is used with Bible Bob's permission.

Look up all Scriptures in your own Bible. Read and/or write the Scriptures on paper. Writing Scriptures on paper slows down your mind and causes the Bible verses to be more deeply burned into your mind.

All Scripture is inspired and true. However, you cannot learn everything at once. Therefore, the three most important Scriptures on this subject are in **bold** type and the next seven most important Scriptures on this subject are underlined.

----

1.   I expect that you have already heard Preacher Paul's message, "Christians Go to Heaven After Death" (chapter 22), or as Preacher Paul further explained, "Successful Christians go to heaven immediately after death." Boy, I was very impressed by Preacher Paul's message. The strong, resonate voice, the podium pounding, the Bible beating, even the way he said "God" ("Gawd"): It sounded good. However, tonight I am going to speak on the subject, "Christians Do Not Go to Heaven After Death." Tonight I am going to show you -- from the Bible -- that successful Christians do *not* go to heaven immediately after death. Grab your Bibles and enjoy the ride!

2.   Note carefully that Preacher Paul did not give a single Scripture which says that any human being is now *in* heaven. (Elijah seem to be an exception, but I will explain the Elijah situation later.) Note the words of Jesus Christ:
  "No one has ever gone into heaven except the one who came from heaven --
  the Son of Man." (**John 3:13** *NIV*)
Do you understand what Jesus said? When Jesus was on Earth he flatly stated that *no* human being had ever gone to heaven. Think about it. Abraham did not go to heaven. Moses did not go to heaven. King David did not go to heaven. None of the prophets (major or minor) went to heaven. Elijah did not go to heaven! Peter, on the day of Pentecost, when the New Testament church began, corroborated Jesus' statement by flatly stating:
  "For David did not ascend to heaven..." (Acts 2:34 *NIV*)
David (King of the tribe of Judah seven years and King of the twelve-tribe nation of Israel 33 years) was dead in the grave (*sheol* in the Hebrew language).

3.   What happened to Elijah? As Preacher Paul pointed out, II Kings 2:11 *NIV* *does* say that "Elijah went up to heaven in a whirlwind." It is necessary to

carefully examine the life of Elijah. The original twelve-tribe nation of Israel over which ruled the kings of Saul, David, and Solomon, was, after Solomon's death, divided into two kingdoms. The House of Israel, with its capital (north) in Samaria, consisted of ten tribes. The House of Judah, with its capital (south) in Jerusalem, consisted of two tribes (Judah and Benjamin). The books of I & II Kings and I & II Chronicles record the history of these two separate kingdoms. At various times God sent prophets, sometimes to encourage and often to warn, to the kings of both of these two kingdoms. Elijah was one of those prophets.

It is necessary to review the length of reigns of the kings of both of these two kingdoms. In the House of Judah, the historical succession of kings was Asa (ruled 41 years), Jehoshaphat (ruled 25 years), and Jehoram (ruled 8 years). In the House of Israel, the historical succession of kings was Omri (ruled 12 years), Ahab (ruled 22 years), Ahaziah (ruled 2 years), and Joram (ruled 12 years). All were father-son relationships except Joram; Joram was Ahaziah's brother.

(To complicate things further, different Bible translations give different names to the same kings.

Person	Name in *KJV*	Name in *NIV*	Name in *REB*
Son of Jehoshaphat (House of Judah)	Jehoram	Jehoram	Joram
Brother of Ahaziah (House of Israel)	Jehoram	Joram	Jehoram

The two names -- Joram and Jehoram -- are essentially the same; one is a variant of the other. The *KJV* translators gave two different people the same name. The *NIV* and *REB* translators made them different so that one can tell the two men apart; however, the *NIV* and *REB* do not agree. This chapter 23 will use the names as given in the *NIV*.)

Elijah was chronologically contemporary with the House of Israel kings Ahab and Ahaziah. (Remember Israel's three-year drought and Elijah's famous confrontation with Ahab at Mt. Carmel?) Elisha, the prophet who came after Elijah, began his work with the House of Israel king Joram. The transfer of official prophetic authority from Elijah to Elisha occurred about the time of the transfer of kingdom from Ahaziah to Joram. Note that Joram was ruling seven years before Jehoram began to rule.

Note carefully this verse:
"Jehoram received a letter from Elijah the prophet, which said..."
(II Chronicles 21:12 *NIV*)
If you read this letter (verses 12-15) you will see that it is a warning from God, a typical message from a prophet of God.

Consider this letter to Jehoram. This letter was written at least seven years *after* Elijah "went up to heaven." Elijah sent a letter to Jehoram at least seven years after he "went up to heaven"! How can this be? How much mail have you heard of either going up to heaven or coming down from heaven? *No* mail is coming from heaven. Mail comes only from Earth. II Chronicles 21:12 means that, even though Elisha was the main prophet of God at this time, Elijah was still on Earth writing and sending letters.

Jesus said:
> "...the Scripture cannot be broken..." (John 10:35 *NIV*)

Yes, the Scripture *cannot* be broken. There are *no* errors in the Word of God. The Bible is true! Every Scripture can fit together into a single truth. So, what is the explanation? How can Elijah have sent a letter on Earth at least seven years *after* he "went up to heaven"?

There are *three* heavens mentioned in the Bible: The English word "heaven" is used to describe *three* different places.

The First Heaven is the atmosphere of gases surrounding Earth, where clouds are and where birds fly:
> "...the floodgates of the heavens were opened. And rain fell on earth forty days and forty nights." (Genesis 7:11-12 *NIV*)

The Second Heaven is outer space where the planets and stars are:
> "The stars of heaven and their constellations
>   will not show their light..." (Isaiah 13:10 *NIV*)

The Third Heaven is where God and Jesus Christ reside:
> "How you have fallen from heaven,
>   O morning star, son of the dawn!..." (Isaiah 14:12 *NIV*)

Of these three heavens, the one which Elijah "went up to" was the First Heaven. Elijah was God's main prophet, and he was burned-out in his job. Elijah wanted to retire. God granted Elijah's request and replaced Elijah with Elisha. Elijah "went up to heaven" in the clouds (First Heaven) and then returned to Earth to live at another location on Earth. At this location Elijah wrote a letter to Jehoram at least seven years later.

In John 3:13 -- and throughout the Bible -- Jesus Christ was right: *No* man has gone up to heaven! The "heaven" Jesus referred to in John 3:13 was the Third Heaven. Elijah did *not* go to the heaven (Third Heaven) where God resides.

What *proof* is there that the Bible speaks of three heavens? The Bible uses the term "third heaven" only once:
> "I know a man in Christ who fourteen years ago was caught up to the third heaven..." (**II Corinthians 12:2** *NIV*)

Paul describes heavenly revelations he received. Since the Bible uses the term "third heaven," there must be a First Heaven and Second Heaven. Looking at the Bible use of the word "heaven," we see that there *is* a First Heaven and Second Heaven.

A major reason why people are confused about "heaven" is that they do not understand that the Bible uses this word to describe *three* different places -- the First Heaven, the Second Heaven, and the Third Heaven. When people use the word "heaven" they usually have in mind the Third Heaven.

4.   Look carefully at the book of Revelation. The book of Revelation was written about 96 AD. Jesus was crucified about 33 AD. The time between the beginning of the New Covenant and the writing of the book of Revelation was, therefore, about sixty years. During this sixty year period a number of Christians died. Some Christians died natural deaths, having lived to normal life expectancy at that time. Other Christians were murdered for their beliefs, having had shorter than normal lives. During this sixty year period hundreds of thousands or even possibly millions of Christians died. According to Preacher Paul these Christians went immediately to heaven (the Third Heaven). The book of Revelation contains a number of detailed descriptions of who and what is in the Third Heaven. Yet the book of Revelation *never* mentions even *one* Christian who was in the Third Heaven after having died during the previous 60 years!

5.   Note carefully that Preacher Paul did not cite any Scriptures which say that man is going *to go* to heaven. In looking at the question of what happens to Christians after death, one must consider where Jesus Christ will be.

> "He will be great and will be called the Son of the Most High. The Lord God
> will give him the throne of his father David, and he will reign over the
> house of Jacob forever; his kingdom will never end." (Luke 1:32-33 *NIV*)

The angel Gabriel was talking to Mary before the Holy Spirit conceived Jesus in her body. Check carefully John 18:36-37; there Jesus told Pilate that he was born to be a king. Jesus Christ will return to Earth to rule as:

> "...KING OF KINGS AND LORD OF LORDS." (Revelation 19:16 *NIV*)

The angels which were present when Jesus first ascended to heaven made this statement:

> "'Men of Galilee,' they said, 'why do you stand here looking into the sky?
> This same Jesus, who has been taken from you into heaven, will come back
> in the same way you have seen him go into heaven.'" (Acts 1:11 *NIV*)

Yes, Jesus will return to rule Earth. The moment of the beginning of the rule of Christ over Earth occurs at the seventh trumpet:

> "The seventh angel sounded his trumpet, and there were loud voices
> in heaven, which said:
> 'The kingdom of the world has become the kingdom of our Lord and
> of his Christ,
> and he will reign for ever and ever.'" (Revelation 11:15 *NIV*)

Jesus' return is described:

> "Look, he is coming with the clouds,
>   and every eye will see him..." (Revelation 1:7 *NIV*)

Jesus will return to Jerusalem and the Mount of Olives:

> "On that day his feet will stand on the Mount of Olives, east of
> Jerusalem..."
>   "The LORD will be king over the whole earth..."

(Zechariah 14:4, 9 *NIV*)

6.   Jesus will return to Earth from heaven. But what about the Christian's reward? Preacher Paul cited several Scriptures which show that the Christian's reward is now *in* heaven. But, does this reward *stay* in heaven?

> "'Behold, I am coming soon! My reward is with me, and I will give to everyone according to what he has done." (**Revelation 22:12** *NIV*)

Jesus said that his reward (the one he will give to Christians) is *with* him. He did *not* say that the Christian's reward is residence in heaven. Jesus will *bring* the Christian's reward with him. Where will Jesus be? Jesus is coming to Earth from heaven. Jesus is bringing the Christian's reward with him from heaven to Earth. Look carefully at Jesus' words (which Preacher Paul also quoted):

> "Do not let your hearts be troubled. Trust in God; trust also in me. In my Father's house are many rooms; if it were not so, I would have told you. I am going there to prepare a place for you. And if I go and prepare a place for you, I will come back and take you to be with me that you also may be where I am." (John 14:1-3 *NIV*)

Preacher Paul *assumed* that Jesus was talking about heaven. However, you cannot find the word heaven in this passage. Jesus is coming to take Christians to where He will be. The Bible has already shown that Jesus is coming to Earth. Jesus has places for Christians on *Earth*. Jesus is bringing the Christian's reward from heaven to Earth.

7.   What will successful Christians do with Christ on Earth? Look carefully at Jesus' message. He continually talked about the Kingdom of God. (For plenty of detail, see chapter 6, "The Kingdom of God: Jesus.") Jesus never once said that successful Christians go to heaven, but he said numerous times that successful Christians enter the Kingdom of God and rule with him on Earth. Daniel confirms Jesus' numerous statements:

> "But the saints of the Most High will receive the kingdom and will possess it forever -- yes, for ever and ever." (Daniel 7:18 *NIV*)
> "until the Ancient of Days came and pronounced judgment in favor of the saints of the Most High, and the time came when they possessed the kingdom." (Daniel 7:22 *NIV*)
> "Then the sovereignty, power and greatness of the kingdoms under the whole heaven will be handed over to the saints, the people of the Most High. His kingdom will be an everlasting kingdom, and all rulers will worship and obey him." (Daniel 7:27 *NIV*)

The saints -- successful Christians -- will rule with Jesus in the Kingdom of God.

> "Blessed are the meek,
>   for they will inherit the earth" (Matthew 5:5 *NIV*)

The meek do not inherit heaven; they inherit *Earth*!

> "To him who overcomes and does my will to the end, I will give authority over the nations --
>   'He will rule them with an iron scepter;
>   he will dash them to pieces like pottery'
> just as I have received authority from my Father." (Revelation 2:26-27 *NIV*)

"You have made them to be a kingdom and priests to serve our God, and they will reign on the earth.'" (Revelation 5:10 *NIV*)
<u>Successful Christians will rule with Jesus in the Kingdom of God on *Earth*.</u>

8.   What about the idea that successful Christians will walk through pearly gates, walk on streets of gold, etc., in heaven? The Bible shows that, later, the Third Heaven is actually coming to earth:
> "Then I saw a new heaven and a new earth, for the first heaven and the first earth had passed away, and there was no longer any sea. I saw the Holy City, the new Jerusalem, coming down out of heaven from God, prepared as a bride beautifully dressed for her husband. And I heard a loud voice from the throne saying, 'Now the dwelling of God is with men, and he will live with them...'" (Revelation 21:1-3 *NIV*)

<u>Christians will eventually be in heaven. However, they won't *go* there. Christians will rule on Earth. Eventually heaven will *come* to Earth!</u>

9.   <u>The apostle Paul explains the resurrection of the saints at Christ's return:</u>
> "According to the Lord's own word, we tell you that we who are still alive, who are left till the coming of the Lord, will certainly not precede those who have fallen asleep. For the Lord himself will come down from heaven, with a loud command, with the voice of the archangel and with the trumpet call of God, and the dead in Christ will rise first. After that, we who are still alive and are left will be caught up together with them in the clouds to meet the Lord in the air. And so we will be with the Lord forever." (I Thessalonians 4:15-17 *NIV*)

Paul describes the coming resurrection as occurring in this manner: (1) Jesus will return at the (seventh) trumpet. (2) The dead in Christ will rise first. (3) Those Christians living on Earth will also rise. (4) Both groups will be with Christ forever! <u>Note that no one goes to heaven and that nothing occurs until Jesus returns. Paul says that Christians remain in the grave until Christ returns. No human has gone to heaven after death or will ever go to heaven!</u>

<u>Bible Bob's Summary.</u> (It is expected that you have already heard Preacher Paul's message (chapter 22) before listening to Bible Bob's message (this chapter 23).) 1. Tonight I am going to show you -- from the Bible -- that successful Christians do *not* go to heaven immediately after death. 2. When Jesus was on Earth he flatly stated that *no* human being had ever gone to heaven. 3. What happened to Elijah? Elijah "went up to heaven" in the clouds (First Heaven) and then returned to earth to live at another location on earth. At this location Elijah wrote a letter to Jehoram at least seven years later. A major reason why people are confused about "heaven" is that they do not understand that the Bible uses this word to describe *three* different places -- the First Heaven, the Second Heaven, and the Third Heaven. 4. The book of Revelation contains a number of detailed descriptions of who and what is in the Third Heaven. Yet the book of Revelation *never* mentions even *one* Christian who was in the Third Heaven after having died during the previous 60 years! 5. Preacher Paul did not cite any Scriptures which say that man is going *to go* to heaven. In looking at the question of what

happens to Christians after death, one must consider where Jesus Christ will be. Jesus will return to rule Earth. 6. The Christian's reward is now *in* heaven. But, does this reward *stay* in heaven? Jesus is bringing the Christian's reward with him from heaven to Earth. Jesus is coming to take Christians to where He will be. The Bible has already shown that Jesus is coming to Earth. Jesus has places for Christians on *Earth*. Jesus is bringing the Christian's reward from heaven to Earth. 7. What will successful Christians do with Christ on Earth? Successful Christians will rule with Jesus in the Kingdom of God on *Earth*. 8. Christians will eventually be in heaven. However, they won't *go* there. Christians will rule on Earth. Eventually heaven will *come* to Earth! 9. The apostle Paul explains the resurrection of the saints at Christ's return. Note that no one goes to heaven and that nothing occurs until Jesus returns. Paul says that Christians remain in the grave until Christ returns. No human has gone to heaven after death or will ever go to heaven!

131

Hell

CHAPTER 24
© 2005, Robert M. Kelley

Look up all Scriptures in your own Bible. Read and/or write the Scriptures on paper. Writing Scriptures on paper slows down your mind and causes the Bible verses to be more deeply burned into your mind.

All Scripture is inspired and true. However, you cannot learn everything at once. Therefore, the three most important Scriptures on this subject are in **bold** type and the next seven most important Scriptures on this subject are underlined.

----

1.   Hell is real. Some people believe that places like "heaven" and "hell" are unreal. In fact, some believe that the Bible itself is myth or fantasy. They are wrong, grievously wrong. The Bible is true and inspired. (See chapter 31, "Proof of the Bible.") In this chapter 24 what the Bible says about hell is summarized.

2.   Many of the popular ideas about hell originated in Dante's *The Divine Comedy*. Dante Alighieri (1265-1321 AD) was an Italian poet. He wrote an epic poem titled *Comedy* in 1321 AD. Later this poem was re-titled *The Divine Comedy*. *The Divine Comedy* describes three places: Paradise (or heaven), Purgatory, and the Inferno (or hell). The Inferno section summarizes Dante's ideas about hell; it is gruesome. The Inferno is filled with ugly scenes of human beings being tortured in innumerable, ingenious ways, forever. If you want to feel depressed, then you should read the Inferno section of *The Divine Comedy*. Preachers for hundreds of years have used Dante's images to gain new converts. Powerful preachers would paint word pictures of the indescribable horrors of hell, then contrast those scenes with the splendor and delights of heaven. "Friend, what future would you prefer: Indescribable tortures in hell forever, or unimaginable pleasures in heaven forever?" The powerful imagery had its effect. Many chose the prospect of heaven, thus adding to Christianity's church organization rolls. Paul Johnson, in his epic work, *History of Christianity*, points out that this heaven vs. hell preaching style was effective in Christianity's growth. However, Dante's ideas came from Dante. The important question about this vital subject is, "What does the Bible say?"

3.   A correct understanding of hell involves examining the Hebrew and Greek words which are translated as the English word "hell" in the *King James Version* (*KJV*) of the Bible. (The *KJV* is used because the reference works associated with it are abundant.) The word "hell" appears 53 times in the *KJV*: 31 times in the Old Testament and 22 times in the New Testament. A thorough examination of these 53 places reveals that "hell" in the Bible has three meanings.

4.   The first meaning of hell is a place where the dead sleep. The Hebrew

word for where the dead sleep is *sheol* (#7585 in the Hebrew and Chaldee Dictionary portion of James Strong's *The Exhaustive Concordance of the Bible*). *Sheol* appears 31 times in the Old Testament. Here is one example rendering of *sheol*:

"For thou wilt not leave my soul in hell..." (Psalm 16:10 *KJV*)

The Greek word for where the dead sleep is *hades* (#86 in the Greek Dictionary of the New Testament portion of James Strong's *The Exhaustive Concordance of the Bible*). *Hades* appears in the New Testament 10 times. Here is one example rendering of *hades*:

"...and the gates of hell shall not prevail against it." (Matthew 16:18 *KJV*)

The hell defined by *sheol* and *hades* is like a meat locker. The dead "sleep," having no consciousness. All residents of this hell are eventually resurrected: (a) Successful New Covenant participants are resurrected spiritually to eternal life. (b) Those who were not called to the New Covenant in their first physical life are resurrected physically to have their offer of the New Covenant. (c) Those who chose to be unsuccessful in the New Covenant are physically resurrected just before being cast into the Lake of Fire for the Second Death. (For more information on groups (b) and (c), see chapter 11, "God's Master Plan: Period Two," and chapter 25, "Immortal Soul.")

5.   The second meaning of hell is a place of fire, damnation, eternal destruction (of people). The Greek word for a place of fire, damnation, and eternal destruction is *gehenna* (#1067 in the Greek Dictionary of the New Testament portion of James Strong's *The Exhaustive Concordance of the Bible*). *Gehenna* appears in the New Testament 11 times. Here is one example rendering of *gehenna*:

"And fear not them which kill the body, but are not able to kill the soul: but rather fear him which is able to destroy both soul and body in hell."
(**Matthew 10:28** *KJV*)

The hell defined by *gehenna* is the Lake of Fire. Human beings are cast into the Lake of Fire. The Lake of Fire is a one-time occurrence. People cast into the Lake of Fire die almost immediately, suffering the Second Death.

6.   The third meaning of hell is a place where angels that sinned are punished. The Greek word for a place where angels that sinned are punished is *tartaros* (#5020 in the Greek Dictionary of the New Testament portion of James Strong's *The Exhaustive Concordance of the Bible*). *Tartaros* appears only once in the New Testament:

"For if God spared not the angels that sinned, but cast them down to hell..." (II Peter 2:4 *KJV*)

The hell defined by *tartaros* is the hell where Satan and demons are cast. This hell lasts forever.

(For more information on *tartaros*, see chapter 20, "Satan and Demons.")

7.   The remainder of this chapter 24 will deal with the second meaning of hell: a place of fire, damnation, and eternal destruction. This hell (*gehenna*) is called, in the Bible, the Lake of Fire:

"And death and hell were cast into the lake of fire. This is the second death. And whosoever was not found written in the book of life was cast into the lake of fire." (**Revelation 20:14-15** *KJV*)

8.   <u>A major fact about hell is that hell is a place of eternal death</u>. A major misconception about hell is that it is a place of eternal punish*ing*. Dante's *The Divine Comedy* portrays a place where torture by fire goes on forever. This is Dante's idea. However, the Bible shows that the Lake of Fire is a place of eternal punish*ment*: eternal death. Revelation 20:14 says "second death." Note what Paul says:
> "For the wages of sin is death..." (<u>Romans 6:23</u> *KJV*)

The wages of sin is not torture or suffering. The wages of sin is *death*. Death is the cessation of life. Some people define death as "separation from God." However, you cannot find this definition in a dictionary. Death is the cessation or end of life.

Newspapers commonly report that certain persons were burned to death in house fires. These human beings were burned to death relatively quickly. The same experience occurs in the Lake of Fire. When a physical human being is cast into the Lake of Fire, death will occur very quickly.

Although death in house fires and death in the Lake of Fire both occur quickly, there is a major difference between them. Death by house fire is one form of the *First* Death. Death in the Lake of Fire is the *Second Death* (Revelation 20:14 *KJV*). The Second Death lasts for all eternity.

God is *not* a sadistic monster who delights in torturing people. Hear what God Himself says:
> "Have I any pleasure at all that the wicked should die? saith the Lord GOD..." (Ezekiel 18:23 *KJV*)
> "For I have no pleasure in the death of him that dieth, saith the Lord GOD..." (Ezekiel 18:32 *KJV*)
> "Say unto them, As I live saith the Lord GOD, I have no pleasure in the death of the wicked..." (<u>Ezekiel 33:11</u> *KJV*)

Note, God says that the wicked will *die*. The end of the wicked is death, not punishing. The idea that God tortures people endlessly in the fires of hell is a man-made idea. One *cannot* find this idea in the Bible!

God is merciful:
> "...God is love." (<u>I John 4:8</u> *KJV*)

The idea that God tortures people endlessly in fire is totally inconsistent with the fact that God is love.

(For more information on God's destruction of those who are unsuccessful in the New Covenant, see chapter 25, "Immortal Soul.")

9.   Malachi, among others, describes the Lake of Fire:
> "For, behold, the day cometh, that shall burn as an oven; and all the proud, yea, and all that do wickedly, shall be stubble: and the day that cometh shall burn them up, saith the LORD of hosts, that it shall leave them neither root nor branch."
> "And ye shall tread down the wicked; for they shall be ashes under the

soles of your feet in the day that I shall do this, saith the LORD of hosts." (**Malachi 4:1, 3** *KJV*)

In the Lake of Fire the wicked are burned to death. They become ashes. (For more information on the Lake of Fire, see chapter 11, "God's Master Plan: Period Two.")

10.   The Lake of Fire is a one-time event. The Lake of Fire occurs at the end of God's Master Plan Period Two. At the end of God's Master Plan Period Two all human beings who will ever live will already have lived and been given the offer of the New Covenant. This offer may have occurred when they physically lived on Earth the first time, or when they were physically resurrected to physically live a second time. (Being physically resurrected to have the offer of the New Covenant will occur a lot in God's Master Plan Period Two.) Those reserved for the Lake of Fire have physically lived earlier, died, and been kept "on ice" in the grave (hell, first meaning), reserved for the Lake of Fire. When the Lake of Fire begins, those reserved for it are resurrected from the grave with physical bodies and cast into the Lake of Fire to be (eternally) destroyed in the Second Death. (Those successful in the New Covenant have already been resurrected with eternal, spirit bodies.)

11.   Some people are confused by the Biblical terms "eternal damnation" and "eternal fire." These two terms each appear only once in the (*KJV*) New Testament:

> "But he that shall blaspheme against the Holy Ghost has never forgiveness, but is in danger of eternal damnation:" (Mark 3:29 *KJV*)

Jesus' use of the term "eternal damnation" means that those who blaspheme against the Holy Spirit will suffer eternal death, the Second Death. Death in the Lake of Fire is eternally irrevocable. Death in the Lake of Fire is "eternal damnation."

> "Even as Sodom and Gomorrha, and the cities about them in like manner, giving themselves over to fornication, and going after strange [margin: Gr. *other*] flesh, are set forth for an example, suffering the vengeance of eternal fire." (Jude 7 *KJV*)

Jude's example of "eternal fire" is the destruction of Sodom and Gomorrah. The human beings in Sodom and Gomorrah did not suffer eternally. They were burned to death in a matter of minutes. After burning Sodom, Gomorrah, and the cities of the plain, this "eternal fire" was totally *out*. This is exactly what will happen with the Lake of Fire: When the surface of Earth and atmosphere have been consumed, the fire will be out.

(History and archaeology confirm that the "eternal fire" of Sodom and Gomorrah is out. Adam Clarke, LLD, FSA, in his *The Holy Bible with a Commentary and Critical Notes* says that Sodom, Gomorrah, and the cities of the plain comprise what is now known as the Dead Sea, which is approximately 70 miles long and 18 miles wide. Modern archaeological evidence of this belief appeared in the April 3-9, 2000, edition of *The Washington Times, National Weekly Edition*, on page 25.)

12.   The Lake of Fire is a part of the "day of the Lord," described by Peter:

> "But the day of the Lord will come as a thief in the night; in the which the

heavens shall pass away with a great noise, and the elements shall melt with fervent heat, the earth also and the works that are therein shall be burned up." (II Peter 3:10 *KJV*)

Summary. 1. Hell is real. 2. Many of the popular ideas about hell originated in Dante's *The Divine Comedy*. 3. A correct understanding of hell involves examining the Hebrew and Greek words which are translated as the English word "hell" in the *King James Version* (*KJV*) of the Bible. The word "hell" appears 53 times in the *KJV*. A thorough examination of these 53 places reveals that "hell" in the Bible has three meanings. 4. The first meaning of hell is a place where the dead sleep. 5. The second meaning of hell is a place of fire, damnation, eternal destruction (of people). 6. The third meaning of hell is a place where angels that sinned are punished. 7. The remainder of this chapter 24 will deal with the second meaning of hell: a place of fire, damnation, and eternal destruction. This hell (*gehenna*) is called, in the Bible, the Lake of Fire. 8. A major fact about hell is that hell is a place of eternal death. 9. In the Lake of Fire the wicked are burned to death. They become ashes. 10. The Lake of Fire is a one-time event. 11. Some people are confused by the Biblical terms "eternal damnation" and "eternal fire." Death in the Lake of Fire is "eternal damnation." After burning Sodom, Gomorrah, and the cities of the plain, this "eternal fire" was totally *out*. 12. The Lake of Fire is a part of the "day of the Lord."

Immortal Soul

CHAPTER 25
© 2005, Robert M. Kelley

Look up all Scriptures in your own Bible. Read and/or write the Scriptures on paper. Writing Scriptures on paper slows down your mind and causes the Bible verses to be more deeply burned into your mind.

All Scripture is inspired and true. However, you cannot learn everything at once. Therefore, the three most important Scriptures on this subject are in **bold** type and the next seven most important Scriptures on this subject are underlined.

---

1.   The concept of the immortal soul is a pagan idea which originated in antiquity. The immortal soul concept appears in history about the time of Socrates (470-399 BC) and his disciple Plato (428-348 BC). Socrates and Plato were both Greek philosophers. The immortal soul concept is the belief that a human being is composed of two parts: (a) the body, which is physical and can die, and (b) the soul, which is spiritual in nature and lives forever.

2.   However, the purpose of *Learn What the Bible* Really *Says -- Fast!* is to determine what the *Bible* says about a particular subject. The term "immortal soul" nowhere appears in these popular Bible translations: *KJV, NIV,* and *NRSV*. In these same translations the term "immortality" is used only to describe God or successful Christians who have been resurrected with spirit bodies.

3.   God describes man as a creation of flesh:
"And the LORD God formed man of the dust of the ground, and breathed into his nostrils the breath of life; and man became a living soul."
(Genesis 2:7 *KJV*)
"And God created great whales, and every living creature that moveth..."
"And God said, Let the earth bring forth the living creature after his kind..." (Genesis 1:21, 24 *KJV*)
In describing His creation, God inspired the *same* Hebrew word, *nephesh* (#5315 in the Hebrew and Chaldee Dictionary portion of James Strong's *The Exhaustive Concordance of the Bible*) to be used for both the English word "soul" in Genesis 2:7 and "creature" in Genesis 1:21, 24. If Adam and the animals were intrinsically different in nature, would not God have inspired *different* Hebrew words for each? The inspired Hebrew defines both Adam and the animals as physical, fleshly entities.
God describes man as having a temporary existence:
"...for dust thou art, and unto dust shalt thou return." (Genesis 3:19 *KJV*)
God defines life essence as existing in physical blood, not in a soul:
"But flesh with the life thereof, which is the blood thereof, shall ye not eat."

(Genesis 9:4 *KJV*)

4. <u>When a human being dies (First Death), he or she goes to the grave and</u> <u>"sleeps" (having no consciousness) until a resurrection</u> (like the ones in I Corinthians 15:52 and Revelation 20:4-15):

> "For in death there is no remembrance of thee: in the grave who shall give thee thanks?" (Psalm 6:5 *KJV*)
>
> "His breath goeth forth, he returneth to his earth; in that very day his thoughts perish." (<u>Psalm 146:4</u> *KJV*)
>
> "For that which befalleth the sons of men befalleth beasts; even one thing befalleth them: as the one dieth, so dieth the other; yea, they have all one breath; so that a man hath no preeminence above a beast: for all is vanity." (Ecclesiastes 3:19 *KJV*)
>
> "For the living know that they shall die: but the dead know not any thing..." (<u>Ecclesiastes 9:5</u> *KJV*)
>
> "Whatsoever thy hand findeth to do, do it with thy might; for there is no work, nor device, nor knowledge, nor wisdom, in the grave, whither thou goest." (Ecclesiastes 9:10 *KJV*)

(For more information about what happens to a human being after death, see chapters 22 & 23, "Christians Go to Heaven After Death" and "Christians Do Not Go to Heaven After Death.")

5. <u>If a human being rejects God's way, he or she will die both physically and</u> <u>spiritually -- forever</u>:

> "But of the fruit of the tree which is in the midst of the garden, God hath said, Ye shall not eat of it, neither shall ye touch it, lest ye die." (Genesis 3:3 *KJV*)
>
> "...the soul that sinneth, it shall die." (<u>Ezekiel 18:4</u> *KJV*)
>
> "The soul that sinneth, it shall die..." (Ezekiel 18:20 *KJV*)
>
> "For the wages of sin is death..." (<u>Romans 6:23</u> *KJV*)
>
> "And fear not them which kill the body, but are not able to kill the soul: but rather fear him which is able to destroy both soul and body in hell." (**Matthew 10:28** *KJV*)

Note carefully: God has said that those who persist in sin will die, both physically and spiritually. Human beings can kill only the body (First Death). However, God can kill both the body and soul (Second Death). As Jesus said in Matthew 10:28 *KJV*, God "is able to destroy both soul and body in hell [Greek *gehenna*]," the Lake of Fire.

6. <u>God will kill human bodies and souls in the Lake of Fire.</u> <u>God calls death in</u> <u>the Lake of Fire the Second Death.</u> The Lake of Fire is a one-time event:

> "And death and hell were cast into the lake of fire. This is the second death. And whosoever was not found written in the book of life was cast into the lake of fire." (**Revelation 20:14-15** *KJV*)

(For more information on the Lake of Fire, see chapter 11, "God's Master Plan: Period Two," and chapter 24, "Hell.")

People are burned to death in the Lake of Fire:

"And ye shall tread down the wicked; for they shall be ashes under the souls of your feet in the day that I shall do this, saith the LORD of hosts." (**Malachi 4:3** *KJV*)

Those burned in the Lake of Fire are *not* tormented forever; they are burned immediately and become ashes!

"...they shall be as though they had not been." (Obadiah 16 *KJV*)

Those who are cast into the Lake of Fire will be destroyed forever. It will be as if they had never existed. The Second Death is a horrible fate: to have one's existence totally and irrevocably terminated.

7.   The immortal soul concept is another one of Satan's lies:
"And the serpent said unto the woman, Ye shall not surely die:" (Genesis 3:4 *KJV*)

Satan essentially said, "You won't die: You have an immortal soul!" The immortal soul concept is the first of Satan's lies recorded in the Bible. Satan and his demons have been promoting the immortal soul doctrine ever since. (Did Socrates get his immortal soul concept from Satan the Devil?) Human beings have been warned about doctrines of demons:

"Now the Spirit speaketh expressly, that in the latter times some shall depart from the faith, giving heed to seducing spirits, and doctrines of devils;" (I Timothy 4:1 *KJV*)

Summary. 1. The concept of the immortal soul is a pagan idea which originated in antiquity. The immortal soul concept is the belief that a human being is composed of two parts: (a) the body, which is physical and can die, and (b) the soul, which is spiritual in nature and lives forever. 2. The term "immortal soul" nowhere appears in these popular Bible translations: *KJV*, *NIV*, and *NRSV*. 3. God describes man as a creation of flesh. 4. When a human being dies (First Death), he or she goes to the grave and "sleeps" (having no consciousness) until a resurrection. 5. If a human being rejects God's way, he or she will die both physically and spiritually -- forever. 6. God will kill human bodies and souls in the Lake of Fire. God calls death in the Lake of Fire the Second Death. 7. The immortal soul concept is another one of Satan's lies. Human beings have been warned about doctrines of demons.

Bible Prophecy Basics

CHAPTER 26

© 2005, Robert M. Kelley

Look up all Scriptures in your own Bible. Read and/or write the Scriptures on paper. Writing Scriptures on paper slows down your mind and causes the Bible verses to be more deeply burned into your mind.

All Scripture is inspired and true. However, you cannot learn everything at once. Therefore, the three most important Scriptures on this subject are in **bold** type and the next seven most important Scriptures on this subject are underlined.

---

1.   Prophecy is the foretelling of future events. Bible prophecy is the foretelling of future events in the Bible. Some people are afraid of Bible prophecy. This fear expresses itself in statements like, "No one can understand prophecy." If human beings are not supposed to understand prophecy, then why did God put it in the Bible? God has placed prophecy in the Bible. God wants human beings to understand this part of His Word.

2.   Prophecy appears, here and there, throughout most of the Bible. However, the three areas of the Bible which deal most with Bible prophecy are: (a) the book of Revelation, (b) the book of Daniel, and (c) the "Olivet Prophecy" of Jesus Christ (in Matthew 24, Mark 13, and Luke 21).

3.   The book of Revelation is special in Bible prophecy. Note the first verse of the book of Revelation:

> "The Revelation of Jesus Christ, which God gave unto him, to shew unto his servants things which must shortly come to pass; and he sent and signified it by his angel unto his servant John:" (Revelation 1:1 *KJV*)

Consider the situation of the Christian church at the time of the writing of the book of Revelation, about 96 AD. Early Christians had been expecting the second coming of Jesus Christ to rule Earth in the Kingdom of God shortly after Christ's ascent to heaven (the Third Heaven, recorded in Acts 1). However, more than 60 years had transpired and Christ had *not* returned. In addition, the church had been heavily persecuted. Eleven of the twelve original apostles had died; many, if not most, had been tortured and/or executed. Only the apostle John was left. John, now near the end of his physical life, had been exiled to the island of Patmos because he still preached the gospel of the Kingdom of God. Yes, the current situation was discouraging. There seemed to be no hope.

Jesus Christ, Head of the church, knew that the church needed to be encouraged. At this crucial time in church history Jesus Christ sent His angel to the apostle John to reveal "things which must shortly come to pass." Jesus delivered Revelation to *encourage* and *inspire* the church! Jesus knew that not only did the Christians living at 100 AD need encouragement, but also those who would live

143

during the next 1900 years, to about 2000 AD, when many of the dramatic events of Revelation would be occurring. All Christians need *vision*.

In addition, the book of Revelation is the only Bible book (of 66) that has a special warning attached to it:

> "For I testify unto every man that heareth the words of the prophecy of this book, If any man shall add unto these things, God shall add unto him the plagues that are written in this book:
> And if any man shall take away from the words of the book of this prophecy, God shall take away his part out of the book of life, and out of the the holy city, and from the things which are written in this book."
> (Revelation 22:18-19 *KJV*)

The book of Revelation is so important for Christians to understand that God warns that anyone who deletes any part of this book will suffer eternal death (the Second Death) in the Lake of Fire!

4.   <u>Bible prophecy serves multiple purposes</u>. It is true that Revelation and other prophetic Biblical passages sometimes describe some very wonderful and some very grisly future events. However, prophecy is very important to people who seek God for several reasons: (a) Prophecy shows that God's Master Plan will be totally fulfilled. (b) Prophecy shows that good will eventually prevail over evil. (c) Prophecy reveals the reward of the New Covenant participant. The final end is one of eternal life and glory for each New Covenant participant. Prophecy is inspiring!

5.   <u>Bible prophecy is a major proof of God</u>. God showed the Israelites why He is superior to all idols:

> "Produce your cause [margin: Heb. *Cause to come near*], saith the LORD; bring forth your strong reasons, saith the King of Jacob.
> Let them bring them forth, and shew us what shall happen: let them shew the former things, what they be, that we may consider them [margin: Heb. *set our heart upon them*], and know the latter end of them; or declare us things for to come.
> Shew the things that are to come hereafter, that we may know that ye are gods: yea, do good, or do evil, that we may be dismayed, and behold it together." (**Isaiah 41:21-23** *KJV*)

Only God can predict the future and then cary out that prediction. Bible prophecy has a 100% fulfillment record. Bible prophecy is proof that God is God.

6.   After Jesus lived his life as a human being, was murdered and resurrected, He returned to visit his disciples. On the road to Emmaus, Jesus talked with two of them:

> "Then he said unto them, O fools, and slow of heart to believe all that the prophets have spoken:
> Ought not Christ to have suffered these things, and to enter into his glory?
> And beginning at Moses and all the prophets, he expounded unto them in all the scriptures the things concerning himself." (Luke 24:25-27 *KJV*)

Later He met with the twelve:

"And he said unto them, These are the words which I spake unto you, while I was yet with you, that all things must be fulfilled, which were written in the law of Moses, and in the prophets, and in the psalms, concerning me.
Then opened he their understanding, that they might understand the scriptures,
And said unto them, Thus it is written, and thus it behoved Christ to suffer, and to rise from the dead the third day." (**Luke 24:44-46** *KJV*)
Jesus' proof to the twelve disciples that he was the Messiah was that he had fulfilled the Old Testament prophecies concerning the Messiah. <u>Bible prophecy is proof that Jesus is the Messiah</u>.

7.   An area of confusion for people who study Bible prophecy is the identity of the nations and peoples mentioned. <u>Many people confuse Israel with Judah (nations) and Israelites with Jews (persons)</u>. Some people believe that Israelites and Jews are synonymous. Nothing could be further from the truth. These people are confused by many Bible verses. Here is one example:
"Then Rezin king of Syria and Pekah son of Remaliah king of Israel came up to Jerusalem to war: and they besieged Ahaz, but could not overcome him." (<u>II Kings 16:5</u> *KJV*)
The Jews were in Jerusalem. Ahaz was king of the Jews. (The word "Jew" first appears in the *KJV* in II Kings 16:6, the next verse.) Remaliah, king of Israel, was warring against the Jews in Jerusalem. <u>Israel was warring against the Jews</u>!
Israel was the name given to Jacob. Jacob had twelve sons. Each son became a tribe. Eventually the descendants of Jacob or Israel became a nation. This nation was the twelve-tribe nation of Israel. At the time of Samuel, the form of government of the twelve-tribe nation of Israel was changed from a theocracy (ruled by God) administered by judges to a kingdom (ruled by a physical king). The first three kings were Saul, David, and Solomon. After Solomon's reign the nation split. Ten of the twelve tribes formed a new nation, called the House of Israel with its capital eventually in Samaria (in the north). The remaining two tribes (Judah and Benjamin) formed a new nation, called the House of Judah with its capital in Jerusalem (in the south).
The Bible books of I & II Kings and I & II Chronicles detail the history of these two separate nations.
Confusion between Israelites and Jews is very common. <u>An Israelite is a genealogical descendant of one of the twelve tribes of Israel</u>. <u>A Jew is a genealogical descendant of Judah</u>. Judah was one of the twelve sons of Israel (originally named Jacob). Judah's descendants -- and *only* Judah's descendants -- are Jews. These famous Old Testament persons were Jews: Judah, Caleb, David, Solomon, Isaiah, and Daniel. However, <u>these famous Old Testament persons were *not* Jews: Abraham, Isaac, Jacob, Moses, Aaron, Joshua, Gideon, Samson, Ruth, Saul, Ezra, Job, Jeremiah, and Ezekiel</u>.
<u>Calling all Israelites Jews betrays a colossal ignorance of Bible history</u>.

8.   Whenever you see or hear the word "Jew" make sure you know exactly who is being discussed.
Originally, and up to the time of the creation of the House of Judah, the term "Jew" meant *only* a genealogical descendant of Judah, the son of Jacob (also called Israel).
After the creation of the House of Judah, the term Jew was used for any citizen of the House of Judah. This was done even though, as discussed above, the House of Judah consisted of the tribes of Judah, Benjamin, and later some Levites. An example of calling citizens of the House of Judah "Jews" occurs in II Kings 16:6, cited above.
Later the term "Jew" was often applied to anyone who was an Old Covenant participant. This probably occurred because, of the twelve tribes of Israel, historically the tribe of Judah kept the Old Covenant more than the other tribes.
Today many people call themselves "Jews" who are neither genealogically descended from Judah nor Old Covenant participants. These "Jews" identify with Jewish *culture*.
The example of the apostle Paul is illustrative of the use of the term "Jew."
The apostle Paul called himself a Jew:
> "I am verily a man which am a Jew, born in Tarsus, a city in Cilicia, yet brought up in this city at the feet of Gamaliel..." (Acts 22:3 *KJV*)
At other times Paul called himself a Pharisee:
> "...I am a Pharisee, the son of a Pharisee..." (Acts 23:6 *KJV*)
In actual fact Paul was *not* a genealogical Jew but, instead, a Benjaminite:
> "Circumcised the eighth day, of the stock of Israel, of the tribe of Benjamin, an Hebrew of the Hebrews; as touching the law, a Pharisee;" (Philippians 3:5 *KJV*)
Paul used whatever term was appropriate to tell others about the Kingdom of God:
> "For though I be free from all men, yet have I made myself servant unto all, that I might gain the more.
> And unto the Jews I became as a Jew, that I might gain the Jews; to them that are under the law, as under the law, that I might gain them that are under the law;
> To them that are without law, as without law, (being not without law to God, but under the law to Christ,) that I might gain them that are without law.
> To the weak became I as weak, that I might gain the weak: I am made all things to all men, that I might by all means save some."
> (I Corinthians 9:19-22 *KJV*)
In actual fact Paul was a former Old Covenant participant, but now a New Covenant participant.

9.   Many people confuse the Israel of the Bible with the political nation created in 1948 AD called "Israel." In 1948 a group of Zionist Jews formed a new nation in Palestine. These Zionist Jews decided to name their new nation "Israel." This fact of recent history has created confusion for Bible students. Jews live in the new nation of Israel. However, the *political* nation of Israel should not be

---

confused with the *Biblical* nation of Israel.

Jews naming their new nation "Israel" is equivalent to California naming itself the United States of America. California is only one state of 50 states in the US. California has *no* right to name itself the US! Jews are only one tribe of the twelve tribes in the original nation of Israel. Jews have *no* right to name their nation Israel!

Some people believe that the political nation of Israel is *synonymous* with the Biblical nation of Israel. Nothing could be further from the truth. These same people believe that political Israel has fulfilled some of the future prophecies of Biblical Israel. These events have *not* yet occurred. All of the prophecies of the future restoration of Biblical Israel will not begin to be fulfilled until Jesus Christ returns to rule Earth in the Millennium.

Christian groups visiting political Israel are told that political Israel has fulfilled many of the (primarily) Old Testament prophecies of Biblical Israel. These visiting Christians, not being Bible scholars, are totally *duped* by these stories. For example, Isaiah 35:1-2 tells of the desert someday blossoming like the rose. Israeli tour guides tell Christian tour groups that the current Israeli practice of irrigation in some regions is a fulfillment of this prophecy. This is totally false! When water *does* come to the desert, *God* will do it. God will bring water to the desert by performing supernatural miracles.

(Note: Unless stated otherwise, the use of the word "Israel" in this book *always* refers to Biblical Israel.)

Can you begin to see why so many people are confused about Bible prophecy?

10.   Bible prophecy shows that Earth will never be destroyed. It is a popular belief that some day Earth will be destroyed or that all life on Earth will be destroyed. This belief results in great plots for books and movies. However, the Bible shows that this belief is totally *false*. There probably *will* be nuclear wars. Gigantic natural disasters such as earthquakes *will* strike Earth. The seven last plagues (described in Revelation) *will* kill many people on Earth. However, Earth will *never* be destroyed and all life on Earth will *not* be destroyed. Earth will be rebuilt in the Millennium. (See chapters 27 & 28, "The Millennium" and "Life in the Millennium.") Earth will one day become the center of the universe. (See chapter 12, "God's Master Plan: Period Three.")

11.   Bible prophecy is exciting. It is exciting to learn of future events which absolutely *will* be fulfilled. It is exciting to learn true information of which most other human beings are totally unaware. However, one can become vain and proud about Bible prophecy knowledge. God has a warning for Bible prophecy students:

> "And though I have the gift of prophecy, and understand all mysteries, and all knowledge; and though I have all faith, so that I could remove mountains, and have not charity, I am nothing."
> "...but whether there be prophecies, they shall fail..."
> **(I Corinthians 13:2, 8 *KJV*)**

One can know all prophecies and still be nothing! As Paul also pointed out, all prophecies will fail: When a prophecy is fulfilled, it fails. When all Bible prophecies are fulfilled there will be no more prophecies! Concentrating your Bible study and thinking on prophecy alone is setting yourself up for spiritual disaster. If God wanted humans to learn only prophecy, then the Bible would consist of only prophecies. You need to know the entire Bible, not just prophecy. <u>The goal of the headed-for-success Christian must be the Kingdom of God, not Bible prophecy knowledge</u>.

<u>Summary</u>. 1. Some people are afraid of Bible prophecy. God has placed prophecy in the Bible. God wants human beings to understand this part of His Word. 2. The three areas of the Bible which deal most with Bible prophecy are: (a) the book of Revelation, (b) the book of Daniel, and (c) the "Olivet Prophecy" of Jesus Christ. 3. The book of Revelation is special in Bible prophecy. Jesus delivered Revelation to *encourage* and *inspire* the church. All Christians need *vision*. 4. Bible prophecy serves multiple purposes. 5. Bible prophecy is a major proof of God. 6. Bible prophecy is proof that Jesus is the Messiah. 7. Many people confuse Israel with Judah (nations) and Israelites with Jews (persons). Israel was warring against the Jews! An Israelite is a genealogical descendant of one of the twelve tribes of Israel. A Jew is a genealogical descendant of Judah. These famous Old Testament persons were *not* Jews: Abraham, Isaac, Jacob, Moses, Aaron, Joshua, Gideon, Samson, Ruth, Saul, Ezra, Job, Jeremiah, and Ezekiel. Calling all Israelites Jews betrays a colossal ignorance of Bible history. 8. Whenever you see or hear the word "Jew" make sure you know exactly who is being discussed. Originally, and up to the time of the creation of the House of Judah, the term "Jew" meant only a genealogical descendant of Judah, the son of Jacob (also called Israel). After the creation of the House of Judah, the term Jew was used for any citizen of the House of Judah. Later the term "Jew" was often applied to anyone who was an Old Covenant participant. Today many people call themselves "Jews" who are neither genealogically descended from Judah nor Old Covenant participants. These "Jews" identify with Jewish *culture*. 9. Many people confuse the Israel of the Bible with the political nation created in 1948 AD called "Israel." However, the *political* nation of Israel should not be confused with the *Biblical* nation of Israel. These same people believe that *political* Israel has fulfilled some of the future prophecies of *Biblical* Israel. These events have *not* yet occurred. 10. Bible prophecy shows that Earth will never be destroyed. 11. The goal of the headed-for-success Christian must be the Kingdom of God, not Bible prophecy knowledge.

The Millennium

CHAPTER 27

© 2005, Robert M. Kelley

Look up all Scriptures in your own Bible. Read and/or write the Scriptures on paper. Writing Scriptures on paper slows down your mind and causes the Bible verses to be more deeply burned into your mind.

All Scripture is inspired and true. However, you cannot learn everything at once. Therefore, the three most important Scriptures on this subject are in **bold** type and the next seven most important Scriptures on this subject are underlined.

----

1.   What is the Millennium? A millennium is a period of 1,000 years. The term "Millennium" refers to the 1,000-year period during which Jesus Christ will rule Earth. When Jesus Christ returns to earth, He is not coming as a humble carpenter who will allow himself to be put to death. That was the manner of his first coming. When Jesus Christ returns (His second coming) He will return as:
   "...KING OF KINGS, AND LORD OF LORDS." (Revelation 19:16 *KJV*)

2.   The Bible clearly shows that Jesus will return to rule Earth for 1,000 years:
   "And I saw thrones, and they sat upon them, and judgment was given
   unto them: and I saw the souls of them that were beheaded for the witness
   of Jesus, and for the word of God, and which had not worshipped the beast,
   neither his image, neither had received his mark upon their foreheads, or
   in their hands; and they lived and reigned with Christ a thousand years.
   But the rest of the dead lived not again until the thousand years were
   finished. This is the first resurrection.
   Blessed and holy is he that hath part in the first resurrection: on such the
   second death hath no power, but they shall be priests of God and of Christ,
   and shall reign with him a thousand years." (**Revelation 20:4-6** *KJV*)
Christians who have remained faithful to God will, at the time of Christ's return,
be resurrected with spirit bodies (as defined in I Corinthians 15) and will rule
with Christ for 1,000 years.
The Millennium is the first part of God's Master Plan Period Two.

3.   Scriptures (including the one above) show that Christians will rule with
Christ on Earth during this 1,000-year period:
   "And hast made us unto our God kings and priests: and we shall reign on
   the earth." (**Revelation 5:10** *KJV*)
Jesus shows that the meek will inherit not heaven, but Earth:
   "Blessed are the meek: for they shall inherit the earth." (Matthew 5:5 *KJV*)
(For abundant Scriptures which clearly show that successful Christians with
resurrected, spirit bodies will rule with Christ on Earth during Christ's 1,000-

year rule, see chapter 23, "Christians Do Not Go to Heaven After Death.")

4.   Some Scriptures say that the Christian's reward is *in* heaven, but note that this reward does not *stay* in heaven:

> "And, behold, I come quickly; and my reward is with me, to give to every man according as his work shall be." (Revelation 22:12 *KJV*)

Jesus is returning from heaven (the Third Heaven) to Earth. <u>The Christian's reward is in heaven.</u> <u>Jesus will bring this reward from heaven to Earth.</u> <u>This reward is eternal life and ruling in the Kingdom of God on Earth with Jesus in the Millennium.</u>

5.   <u>Why is it that many people believe that the reward of the Christian is to go to heaven?</u> Some people have the idea that Christians go to heaven for an eternal life of leisure. Where do they get this idea? <u>This may be a popular idea.</u> <u>However, this idea cannot be found in the Bible!</u> No Christian leader whose life is recorded in the Bible -- the twelve apostles, Paul, or Christ himself -- ever said that the reward of the Christian is to go to heaven. (Be sure to see chapters 22 & 23, "Christians Go to Heaven After Death" and "Christians Do Not Go to Heaven After Death.")

6.   <u>God will resurrect King David of ancient Israel to rule over Israel in the Millennium:</u>

> "And I will set up one shepherd over them, and he shall feed them, even my servant David; he shall feed them, and he shall be their shepherd.
> And I the LORD will be their God, and my servant David a prince among them..." (Ezekiel 34:23-24 *KJV*)
> "And David my servant shall be king over them; and they all shall have one shepherd..."
> "...and my servant David shall be their prince for ever."
> (Ezekiel 37:24, 25 *KJV*)

7.   <u>The twelve apostles of the New Testament church will rule over the twelve tribes of Israel in the Millennium:</u>

> "Then answered Peter and said unto him, Behold, we have forsaken all, and followed thee; what shall we have therefore?
> And Jesus said unto them, Verily I say unto you, That ye which have followed me, in the regeneration when the Son of man shall sit in the throne of his glory, ye also shall sit upon twelve thrones, judging the twelve tribes of Israel." (**Matthew 19:27-28** *KJV*)

8.   Originally God placed man in charge of Earth:

> "And God blessed them, and God said unto them, Be fruitful, and multiply, and replenish the earth, and subdue it: and have dominion over the fish of the sea, and over the fowl of the air, and over every living thing that moveth [margin: Heb. *creepeth*] upon the earth." (Genesis 1:28 *KJV*)
> "And the LORD God took the man [margin: Or, *Adam*], and put him into

the Garden of Eden to dress it and to keep it." (Genesis 2:15 *KJV*)
However, what has happened? Has man properly developed Earth? <u>For at least 6,000 years human beings, under the inspiration of Satan the Devil, have been damaging and destroying Earth.</u> Man, under the influence of Satan, has made a mess of Earth. Note what God says about those who destroy Earth:

> "And the nations were angry, and thy wrath is come, and the time of the dead, that they should be judged, and that thou shouldest give reward unto thy servants the prophets, and to the saints, and them that fear thy name, small and great; and shouldest destroy them which destroy [margin: Or, *corrupt*] the earth." (<u>Revelation 11:18</u> *KJV*)

9.   <u>The amazing, wonderful truth is that successful Christians, with resurrected, spirit bodies, will assist Jesus in cleaning up, rebuilding, and renewing the entire Earth.</u> Under Christ, Christians will have the opportunity to truly make things right!
This is why the very first thing Jesus told all people to pray for (in the model prayer called by some the "Lord's Prayer") was:

> "Thy kingdom come..." (<u>Matthew 6:10</u> *KJV*)

God's Kingdom -- the Kingdom of God -- will come to Earth during the Millennium.
Jesus is coming to save man from man, and Earth from man.

10.   <u>Many people today believe that they are "saving Earth." They do not know what they are talking about!</u> Innocent school children are religiously taught to sort and recycle household trash. Their equally duped teachers do not tell these children that household trash comprises about 2% of total trash. You can recycle household trash forever while planet Earth goes to pollution hell.
Human beings are not going to "save Earth." Human beings do not have the power to save Earth, their nation, their state, their city, their neighborhood, or themselves!

11.   <u>There is a darker side of some whose sole motivation is to, themselves, "save Earth." Some of these people are involved in nature worship.</u> Paul describes, in Romans 1, how nature worship began:

> "Professing themselves to be wise, they became fools,
> And changed the glory of the uncorruptible God into an image made like to corruptible man, and to birds, and four-footed beasts, and creeping things." (Romans 1:22-23 *KJV*)
> "Who changed the truth of God into a lie, and worshipped and served the creature more [margin: Or, *rather*] than the Creator, who is blessed for ever. Amen." (<u>Romans 1:25</u> *KJV*)

If one looks carefully at the eco-freak movement, one can see interesting behaviors. Many eco-freaks value animal life over human life. Many eco-freaks envision an Earth in which billions of living people must die. Many eco-freaks are simply nature worshippers!

12.   One of the great truths of all eternity is that man needs God. Those who believe that man will save himself are as foolish as those who believe that God did not create man or that man created himself. Eventually, those human beings who do not learn that man needs God will be consigned to the Lake of Fire for the Second Death! God will save man. God will save Earth. God will save Earth by putting Jesus Christ in charge of Earth in the Millennium.

13.   How does the Millennium relate to the Kingdom of God? The Kingdom of God is the rule of God. The Kingdom of God has always existed and will always exist. The rule of God can be over any domain: an individual human being, angels, the Third Heaven, etc. This rule can occur at any time: before man was created, during the Old Testament & New Testament periods (which are in God's Master Plan Period One), during God's Master Plan Period Two, or during God's Master Plan Period Three. The Millennium is one (of many) manifestations of the Kingdom of God. In the Millennium Jesus Christ, the Messiah, will head the Kingdom of God over all Earth.

14.   In the Millennium the Kingdom of God will be over all human beings living on Earth. What human beings will be living on Earth in the Millennium? Human beings living on Earth in the Millennium are those who have survived from God's Master Plan Period One and the descendants of those survivors.

15.   Israelites (all twelve tribes) in the Old Testament period looked forward to the Millennium. It is easy to see why. When King Solomon ruled the twelve-tribe nation of Israel, he essentially ruled most of the civilized world. Later, conditions deteriorated for the Israelites. About 721 BC the House of Israel (ten tribes) went into captivity to the Assyrians. The people were moved to other nations, eventually to be known as the "Lost Ten Tribes of Israel." About 586 BC the House of Judah (two tribes, Judah and Benjamin) went into captivity to the Babylonians. The people were moved to Babylon. After seventy years a few Jews (of the tribe of Judah) and Levites returned to Jerusalem to rebuild the temple and city walls. In summary, the twelve-tribe nation of Israel has had a difficult history. During centuries of slavery, the Israelites, as underdogs, looked forward to the fulfillment of the Millennium prophecies. The Old Testament pictures of the Millennium show an Israel once again leading all other nations. (Note: See chapter 26, "Bible Prophecy Basics," about the difference between *political* Israel and *Biblical* Israel.)

16.   The major and minor prophetic books of the Old Testament are loaded with pictures of what life will be like in the Millennium. Basically, the entire Earth will be rebuilt. This is an exciting story, one too big for this chapter 27. See chapter 28, "Life in the Millennium."

Summary. 1. The term "Millennium" refers to the 1,000-year period in which Jesus Christ will rule Earth. 2. Christians who have remained faithful to God will, at the time of Christ's return, be resurrected with spirit bodies (as defined in I Corinthians 15) and will rule with Christ for 1,000 years. The Millennium is the first part of God's Master Plan Period Two. 3. Scriptures (including the one above) show that Christians will rule with Christ on Earth during this 1,000-year period. 4. The Christian's reward is in heaven. Jesus will bring this reward from heaven to Earth. This reward is eternal life and ruling in the Kingdom of God on Earth with Jesus in the Millennium. 5. Why is it that many people believe that the reward of the Christian is to go to heaven? This may be a popular idea. However, this idea cannot be found in the Bible! 6. God will resurrect King David of ancient Israel to rule over Israel in the Millennium. 7. The twelve apostles of the New Testament church will rule over the twelve tribes of Israel in the Millennium. 8. For at least 6,000 years human beings, under the inspiration of Satan the Devil, have been damaging and destroying Earth. 9. The amazing, wonderful truth is that successful Christians, with resurrected, spirit bodies, will assist Jesus in cleaning up, rebuilding, and renewing the entire Earth. 10. Many people today believe that they are "saving Earth." They do not know what they are talking about! 11. There is a darker side of some whose sole motivation is to, themselves, "save Earth." Some of these people are involved in nature worship. 12. One of the great truths of all eternity is that man needs God. 13. How does the Millennium relate to the Kingdom of God? The Millennium is one (of many) manifestations of the Kingdom of God. 14. In the Millennium the Kingdom of God will be over all human beings living on Earth. 15. The Old Testament pictures of the Millennium show an Israel once again leading all other nations. 16. The major and minor prophetic books of the Old Testament are loaded with pictures of what life will be like in the Millennium.

Life in the Millennium

CHAPTER 28

© 2005, Robert M. Kelley

Look up all Scriptures in your own Bible. Read and/or write the Scriptures on paper. Writing Scriptures on paper slows down your mind and causes the Bible verses to be more deeply burned into your mind.

All Scripture is inspired and true. However, you cannot learn everything at once. Therefore, the three most important Scriptures on this subject are in **bold** type and the next seven most important Scriptures on this subject are underlined.

----

1.   If you have not done so, be sure to see chapter 27, "The Millennium." Chapter 27 establishes the framework for the Millennium. This chapter 28 provides the detail of what life will be like in the Millennium.

2.   Consider this moment in time. The beginning of the Millennium marks the beginning of God's Master Plan Period Two. Earth has just endured approximately 6,000 years of man's rule (God's Master Plan Period One). During this approximate 6,000 years man has been under the constant influence of Satan the Devil. Most of God's Master Plan Period One can be characterized as man's misrule. The end of God's Master Plan Period One witnessed many of the events predicted in the book of Revelation. Huge wars have occurred. The seven last plagues have destroyed much of Earth (both people and property). Those human beings still alive have suffered greatly and are still shell-shocked. At this precise moment Jesus Christ has returned from the Third Heaven, the Christian saints have been resurrected (dead ones first, living ones second), Satan has been bound, and Jesus begins His rule.

3.   When Jesus returns to rule Earth He will arrive on the Mount of Olives, near Jerusalem:
>   "And his feet shall stand in that day upon the mount of Olives, which
>   is before Jerusalem on the east..." (Zechariah 14:4 *KJV*)
Note carefully that when Jesus originally ascended into the Third Heaven, he left Earth from the Mount of Olives:
>   "And when he had spoken these things, while they beheld, he was taken
>   up; and a cloud received him out of their sight.
>   And while they looked stedfastly toward heaven as he went up, behold, two
>   men stood by them in white apparel;
>   Which also said, Ye men of Galilee, why stand ye gazing up into heaven?
>   this same Jesus, which is taken up from you into heaven, shall so come in
>   like manner as ye have seen him go into heaven.
>   Then returned they unto Jerusalem from the mount called Olivet, which is
>   from Jerusalem a sabbath day's journey." (Acts 1:9-12 *KJV*)

Jesus left Earth from the Mount of Olives. When Jesus returns to Earth He will "land" on the Mount of Olives. Zechariah continues his prophecy of Christ's return:

"...and the LORD my God shall come, and all the saints with thee."

"And the LORD shall be king over all the earth..." (Zechariah 14:5, 9 *KJV*) Other prophecies describe Christ's triumphant return to rule Earth from Jerusalem:

"O Zion, that bringest good tidings [margin: Or, *O thou that tellest good tidings to Zion*], get thee up into the high mountain; O Jerusalem that bringest good tidings, lift up thy voice with strength; lift it up, be not afraid; say unto the cities of Judah, Behold your God!

Behold, the Lord GOD will come with strong hand, and his arm shall rule for him: behold, his reward is with him, and his work [margin: Or, *recompense for his work*] before him." (Isaiah 40:9-10 *KJV*)

4.   <u>Isaiah gives more detail about Christ's rule</u>:

"And there shall come forth a rod out of the stem of Jesse, and a Branch shall grow out of his roots:

And the spirit of the LORD shall rest upon him, the spirit of wisdom and understanding, the spirit of counsel and might, the spirit of knowledge and of the fear of the LORD;

And shall make him of quick understanding in the fear of the LORD: and he shall not judge after the sight of his eyes, neither reprove after the hearing of his ears:

But with righteousness shall he judge the poor, and reprove with equity for the meek of the earth: and he shall smite the earth with the rod of his mouth, and with the breath of his lips shall he slay the wicked.

And righteousness shall be the girdle of his loins, and faithfulness the girdle of his reins." (<u>Isaiah 11:1-5</u> *KJV*)

5.   To the prophets were revealed glimpses of life in the Millennium. Here is an overview of life in the Millennium:

"And it shall come to pass in the last days, that the mountain of the LORD's house shall be established [margin: Or, *prepared*] in the top of the mountains, and shall be exalted above the hills; and all nations shall flow unto it.

And many people shall go and say, Come ye, and let us go up to the mountain of the LORD, to the house of the God of Jacob; and he will teach us of his ways, and we will walk in his paths: for out of Zion shall go forth the law, and the word of the LORD from Jerusalem.

And he shall judge among the nations, and shall rebuke many people: and they shall beat their swords into plowshares, and their spears into pruninghooks [margin: Or, *scythes*]: nation shall not lift up sword against nation, neither shall they learn war any more."

(Isaiah 2:2-4 *KJV*)

This same passage is repeated in Micah 4:1-3. Micah 4 adds one more thought:

"But they shall sit every man under his vine and under his fig tree; and none shall make them afraid: for the mouth of the LORD of hosts hath spoken it." (Micah 4:4 *KJV*)

Symbols are used in this prophecy. "Mountains" means nations. "Hills" means smaller national entities. Note what is happening in this famous summary of life in the Millennium. <u>God's government, with headquarters in Jerusalem, will be over all nations.</u> <u>The law of God, not man's laws, will be applied to all Earth.</u> <u>God, not the United Nations, will settle disputes between nations.</u> <u>There will be no more war or human military soldiers or weapons.</u>

Zechariah corroborates Isaiah and Micah:

"Thus saith the LORD; I am returned unto Zion, and will dwell in the midst of Jerusalem: and Jerusalem shall be called a city of truth; and the mountain of the LORD of hosts the holy mountain." (Zechariah 8:3 *KJV*)

6. <u>Major physical changes -- land healing -- will occur on Earth:</u>
    "The wilderness and the solitary place shall be glad for them; and the desert shall rejoice, and blossom as the rose.
    It shall blossom abundantly, and rejoice even with joy and singing: the glory of Lebanon shall be given unto it, the excellency of Carmel and Sharon, they shall see the glory of the LORD, and the excellency of our God." (<u>Isaiah 35:1-2</u> *KJV*)

Isaiah speaks of additional changes:

"The voice of him that crieth in the wilderness, Prepare ye the way of the LORD, make straight in the desert a highway for our God.
Every valley shall be exalted, and every mountain and hill shall be made low: and the crooked shall be made straight [margin: Or, *a straight place*], and the rough places plain [margin: Or, *a plain place*]:" (Isaiah 40:3-4 *KJV*)

7. <u>God will bring water, even to places which have never known it:</u>
    "...in the wilderness shall waters break out, and streams in the desert." (Isaiah 35:6 *KJV*)
    "When the poor and needy seek water, and there is none, and their tongue faileth for thirst, I the LORD will hear them, I the God of Israel will not forsake them.
    I will open rivers in high places, and fountains in the midst of the valleys: I will make the wilderness a pool of water, and the dry land springs of water." (<u>Isaiah 41:17-18</u> *KJV*)
    "...I will cause the shower to come down in his season; there shall be showers of blessing." (Ezekiel 34:26 *KJV*)
    "Be glad then, ye children of Zion, and rejoice in the LORD your God: for he hath given you the former rain moderately, and he will cause to come down for you the rain, the former rain, and the latter rain in the first month." (Joel 2:23 *KJV*)

8. <u>The land will yield abundant crops:</u>
    "Therefore they shall come and sing in the height of Zion, and shall flow together to the goodness of the LORD, for wheat, and for wine, and for oil,

and for the young of the flock and of the herd: and their soul shall be as a watered garden; and they shall not sorrow any more at all."
(Jeremiah 31:12 *KJV*)

"And the tree of the field shall yield her fruit, and the earth shall yield her increase..." (Ezekiel 34:27 *KJV*)

"...I will call for the corn, and will increase it, and lay no famine upon you. And I will multiply the fruit of the tree, and the increase of the field, that ye shall receive no more reproach of famine among the heathen."
(Ezekiel 36:29-30 *KJV*)

"Yea, the LORD will answer and say unto his people, Behold I will send you corn, and wine, and oil, and ye shall be satisfied therewith: and I will no more make you a reproach among the heathen:" (Joel 2:19 *KJV*)

"Fear not, O land; be glad and rejoice: for the LORD will do great things. Be not afraid, ye beasts of the field: for the pastures of the wilderness do spring, for the tree beareth her fruit, the fig tree and the vine do yield their strength." (Joel 2:21-22 *KJV*)

"Behold, the days come, saith the LORD, that the plowman shall overtake the reaper, and the treader of grapes him that soweth seed; and the mountains shall drop sweet [margin: Or, *new*] wine, and all the hills shall melt." (Amos 9:13 *KJV*)

"...they shall plant vineyards, and drink the wine thereof; they shall also make gardens, and eat the fruit of them." (Amos 9:14 *KJV*)

9.   Trees and forests will be restored:
"I will plant in the wilderness the cedar, the shittah tree, and the myrtle, and the oil tree; I will set in the desert the fir tree, and the pine, and the box tree together." (Isaiah 41:19 *KJV*)

10.   The nature of animals will be changed from dangerous to friendly:
"The wolf also shall dwell with the lamb, and the leopard shall lie down with the kid; and the calf and the young lion and the fatling together; and a little child shall lead them.
And the cow and the bear shall feed; their young ones shall lie down together: and the lion shall eat straw like the ox.
And the sucking child shall play on the hole of the asp, and the weaned child shall put his hand on the cockatrice' [margin: Or, *adder's*] den.
They shall not hurt nor destroy in all my holy mountain: for the earth shall be full of the knowledge of the LORD, as the waters cover the sea."
(Isaiah 11:6-9 *KJV*)

"The wolf and the lamb shall feed together, and the lion shall eat straw like the bullock: and dust shall be the serpent's meat. They shall not hurt nor destroy in all my holy mountain, saith the LORD." (Isaiah 65:25 *KJV*)

11.   People will be healed:
"Then the eyes of the blind shall be opened, and the ears of the deaf shall be unstopped.
Then shall the lame man leap as an hart, and the tongue of the dumb

sing..." (Isaiah 35:5-6 *KJV*)

12. Cities will be rebuilt:
"...the cities shall be inhabited; and the wastes shall be builded:"
(Ezekiel 36:10 *KJV*)
"Thus saith the Lord GOD; In the day that I shall have cleansed you from all your iniquities I will also cause you to dwell in the cities, and the wastes shall be builded.
And the desolate land shall be tilled, whereas it lay desolate in the sight of all that passed by.
And they shall say, This land that was desolate is become like the garden of Eden; and the waste and desolate and ruined cities are become fenced, and are inhabited.
Then the heathen that are left round about you shall know that I the LORD build the ruined places, and plant that that was desolate: I the LORD have spoken it, and I will do it." (Ezekiel 36:33-36 *KJV*)

13. Children and the elderly will live securely:
"Thus saith the LORD of hosts; There shall yet old men and old women dwell in the streets of Jerusalem, and every man with his staff in his hand for very age [margin: Heb. *multitude of days*].
And the streets of the city shall be full of boys and girls playing in the streets thereof." (Zechariah 8:4-5 *KJV*)

14. The twelve-tribe nation of Israel will be gathered. At the time of Samuel the twelve-tribe nation of Israel became a kingdom. Three kings ruled: Saul, David, and Solomon. After Solomon's death, Israel divided into two kingdoms. The House of Israel, with its capital (north) in Samaria, consisted of ten tribes. The House of Judah, with its capital (south) in Jerusalem, consisted of two tribes (Judah and Benjamin). The books of I & II Kings and I & II Chronicles record the two separate histories of these two kingdoms. Each kingdom was conquered in war; most of the citizens became slaves and were marched away into captivity. The House of Israel was conquered by the Assyrians about 721 BC; these ten tribes were marched into Assyria. The House of Judah was conquered by the Babylonians about 586 BC; these two tribes were marched into Babylon. A few Jews (of the tribe of Judah) and Levites returned to Jerusalem from Babylon to rebuild the city walls and temple. Most of the twelve tribes (including Judah) remained in lands far away from Palestine and were scattered throughout a number of nations. In the Millennium the remnants of these scattered twelve tribes will be gathered from other nations and brought to Palestine:
"And it shall come to pass in that day, that the Lord shall set his hand again the second time to recover the remnant of his people, which shall be left, from Assyria, and from Egypt, and from Pathros, and from Cush, and from Elam, and from Shinar, and from Hamath, and from the islands of the sea.
And he shall set up an ensign for the nations, and shall assemble the outcasts of Israel, and gather together the dispersed of Judah from the four

corners [margin: Heb. *wings*] of the earth." (Isaiah 11:11-12 *KJV*)
"Behold, I will gather them out of all countries, whither I have driven them in mine anger, and in my fury, and in great wrath; and I will bring them again unto this place, and I will cause them to dwell safely." (Jeremiah 32:37 *KJV*)
"For I will take you from among the heathen, and gather you out of all countries, and will bring you into your own land." (Ezekiel 36:24 *KJV*)
(Note: See chapter 26, "Bible Prophecy Basics," about the difference between *political* Israel and *Biblical* Israel.)

15.   The New Covenant will be offered freely. This example is given of the New Covenant being offered to the gathered twelve-tribe nation of Israel (see Ezekiel 36:24 above):
"A new heart also will I give you, and a new spirit will I put within you: and I will take away the stony heart out of your flesh, and I will give you an heart of flesh.
And I will put my spirit within you, and cause you to walk in my statutes, and ye shall keep my judgments, and do them." (**Ezekiel 36:26-27** *KJV*)
Receiving the Holy Spirit is becoming a New Covenant participant. (For more information, see chapter 5, "The New Covenant.") People living on earth in the Millennium will be offered the New Covenant.

16.   The *physical* resurrections of people who have physically lived on the earth during God's Master Plan Period One occur in God's Master Plan Period Two. However, these resurrections occur *after* the Millennium:
"But the rest of the dead lived not again until the thousand years were finished..." (Revelation 20:5 *KJV*)
(For more detail on the *physical* resurrection of people (in God's Master Plan Period Two) who have lived physically before (in God's Master Plan Period One), see chapter 11, "God's Master Plan: Period Two.")
Consider what Earth will look like at the end of the Millennium. Jesus Christ will have spent 1,000 years leading former Christians (now with resurrected, spirit bodies) in the clean-up and rebuilding of Earth. Earth will be a beautiful place, with healed land, water, and peoples. The messes of 6,000 years of Satan-influenced life will have been cleaned up. No wars will occur. Military-trained warriors will not exist. World peace will prevail. Rotten government will be a bad-dream memory. Food and prosperity will prevail world-wide. Thick steaks and fine wines will be abundant.
Can you imagine the reactions of people who have been physically resurrected from God's Master Plan Period One? They will be thrilled to be in such a new world!

Summary. 1. This chapter 28 provides the detail of what life will be like in the Millennium. 2. Consider this moment in time. 3. When Jesus returns to rule Earth He will arrive on the Mount of Olives, near Jerusalem. 4. Isaiah gives more detail about Christ's rule. 5. God's government, with headquarters in Jerusalem, will be over all nations. The law of God, not man's laws, will be applied to all Earth. God, not the United Nations, will settle disputes between nations. There will be no more war or human military soldiers or weapons. 6. Major physical changes -- land healing -- will occur on Earth. 7. God will bring water, even to places which have never known it. 8. The land will yield abundant crops. 9. Trees and forests will be restored. 10. The nature of animals will be changed from dangerous to friendly. 11. People will be healed. 12. Cities will be rebuilt. 13. Children and the elderly will live securely. 14. The twelve-tribe nation of Israel will be gathered. 15. The New Covenant will be offered freely. People living on earth in the Millennium will be offered the New Covenant. 16. The *physical* resurrections of people occur *after* the Millennium. Consider what Earth will look like at the end of the Millennium. Can you imagine the reactions of people who have been physically resurrected from God's Master Plan Period One? They will be thrilled to be in such a new world!

Satan's One-World Government

CHAPTER 29
© 2005, Robert M. Kelley

Look up all Scriptures in your own Bible. Read and/or write the Scriptures on paper. Writing Scriptures on paper slows down your mind and causes the Bible verses to be more deeply burned into your mind.

All Scripture is inspired and true. However, you cannot learn everything at once. Therefore, the three most important Scriptures on this subject are in **bold** type and the next seven most important Scriptures on this subject are underlined.

----

1.   Christ is coming to institute God's one-world government over Earth in the Millennium. (Chapter 27, "The Millennium," shows how God's one-world government will be established. Chapter 28, "Life in the Millennium," provides the detail of what life will be like in God's one-world government.) However, chapter 20, "Satan and Demons," shows that Satan loves to *counterfeit* things of God. Satan has known for eons of time about God's coming world-ruling government in the Millennium. Therefore Satan, the counterfeiter of things of God, has been working hard for almost 6,000 years to influence man to create an in-defiance-of-God world government. Satan has been inspiring and is continuing to inspire leaders, politicians, thinkers, and writers to talk about, promote, and work to create *his* one-world government. The Bible shows that near the end of Satan's 6,000-year invisible rule (in God's Master Plan Period One) Satan will *succeed* in creating a Satanic one-world government just before Christ returns to institute God's one-world government in the Millennium. Satan's counterfeit world government will promise peace and *look* good.

2.   In describing Satan's coming one-world government the Bible uses terms like "Beast," "False Prophet," "Babylon," and "Ten Kings." These Bible terms will be defined and explained later. People working for Satan's coming one-world government have commonly used the term "New World Order." Many people have "caught on" to the New World Order term. In recent years those working for Satan's coming one-world government have used the word "global" a lot. I choose to call this coming ugly political and governmental entity what the Bible says it is: Satan's One-World Government (SOWG). This chapter 29, "Satan's One-World Government," will use SOWG to refer to Satan's coming one-world government. Is SOWG being forced on the world through the United Nations (UN), the North Atlantic Treaty Organization (NATO), or the United States of America (US)?

3.   SOWG is known from Bible prophecy. The prophetic part of the Old

Testament (called the Prophets) consists of the Major Prophets (Isaiah, Jeremiah, Ezekiel), and the Minor Prophets (twelve books). However, prophetic statements appear throughout the Bible. The areas of the Bible which deal most in Bible prophecy are given in chapter 26, "Bible Prophecy Basics." Most of the information on SOWG comes from these areas.

4.   SOWG will rule the world:
   "...and power was given him over all kindreds, and tongues, and nations." (**Revelation 13:7** *KJV*)

This is a small statement, but it is powerful. SOWG will rule over "all kindreds, and tongues, and nations." The term *all* is inclusive.

   "...and they worshipped the beast, saying, Who is like unto the beast? who is able to make war with him?" (Revelation 13:4 *KJV*)

There will be *no* power on Earth to challenge SOWG.

   "Thus he said, The fourth beast shall be the fourth kingdom upon earth, which shall be diverse from all kingdoms, and shall devour the whole earth, and shall tread it down, and break it in pieces." (Daniel 7:23 *KJV*)

SOWG will "devour the whole earth" in many ways.

5.   SOWG will control all economic activity on Earth:
   "And he causeth all, both small and great, rich and poor, free and bond, to receive [margin: Gr. *to give them*] a mark in their right hand, or in their foreheads:
   And that no man might buy or sell, save he that had the mark, or the name of the beast, or the number of his name.
   Here is wisdom. Let him that hath understanding count the number of the beast: for it is the number of a man; and his number is Six hundred threescore and six." (Revelation 13:16-18 *KJV*)

Before the present time (near the end of God's Master Plan Period One), it was impossible to understand many of the statements in Revelation. In light of modern technologies it is now possible to physically understand how many statements in Revelation can be fulfilled.

For example, it is rumored that the US Government will start total economic control with uniquely-encoded microchip-embedded ID cards. Each citizen will be forced to carry his or her card at all times. Eventually these microchips can be placed in babies when they are born in hospitals (in their right hands or foreheads). These microchips will have to be passed over scanners for all purchase and sale transactions. In addition, satellites will be able to determine the exact location of every single human being by sensing the microchip embedded in each individual.

Consider what is already in place today. Years ago British authorities had a microchip surgically placed in the oldest son of Prince Charles. This act (but not the location) was announced to the public. If the young crown prince is kidnapped, satellites can immediately identify his exact location. Presently each pet owner can have a microchip placed in his or her pet, for total pet control. (Call your local vet and check it out!)

6.   <u>Satan is at the heart and core of SOWG</u>:
> "...and the dragon gave him his power, and his seat, and great authority."
(Revelation 13:2 *KJV*)

This Scripture says that the "dragon" gave power unto the Beast (SOWG). You don't have to guess what Bible symbols mean. The Bible defines its own symbols:
> "And the great dragon was cast out, that old serpent, called the Devil, and Satan, which deceiveth the whole world..." (Revelation 12:9 *KJV*)

The Bible shows that "dragon," "serpent," "Devil," and "Satan" are the same being. The Bible clearly shows that Satan is behind SOWG.

Satan's empowering the Beast or SOWG is repeated:
> "And they worshipped the dragon which gave power unto the beast: and they worshipped the beast, saying, Who is like unto the beast? who is able to make war with him?" (Revelation 13:4 *KJV*)

(For more information on Satan and his rule over this world, see chapters 20 & 21, "Satan and Demons" and "This is Satan's World.")

7.   <u>SOWG, like all dictatorships, rests upon four pillars: (a) murder, (b) lies, (c) slavery, and (d) anti-God programs</u>. All dictatorships, whether of the Caesars of Rome, of World War II dictators such as Adolph Hitler and Joseph Stalin, or of modern dictators like Idi Amin and Saddam Hussein, possess certain common characteristics. These characteristics are embodied in four pillars. All four of these pillars are required to make a dictatorship work.

8.   <u>Murder is an essential pillar of a dictatorship</u>. Dictatorships rule by fear and intimidation. Those who do not comply completely with a dictator's wishes are threatened, intimidated, harassed, imprisoned, tortured, and murdered. "Rebels" are first threatened and harassed. If rebels are not made compliant by threats and harassment, then they are either imprisoned and tortured, or murdered.

Those who murder follow Satan the Devil:
> "Ye are of your father the devil, and the lusts of your father ye will do. He was a murderer from the beginning, and abode not in the truth, because there is no truth in him. When he speaketh a lie, he speaketh of his own: for he is a liar, and the father of it." (John 8:44 *KJV*)

Satan is a murderer. Is it any wonder that SOWG, the creation of Satan, is a big murder machine?

Dictators murder rebels, snitches (see below), and even loyal supporters. (Once Hitler was in control in Germany he murdered many of his brown-shirt Nazi leaders who helped put him in office.) Dictators murder everyone!

One SOWG leader has publicly said that Earth's population must be reduced from six billion to two billion. According to SOWG, four billion people must *die*. SOWG has, is, and will murder large numbers of people in a number of ways.

In the US over 45 million babies (and millions more who would have been their descendants) have been murdered via abortion since the US Supreme Court Roe v. Wade decision on January 22, 1973.

Hundreds of millions of people have been and will continue to be murdered by the world-wide ban on DDT. DDT has killed no one. However, DDT's ban has allowed killer diseases like malaria to stage a huge comeback.

Killer diseases have been created in scientific laboratories for the purpose of murdering large numbers of people. AIDS is in this group.

What about the new killer diseases identified today, such as West Nile Virus, SARS, Ebola, Mad Cow Disease, Bovine Spongiform Encephalopathy (BSE), and Chronic Wasting Disease (CWD)? Why are these diseases *new*?

9.   <u>Lies are an essential pillar of a dictatorship</u>. The former Soviet Union consisted of fifteen Soviet Socialist Republics. The Union of Soviet Socialist Republics, the USSR, was destroyed by truth. Truth came to Soviet citizens via satellite TV and fax machines. Jesus revealed this fact:

> "And ye shall know the truth, and the truth shall make you free."
> (<u>John 8:32</u> *KJV*)

Those who lie follow Satan the Devil:

> "Ye are of your father the devil, and the lusts of your father ye will do. He was a murderer from the beginning, and abode not in the truth, because there is no truth in him. When he speaketh a lie, he speaketh of his own: for he is a liar, and the father of it." (John 8:44 *KJV*)

Satan is a liar. Is it any wonder that SOWG, the creation of Satan, is a lie machine? Truth to SOWG is like sunshine to a vampire. Sunshine kills vampires and truth kills dictatorships. Dictators fear truth more than anything else. (Truth is more dangerous to them than bullets.) Dictatorships threaten, intimidate, harass, imprison, torture, and murder anyone who tells the truth. In many nations telling the truth is referred to as a "hate crime."

Most people receive the information they believe from the major media networks. Most people believe that they are receiving accurate information from these networks. Nothing could be further from the truth! The mission of the media networks is to make sure that you *never* find out what is truly happening. It is true that media networks *do* lie. However, even worse, most of the real news -- at least 95% -- is *never* reported. Most media space is filled with meaningless stories of trivia. Remember "news" stories like Tanya Harding, O.J. Simpson, Columbine, and the "Washington Sniper"? Media network employees should properly be called "information prostitutes." A sex prostitute will perform any sex act for money. An information prostitute will write or say *anything* for money. At all times -- 24/7 -- *propaganda poop* flows from the media networks. (Be sure to see chapters 13 & 14, "Truth" and "Lies.")

Note that murder and lies are closely related. Jesus Christ mentioned both in the same Bible verse (John 8:44) describing Satan's nature. Satan's murdering is closely related to his lying. A modern manifestation of the close relationship between murder and lying is the practice of referring to a murder as a "suicide." Modern dictators control all media through which to broadcast their propaganda poop. A dictator's committing murder is referred to as a "suicide." The "suicide" claim is the ultimate insult: the public is made to believe that the murder victim took his or her own life.

10.   <u>Slavery is an essential pillar of a dictatorship</u>. The Roman Empire was famous for its slavery system. Stalin's USSR had (and still has) its Gulag slave

camp system. Hitler was noted for his slave camps. China has many slave camps.

SOWG will be heavily involved in slavery:

> "And the merchants of the earth shall weep and mourn over her; for no man buyeth their merchandise any more:
> The merchandise of gold, and silver, and precious stones, and of pearls, and fine linen, and purple, and silk, and scarlet, and all thyine [margin: Or, *sweet*] wood, and all manner vessels of ivory, and all manner vessels of most precious wood, and of brass, and iron, and marble,
> And cinnamon, and odours, and ointments, and frankincense, and wine, and oil, and fine flour, and wheat, and beasts, and sheep, and horses, and chariots, and slaves [margin: Or, *bodies*], and souls of men."
> (<u>Revelation 18:11-13</u> *KJV*)

The greatest prison building boom in the history of Earth has occurred in the US in the last 25 years. However, you haven't heard about it, have you?

The US prison population has increased four-fold since 1985, to over two million. In fact, per capita, more US citizens are incarcerated in prisons today than citizens of the former USSR, China, or any other nation. Many US citizens are in prison for DUI, check-writing, and drug possession/use -- non-violent crime convictions.

In California, 70% of the prison inmates who have received life sentences because of the "three strikes and you're out" law have *never* committed a violent crime. One man received a life sentence for stealing a $5.62 chuck steak to feed his mother and mentally retarded brother. California now spends more money on its prison system than on education.

In the US prison system murderers and other violent offenders are commonly released early (via parole), while non-violent offenders are forced to fulfill their full prison terms. (Parole is not permitted for drug convictions.)

The US prison Gulag has many factories, just like China and the former USSR. US prison workers perform billions of dollars of work annually for Unicorp and many big-name US corporations. Non-violent prisoners make excellent factory workers!

Scores (or hundreds) of thousands of rapes of women and men are committed each week in US prisons; these rapes are neither reported nor recorded.

Also consider that there are different forms of slavery. Slavery concerns degrees of control. Presently all US wireless phone companies are telling the US Government where every customer is at all times. Wireless phone users *pay* to carry US Government tracking devices! The US National Security Agency (NSA) monitors all land telephone, wireless telephone, fax, Internet, microwave, radio, and TV traffic, in part, via Project ECHELON. The US Federal Bureau of Investigation (FBI) is reading all e-mail with Carnivore, its massive surveillance system.

Micro-chips in ID cards and in hands will make every human being geographically locatable at all times.

State-of-the-art electronics makes a degree of slavery possible of which former dictators could only dream.

11.   <u>Anti-God programs are an essential pillar of a dictatorship</u>. People who believe in God are a threat to any dictatorship, whether of Caesar, Stalin, Hitler, or any would-be modern dictator. Belief in God is the heart of marriage and family. The bonds of marriage and family are very strong. Marriage and family bonds provide structure to fight dictatorships. Citizens who are isolated as individuals are easier to control. Dictators know these facts. Therefore they deliberately attack marriages, families, and all God-worshipping structures.

Each ancient Roman citizen was required to make an annual public sacrifice to the Emperor and to the god of Rome. (Early emperors were regarded as men; later emperors were regarded as gods.) When this act was performed the worshipper was given a certificate which was duly signed by local officials. If a citizen could not produce a certificate verifying that the required sacrifice had been made during the last twelve months, he or she could be put to death.

Polycarp (69-155 AD), Bishop of Smyrna, refused to worship the Emperor or Rome. He was executed -- burned at the stake -- on Saturday, February 23, 155 AD, at age 86.

When Mao Tse-tung (1893-1976 AD) took over China, one of his first acts was to reduce the strength of the Chinese marriage. Husbands and wives were forced to publicly denounce each other.

Communism is the major reason why the former USSR has great marriage and family problems today. Citizens were encouraged to "turn in" their neighbors if any anti-state attitude was suspected. Marriage mates were encouraged to spy and "rat" on each other. Alexander Solzhenitsyn (1918- AD) is the famous author of *The Gulag Archipelago* and other books. Solzhenitsyn has carefully documented how dictatorships work, from the perspectives of living both inside and outside the USSR Gulag prison system. He lived in the west for 20 years, then returned to the former USSR. He trashed his first wife (who he says betrayed him to the KGB) and married his typist, a much younger woman.

When Communists target a nation for subversion one of their first acts is to murder all Christian missionaries.

Hitler established youth training programs. German youth were taught to "turn in" their parents if any anti-Nazi attitudes were suspected.

Dictatorships always target youth for education and parents for "re-education."

In US public schools, prayer, the Bible, and the Ten Commandments have been banned. Girls spend time putting condoms on bananas. Students are "dumbed down." High-ability children are forced to work in teams in order to kill their potential high achievement. Homosexuality is promoted as a valid lifestyle.

Programs like DARE encourage children to "rat" on their parents. Some parents are in prison (and their children in foster homes) because their DARE-trained children turned them in for smoking marijuana at home. (For an excellent picture of what is happening in US public schools, read John A. Stormer's book, *None Dare Call It Education*, ISBN 0-914053-12-4.)

The US Internal Revenue Service (IRS) targets mainly churches, Christian organizations, and Christians for audits. The media and entertainment industry work day and night to turn out programs and movies which portray marriage and family as bad. US IRS laws have forced married couples to pay more taxes than unmarried couples for many decades.

12.   Satan's fingerprints are all over SOWG. Satan's influence in the creation of SOWG can be seen in three areas: (a) the selection of SOWG's world capital, (b) the symbol used to represent SOWG, and (c) the dates on which important SOWG events are performed.

13.   Satan's fingerprints can be seen in the selection of SOWG's world capital. What city will be SOWG's world capital? Revelation 11 tells about "two witnesses" who will be very active in the SOWG world capital at the very end of God's Master Plan Period One. These "two witnesses" are given power by God:
> "And I will give power unto my two witnesses and they shall prophecy a thousand two hundred and threescore days, clothed in sackcloth."
> (Revelation 11:3 *KJV*)
These Two Witnesses are given power to harass SOWG leaders in SOWG's capital for 1,260 days or forty-two months or three and one-half years. The Two Witnesses perform a great work for God just before the end of SOWG's rule. After 1,260 days God allows the Two Witnesses to be murdered by Satan's henchmen. Note carefully in which city these murders occur:
> "And their dead bodies shall lie in the street of the great city, which spiritually is called Sodom and Egypt, where also our Lord was crucified."
> (Revelation 11:8 *KJV*)
What is the city "where also our Lord was crucified"? Jesus was crucified in Jerusalem!   SOWG's world capital will be Jerusalem!
Satan knows that the world capital of Jesus Christ ruling the Kingdom of God on Earth will be Jerusalem. Satan, always *counterfeiting* the things of God, has inspired his servants to make Jerusalem SOWG's world capital.

14.   Satan's fingerprints can be seen in the symbol used to represent SOWG. Those who have studied the development of SOWG through the centuries have noted that the one-world-government people identify the pyramid as the SOWG model. Writers and thinkers have identified the pyramid on the back of a $1 Federal Reserve Note as a secret symbol of SOWG. (It is not so secret now.) Since SOWG rests on four pillars, it is entirely appropriate that SOWG be represented by a solid with a square as a base, the pyramid. However, the pyramid symbol has been counterfeited from the description of the Holy City, the New Jerusalem, given in the Bible:
> "And the city lieth foursquare, and the length is as large as the breadth: and he measured the city with the reed, twelve thousand furlongs. The length and the breadth and the height of it are equal."
> (Revelation 21:16 *KJV*)
(Other Scriptures, such as Ephesians 2:20, confirm that this structure is a pyramid.)
The Holy City, the New Jerusalem, which will one day come down to Earth from the Third Heaven (where God and Jesus Christ are now), has the shape of a regular pyramid: It has a square (four-sided) base and a height equal to the side of the square.
Amazing, isn't it? Satan, in his last-gasp attempt to create a world government

in opposition to God via SOWG, has *counterfeited* the model of the Holy City, the New Jerusalem, which will be the headquarters of true world government for all eternity. Satan always *plagiarizes* from God!

15. Satan's fingerprints can be seen in the dates on which important SOWG events are performed. September 11, 2001, was a date used for an important event in SOWG's timetable: the disasters which occurred in both New York City and Washington, DC. Why was September 11 chosen by the perpetrators of these disasters? Why not some other date? September 11 was chosen because it is the real date of Jesus Christ's birth. Jesus Christ was *not* born on December 25. Even neophyte Bible scholars know this. Churches may be confused about the date of Jesus Christ's birth, but Satan is not! Satan knows that Jesus Christ was born on September 11.
The only person in 2,000 years to accurately determine the exact date of Christ's birth is Dr. Ernest L. Martin. Martin shows that Jesus Christ was born on September 11, 3 BC. Astronomy confirms the exactness of this date. All of the detail explaining this discovery is contained in the book *The Star That Astonished the World*, © 1996, Ernest L. Martin, ISBN 0-945657-87-0, 280 pp, soft cover, published by Ask Publications, P.O. Box 25000, Portland, Oregon 97225. Published accounts verify that Dr. Martin made his discovery at least before the end of 1976. Over 600 planetariums around the world have altered their Christmas shows to reflect this new truth.
Satan knows that the *real* King of Kings was born on September 11. Satan, the *counterfeit* King of Kings, inspired his SOWG servants to create havoc on September 11, 2001.

16. Snitches are characteristic of all dictatorships, including SOWG. The average person will do anything to save his or her life. When the average person is threatened by SOWG officials, he or she will "turn in" or "rat on" others to save his or her own skin. These others will include neighbors, friends, and even relatives. When tortured, a victim will often do anything to make the pain temporarily stop. Such persons often give the names of other people, even those who have done nothing against the dictatorship. A snitch is an informer.
Snitches will be very active in SOWG:
> "And then shall many be offended, and shall betray one another, and shall hate one another." (Matthew 24:10 *KJV*)
> "Now the brother shall betray the brother to death, and the father the son; and children shall rise up against their parents, and shall cause them to be put to death." (Mark 13:12 *KJV*)
Jesus said this about snitches:
> "For whosoever will save his life shall lose it: and whosoever will lose his life for my sake shall find it." (Matthew 16:25 *KJV*)
The US President has asked Americans to become snitches on their fellow Americans, via the TIPS program. At its height of power, East Germany had one (paid) government snitch per 100 citizens. The US President wants one (paid) US snitch per 10 citizens -- *ten times* the number of one of the greatest hell-holes in world history!

The sad fact about snitches is that once the dictator is in full control, he will murder all snitches. The dictator reasons, "If this person turned on his friends and relatives to save his skin, will not this same person also turn on *me* to save his skin?"

17.   <u>SOWG will force its false religion upon its subjects.</u> <u>Christians will be persecuted, tortured, and murdered</u>:

> "And it was given unto him to make war with the saints, and to overcome them...
> And all that dwell upon the earth shall worship him, whose names are not written in the book of life of the Lamb slain from the foundation of the world." (Revelation 13:7-8 *KJV*)
> "And he had power to...cause that as many as would not worship the image of the beast should be killed." (<u>Revelation 13:15</u> *KJV*)
> "And the dragon was wroth with the woman, and went to make war with the remnant of her seed, which keep the commandments of God, and have the testimony of Jesus Christ." (Revelation 12:17 *KJV*)

Revelation 12 is a history of the Christian church. "Woman" is another name for the Christian church. "Seed" is Jesus Christ. "Remnant of her seed" are Christians. This last verse shows that Satan will inspire his human servants to murder Christians at the end of God's Master Plan Period One.

> "Then shall they deliver you up to be afflicted, and shall kill you: and ye shall be hated of all nations for my name's sake." (Matthew 24:9 *KJV*)
> "I beheld, and the same horn made war with the saints, and prevailed against them;" (Daniel 7:21 *KJV*)
> "...yea, the time cometh, that whosoever killeth you will think that he doeth God service." (John 16:2 *KJV*)

Satan knows *exactly* who are Christians (have the Holy Spirit) and who are fake Christians (do not have the Holy Spirit). Satan will make sure that *Christians* will be tortured and murdered. Others will be inadvertently lumped in with Christians.

18.   <u>SOWG consists of certain personages and entities: (a) the Beast, (b) the False Prophet, (c) Babylon, and (d) Ten Kings.</u> The Beast is a Bible term for SOWG itself. The False Prophet is a religious leader who will be at the top of SOWG. Babylon describes the way of SOWG. The Ten Kings are the ten top rulers of SOWG.

19.   <u>The Bible term for SOWG is "the Beast."</u> The Beast is described in Revelation 13:1-10 as well as in Revelation chapters 14, 16-18.

20.   <u>The "False Prophet" is a religious leader who will be at the top of SOWG.</u> The False Prophet is spoken of as "another beast" in Revelation 13:11. The False Prophet will perform miracles in order to entice citizens to worship the Beast:

> "And he doeth great wonders, so that he maketh fire come down from heaven on the earth in the sight of men,
> And deceiveth them that dwell on the earth by the means of those miracles

which he had power to do in the sight of the beast; saying to them that dwell on the earth, that they should make an image to the beast, which had the wound by a sword, and did live." (<u>Revelation 13:13-14</u> *KJV*)

In II Kings 1:10, 12 Elijah called fire down from heaven twice. In each instance fire from heaven consumed 51 soldiers. God has given this power to His prophets in the past. However, at the end of God's Master Plan Period One the False Prophet will be able to call fire down from heaven. God is telling human beings in advance that the False Prophet will have this power so that those who seek God will not be deceived.

The False Prophet is mentioned by name in three Scriptures in Revelation:

"And I saw three unclean spirits like frogs come out of the mouth of the dragon, and out of the mouth of the beast, and out of the mouth of the false prophet." (Revelation 16:13 *KJV*)

"And the beast was taken, and with him the false prophet that wrought miracles before him, with which he deceived them that had received the mark of the beast, and them that worshipped his image. These both were cast alive into a lake of fire burning with brimstone." (Revelation 19:20 *KJV*)

"And the devil that deceived them was cast into the lake of fire and brimstone, where the beast and the false prophet are, and shall be tormented day and night for ever and ever." (Revelation 20:10 *KJV*)

Paul talked about the False Prophet doing his thing on Earth before Christ's return:

"That ye be not soon shaken in mind, or be troubled, neither by spirit, nor by word, nor by letter as from us, as that the day of Christ is at hand.

Let no man deceive you by any means: for that day shall not come, except there come a falling away first, and that man of sin be revealed, the son of perdition;

Who opposeth and exalteth himself above all that is called God, or that is worshipped; so that he as God sitteth in the temple of God, shewing himself that he is God.

Remember ye not, that, when I was yet with you, I told you these things?

And now ye know what withholdeth [margin: Or, *holdeth*] that he might be revealed in his time.

For the mystery of iniquity doth already work: only he who now letteth will let, until he be taken out of the way.

And then shall that Wicked be revealed, whom the Lord shall consume with the spirit of his mouth, and shall destroy with the brightness of his coming:

Even him, whose coming is after the working of Satan with all power and signs and lying wonders,

And all deceivableness of unrighteousness in them that perish; because they received not the love of the truth, that they might be saved.

And for this cause God shall send them strong delusion, that they should believe a lie:

That they all might be damned who believed not the truth, but had pleasure in unrighteousness." (II Thessalonians 2:2-12 *KJV*)

Paul wrote to the Christians in Thessalonica about 51 AD. Even at that time some Christians believed that Christ's return was imminent. Therefore Paul reviewed for them the events which will precede Christ's return. Paul mentioned a "man of sin," also called "the son of perdition," who will pretend to be God. Paul called the movement of this man "the mystery of iniquity." Paul described this "Wicked" person as one who will perform miracles by the power of Satan, in order to deceive people. Paul said that Christ will destroy this person when He returns. This person is the False Prophet.

21. <u>Babylon is the way of SOWG</u>. Babylon is described in Revelation 17. The story of Babylon's future destruction is given in Revelation 18.

22. <u>The Ten Kings are the ten top rulers of SOWG</u>:
> "And the ten horns which thou sawest are ten kings, which have received no kingdom as yet; but receive power as kings one hour with the beast. These have one mind, and shall give their power and strength unto the beast.
> These shall make war with the Lamb, and the Lamb shall overcome them: for he is Lord of lords, and King of kings: and they that are with him are called, and chosen, and faithful." (Revelation 17:12-14 *KJV*)

Many have speculated about the identity of the Ten Kings. Some say they are leaders of ten nations in Europe. Others say they are a group of the very rich and powerful and call them the "Illuminati," or enlightened ones. These Ten Kings rule SOWG.

23. <u>Jesus Christ will destroy SOWG when He returns</u>. The beginning of the end for SOWG -- the Beast, False Prophet, Babylon, and the Ten Kings -- occurs when the seventh angel sounds his trumpet:
> "And the seventh angel sounded; and there were great voices in heaven, saying, The kingdoms of this world are become the kingdoms of our Lord, and of his Christ; and he shall reign for ever and ever."
> (Revelation 11:15 *KJV*)

The Bible reveals the location of this last climactic battle for control of Earth, between SOWG and Jesus Christ:
> "And he gathered them together into a place called in the Hebrew tongue Armageddon." (Revelation 16:16 *KJV*)

SOWG will fight against Jesus Christ when He returns. However, Christ will win:
> "These shall make war with the Lamb, and the Lamb shall overcome them: for he is Lord of lords, and King of kings: and they that are with him are called, and chosen, and faithful." (**Revelation 17:14** *KJV*)

Jesus Christ's triumphant return with armies from heaven and war with SOWG are described in Revelation 19:11-21. The outcome of this battle is certain:
> "And I saw the beast, and the kings of the earth, and their armies, gathered together to make war against him that sat on the horse, and against his army.
> And the beast was taken, and with him the false prophet that wrought miracles before him, with which he deceived them that had received the

mark of the beast, and them that worshipped his image. These both were cast alive into a lake of fire burning with brimstone.

And the remnant were slain with the sword of him that sat upon the horse, which sword proceeded out of his mouth: and all the fowls were filled with their flesh." (Revelation 19:19-21 *KJV*)

Entertainment media have persuaded Americans that alien space invaders will come to destroy those on Earth. Movies such as *Independence Day* portray evil space aliens coming to kill earthlings. The truth is that Jesus Christ is coming to destroy an evil, inspired-by-Satan SOWG which will have already enslaved all earthlings! Is Satan influencing entertainment media?

24.   <u>Those who support SOWG will have a terrible end</u>. These people will suffer punishment from God:

"And the third angel followed them, saying with a loud voice, If any man worship the beast and his image, and receive his mark in his forehead, or in his hand,

The same shall drink of the wine of the wrath of God, which is poured out without mixture into the cup of his indignation; and he shall be tormented with fire and brimstone in the presence of the holy angels, and in the presence of the Lamb:

And the smoke of their torment ascendeth up for ever and ever: and they have no rest day nor night, who worship the beast and his image, and whosoever receiveth the mark of his name." (Revelation 14:9-11 *KJV*)

The plagues of God are poured out upon SOWG supporters:

"And I heard a great voice out of the temple saying to the seven angels, Go your ways, and pour out the vials of the wrath of God upon the earth.

And the first went, and poured out his vial upon the earth; and there fell a noisome and grievous sore upon the men which had the mark of the beast, and upon them which worshipped his image." (Revelation 16:1-2 *KJV*)

25.   <u>Christians will have eventual, total, and eternal victory over SOWG</u>:

"And he shall speak great words against the most High, and shall wear out the saints of the most High, and think to change times and laws: and they shall be given into his hand until a time and times and the dividing of time.

But the judgment shall sit, and they shall take away his dominion, to consume and to destroy it unto the end.

And the kingdom and dominion, and the greatness of the kingdom under the whole heaven, shall be given to the people of the saints of the most High, whose kingdom is an everlasting kingdom, and all dominions [margin: Or, *rulers*] shall serve and obey him." (<u>Daniel 7:25-27</u> *KJV*)

"But the saints of the most High [margin: Chald. *high ones*, that is, *things*, or, *places*] shall take the kingdom, and possess the kingdom for ever, even for ever and ever." (Daniel 7:18 *KJV*)

<u>Summary</u>. 1. The Bible shows that near the end of Satan's 6,000-year invisible rule (in God's Master Plan Period One) Satan will *succeed* in creating a Satanic

one-world government just before Christ returns to institute God's one-world government in the Millennium. 2. This chapter 29, "Satan's One-World Government," will use SOWG to refer to Satan's coming one-world government. 3. SOWG is known from Bible prophecy. 4. SOWG will rule the world. 5. SOWG will control all economic activity on Earth. 6. Satan is at the heart and core of SOWG. 7. SOWG, like all dictatorships, rests upon four pillars: (a) murder, (b) lies, (c) slavery, and (d) anti-God programs. 8. Murder is an essential pillar of a dictatorship. 9. Lies are an essential pillar of a dictatorship. 10. Slavery is an essential pillar of a dictatorship. 11. Anti-God programs are an essential pillar of a dictatorship. 12. Satan's fingerprints are all over SOWG. 13. Satan's fingerprints can be seen in the selection of SOWG's world capital. Satan knows that the world capital of Jesus Christ ruling the Kingdom of God on Earth will be Jerusalem. Satan, always *counterfeiting* the things of God, has inspired his servants to make Jerusalem SOWG's world capital. 14. Satan's fingerprints can be seen in the symbol used to represent SOWG. The one-world-government people identify the pyramid as the SOWG model. The Holy City, the New Jerusalem has the shape of a regular pyramid. Satan has *counterfeited* the model of the Holy City, the New Jerusalem. 15. Satan's fingerprints can be seen in the dates used to perform important SOWG events. September 11 was chosen because it is the real date of Jesus Christ's birth. Satan, the *counterfeit* King of Kings, inspired his SOWG servants to create havoc on September 11, 2001. 16. Snitches are characteristic of all dictatorships, including SOWG. 17. SOWG will force its false religion upon its subjects. Christians will be persecuted, tortured, and murdered. 18. SOWG consists of certain personages and entities: (a) the Beast, (b) the False Prophet, (c) Babylon, and (d) Ten Kings. 19. The Bible term for SOWG is "the Beast." 20. The "False Prophet" is a religious leader who will be at the top of SOWG. 21. Babylon is the way of SOWG. 22. The Ten Kings are the ten top rulers of SOWG. 23. Jesus Christ will destroy SOWG when He returns. 24. Those who support SOWG will have a terrible end. 25. Christians will have eventual, total, and eternal victory over SOWG.

The Greatest Sin

CHAPTER 30

© 2005, Robert M. Kelley

Look up all Scriptures in your own Bible. Read and/or write the Scriptures on paper. Writing Scriptures on paper slows down your mind and causes the Bible verses to be more deeply burned into your mind.

All Scripture is inspired and true. However, you cannot learn everything at once. Therefore, the two most important Scriptures on this subject are in **bold** type and the next three most important Scriptures on this subject are underlined.

----

1.   Why is there a chapter on one (and only one) type of sin? Through 40 years of regular Bible reading, Bible study, prayer, and the gift of the Holy Spirit, I have come to see that one sin seems to be paramount. There are many sins and many ways to sin. However, there is one potential sin which seems to be a greater threat than all others. In addition, Christians are more susceptible to this sin than non-Christians. This one sin is a killer. This one sin is the reason why Satan fell. This one sin has toppled kings and TV evangelists. I have meditated a lot on this sin for years. In this chapter I feel compelled to tell you about it. The greatest sin is attributing God's gifts to ourselves.

2.   Consider the sin of attributing God's gifts to ourselves. This sin sounds absurd. It sounds stupid. It sounds like something no thinking person would do. Consider that God has created all things. God created the heavens (all three). The Second Heaven has innumerable galaxies (one estimate is the number ten to the 29th exponential power). Closer to home, God created Earth's solar system with a sun, moon and nine (or ten?) planets. God made the clouds, weather, and seasons on Earth. God made the birds, animals, and sea creatures. God made human beings. God allows a person to live on Earth for a while. Everything one has -- talents, abilities, food, clothing, shelter, freedom, health, time, money, possessions -- all come from God. If a woman is a beauty queen, it is totally due to God having given her beauty. If a man is a sports hero, it is totally due to God having given him the body, strength, agility, training, etc. If a person has great intellectual gifts, it is totally due to God having given that person those gifts. If a person has great musical ability, it is totally due to God having given that person a great voice, great lungs, pitch discrimination, excellent finger coordination, training, etc. All a human being has -- gifts to use for a little while -- comes from God! Logically, it is dumb to attribute God's gifts to ourselves. It is dumb. However, some do it, to their own destruction.

3.   Satan's fall was caused by attributing God's gifts to himself. Satan is the king of sin. Satan *invented* sin. What greater authority on sin could there be than Satan himself? Chapter 20, "Satan and Demons," explains Lucifer's rebellion

against God, which caused Lucifer to become Satan. God explains the reason for Lucifer's rebellion:

> "Thine heart was lifted up because of thy beauty, thou hast corrupted thy wisdom by reason of thy brightness: I will cast thee to the ground, I will lay thee before kings, that they may behold thee." (**Ezekiel 28:17** *KJV*)

Earlier verses in Ezekiel 28 explain the incredible beauty, wisdom, and perfection which God gave to Lucifer when God created Lucifer. Unfortunately, Lucifer attributed God's gifts to himself, and became Satan. <u>Satan, the king of sin, set the wrong example by being the first being to commit the greatest sin</u>.

4.   Every human being has many gifts from God. However, Christians have an additional gift: the Holy Spirit. This fact is why Christians are especially vulnerable to the greatest sin. The Holy Spirit is given to Christians at all times:

> "And I will pray the Father, and he shall give you another Comforter, that he may abide with you forever;
>
> Even the Spirit of truth..." (**John 14:16-17** *KJV*)

Because of the Holy Spirit, Christians can have wonderful thoughts and perform miraculous actions which would be impossible without the Holy Spirit. It is easy for a Christian to attribute those thoughts and actions to himself or herself instead of to God. <u>Christians have an additional major reason to commit the greatest sin</u>!

5.   The Old Testament has many examples of people committing the greatest sin. <u>Moses and Aaron committed the greatest sin</u>. This example is recorded in Numbers 20. The children of Israel desired water. Being faithless, they complained to Moses. God told Moses and Aaron how to handle the situation:

> "And the LORD spake unto Moses, saying,
>
> Take the rod, and gather thou the assembly together, thou, and Aaron thy brother, and speak ye unto the rock before their eyes; and it shall give forth his water, and thou shalt bring forth to them water out of the rock: so thou shalt give the congregation and their beasts drink." (Numbers 20:7-8 *KJV*)

God told Moses and Aaron what to do. However, something different happened:

> "And Moses took the rod from before the LORD, as he commanded him.
>
> And Moses and Aaron gathered the congregation together before the rock, and he said unto them, Hear now, ye rebels; must we fetch you water out of this rock?
>
> And Moses lifted up his hand, and with his rod he smote the rock twice: and the water came out abundantly, and the congregation drank, and their beasts also." (Numbers 20:9-11 *KJV*)

Note carefully what happened. Moses did not *speak* to the rock. Moses *struck* the rock with the staff. Nothing happened. Moses struck the rock with his staff a second time. God decided to back up Moses and Aaron; God caused the water to flow. However, Moses and Aaron did not give God the glory. Moses said, "must *we* fetch you water out of this rock?" Moses and Aaron acted as though Moses and Aaron were supplying the water, not God. God pronounced a punishment:

> "And the LORD spake unto Moses and Aaron, Because ye believed me not, to sanctify me in the eyes of the children of Israel, therefore ye

shall not bring this congregation into the land which I have given them." (Numbers 20:12 *KJV*)

The punishment was later carried out against Aaron:

"Aaron shall be gathered unto his people: for he shall not enter into the land which I have given unto the children of Israel, because ye rebelled against my word at the water of Meribah." (Numbers 20:24 *KJV*)

The punishment was later carried out against Moses:

"And the LORD spake unto Moses that selfsame day, saying,

Get thee up into this mountain, Abarim, unto mount Nebo, which is in the land of Moab, that is over against Jericho; and behold the land of Canaan, which I give unto the children of Israel for a possession:

And die in the mount whither thou goest up, and be gathered unto thy people; as Aaron thy brother died in mount Hor, and was gathered unto his people:

Because ye trespassed against me among the children of Israel at the waters of Meribah-Kadesh, in the wilderness of Zin; because ye sanctified me not in the midst of the children of Israel.

Yet thou shalt see the land before thee; but thou shalt not go thither unto the land which I give the children of Israel." (Deuteronomy 32:48-52 *KJV*)

Moses and Aaron were called by God to lead the children of Israel from Egypt into the promised land. However, because they committed the greatest sin, they did *not* complete their life mission. God punished Moses even though he was a great man in God's Master Plan:

"And there arose not a prophet since in Israel like unto Moses, whom the LORD knew face to face,

In all the signs and the wonders, which the LORD sent him to do in the land of Egypt to Pharaoh, and to all his servants, and to all his land,

And in all that mighty hand, and in all the great terror which Moses shewed in the sight of all Israel." (Deuteronomy 34:10-12 *KJV*)

6. Did Samson commit the greatest sin? This example is recorded in Judges 15. Samson had been tied up and delivered to the Philistines:

"And when he came unto Lehi, the Philistines shouted against him: and the Spirit of the LORD came mightily upon him, and the cords that were upon his arms became as flax that was burnt with fire, and his bands loosed [margin: Heb. *were melted*] from off his hands.

And he found a new [margin: Heb. *moist*] jawbone of an ass, and put forth his hand, and took it, and slew a thousand men therewith.

And Samson said, With the jawbone of an ass, heaps upon heaps, with the jaw of an ass have I slain a thousand men.

And it came to pass, when he had made an end of speaking, that he cast away the jawbone out of his hand, and called that place Ramathlehi [margin: That is, *the lifting up of the jawbone*, or *casting away of the jawbone*].

And he was sore athirst, and called on the LORD, and said, Thou hast given this great deliverance into the hand of thy servant: and now shall I die for thirst, and fall into the hand of the uncircumcised?

But God clave an hollow place that was in the jaw [margin: Or, *Lehi*], and there came water thereout; and when he had drunk, his spirit came again, and he revived: wherefore he called the name thereof Enhakkore [margin: That is, *the well of him that called*, or *cried*], which is in Lehi unto this day." (<u>Judges 15:14-19</u> *KJV*)

In the many examples in the Bible (mainly in the Old Testament) when God gave a great victory to a leader, there is *no* other instance in which that leader suddenly became thirsty. Is it possible that Samson mentally gave *himself* credit for the victory? Note Samson's words, "now shall I die...?" Are these the words of a humble person? Did God see Samson's thoughts and decide to make Samson realize that his every breath depended upon moment-by-moment help from God? Did Samson commit the greatest sin?

7.   <u>The Old Testament is loaded with examples of people who committed the greatest sin</u>. Examples are Saul and Solomon, the first and third kings of the twelve-tribe nation of Israel. The kings of the ten-tribe House of Israel and two-tribe (Judah and Benjamin) House of Judah provide additional examples. Hezekiah of the House of Judah is an example. *Learn What the Bible* Really *Says -- Fast!* is not exhaustive. *Learn What the Bible* Really *Says -- Fast!* does not provide *every* proof or example which could be cited. The purpose of *Learn What the Bible* Really *Says -- Fast!* is to provide only the basics.

<u>Summary</u>. 1. The greatest sin is attributing God's gifts to ourselves. 2. Logically, it is dumb to attribute God's gifts to ourselves. 3. Satan, the king of sin, set the wrong example by being the first being to commit the greatest sin. 4. Christians have an additional major reason to commit the greatest sin! 5. Moses and Aaron committed the greatest sin. 6. Did Samson commit the greatest sin? 7. The Old Testament is loaded with examples of people who committed the greatest sin.

Proof of the Bible

CHAPTER 31
© 2005, Robert M. Kelley

Look up all Scriptures in your own Bible. Read and/or write the Scriptures on paper. Writing Scriptures on paper slows down your mind and causes the Bible verses to be more deeply burned into your mind.

All Scripture is inspired and true. However, you cannot learn everything at once. Therefore, the three most important Scriptures on this subject are in **bold** type and the next three most important Scriptures on this subject are underlined.

----

1.   Proving the veracity of the Bible is an important matter. I (and others) have said that the Bible is the inspired word of God. Because the entirety of the Bible is inspired by the Holy Spirit, the Bible is true. The Bible is the *only* source of knowledge which you can intrinsically know to be totally true. These are tall claims. However, one must be able to *prove* these claims. The reading and studying of the Bible (with or without *Learn What the Bible* Really *Says -- Fast!*) is premised on the assumption that the Bible is true and therefore worthy of your study time. This chapter 31, "Proof of the Bible," deals with proving (the veracity of) the Bible.

2.   The Bible proclaims itself to be the Word of God. Paul said that all Scripture is inspired:
   "All scripture is given by inspiration of God, and is profitable for doctrine, for reproof, for correction, for instruction in righteousness:"
   (**II Timothy 3:16** *KJV*)
Jesus said that God's words are truth:
   "Sanctify them through thy truth: thy word is truth." (**John 17:17** *KJV*)
Jesus said that even though physical things are temporary, his words, spoken under the guidance of the Holy Spirit, are eternal:
   "Heaven and earth shall pass away, but my words shall not pass away."
   (Matthew 24:35 *KJV*)
When Jesus was involved in an argument with Israelites about Scripture, Jesus reminded them that the Word of God is true and consistent; there are no contradictions:
   "...the scripture cannot be broken;" (**John 10:35** *KJV*)
Paul pointed out that when there is a conflict between what men say and what God says, God is always right:
   "...let God be true, but every man a liar..." (Romans 3:4 *KJV*)
Paul urged Christians to hold on to what can be proved:
   "Prove all things; hold fast that which is good." (I Thessalonians 5:21 *KJV*)

3.   The Bible has internal proofs: Different men, writing at different locations

and separated by hundreds or thousands of years, wrote the same particulars and details about the same subjects.

One example of internal proofs is the prophecies about Jesus coming to Earth (both his first coming and second coming). From Genesis 3:15, through the Law books, the Writings, and the Prophets (both major and minor), are many Scriptures which discuss the particulars and details of Christ's first and second comings. These Scriptures corroborate each other in defining the same particulars and details. (Books are available which abundantly document these particulars and details.)

Another example of internal proofs is the prophecies of the Millennium, the 1,000-year period when Christ will rule Earth. The Writings and the Prophets (both major and minor) give corroborating particulars on the same facets of life in the Millennium. (See chapter 28, "Life in the Millennium.")

Another example of internal proofs is the corroboration of details about the New Heavens & Earth in Isaiah 65 and Revelation 21 & 22. How could the apostle John in Revelation add details to Isaiah 65 unless the Holy Spirit and/or Jesus Christ revealed this knowledge to him?

The pattern of the Bible is that bits and pieces of information on the same subject are scattered throughout the Bible. These bits and pieces of information complement, reinforce, and corroborate each other. Abundant internal proofs verify the Bible.

4.   History proves the Bible. History verifies the Biblical account. In secular human history Biblical historical accounts are verified.

5.   Archaeology proves the Bible. Archaeology is a field of work in which people dig down in the ground many layers to obtain and study the artifacts of past ages. Where this has been done the archaeological record verifies the Bible. One well known archaeologist who has performed extensive archaeological work in Palestine is Kathleen Kenyon (1906-1978 AD). Kenyon performed a lot of archaeological work in the area of Jericho, a town famous in Bible history. In recent decades archaeological expeditions have found what is believed to be remnants of Noah's Ark near Mt. Ararat in Turkey. Sometimes in archaeological work initial attempts to locate a Biblical city or town are unsuccessful: The city or town cannot be found. However, often later archaeological work results in the finding of the originally-sought destination.

6.   Fulfilled Bible prophecy proves the Bible. One example is Daniel 11, the longest and most detailed single Bible prophecy. Daniel lived about 605-530 BC. However, the prophecy which God revealed to Daniel which is recorded in Daniel 11 details human history from Daniel's time to the return of Jesus Christ to rule Earth in the Millennium. Historians have identified the fulfillment of every single detail of all 45 verses in Daniel 11 from ancient times, except for a few events at the end of God's Master Plan Period One which have not yet occurred. There are many examples of fulfilled Bible prophecy. Daniel 11 is the largest example. Bible prophecy has a 100% fulfillment rate.

Compare Bible prophecy with the work of Nostradamus (1503-1566 AD).

Nostradamus was a French physician and astrologer. He wrote his prophecies in his book *Centuries*, published in 1555 AD. *Centuries* is very popular today. Nostradamus' prophecies have about a 50% fulfillment rate. Who will you believe -- Nostradamus or God in the Bible? Be sure to see chapter 26, "Bible Prophecy Basics." Chapter 26 clearly shows that prophecy is a major proof of God and that prophecy proves that Jesus is the Messiah.

7.   <u>Other examples of fulfilled Bible prophecy abound, such as Egypt and Babylon</u>. Ezekiel 30 contains a prophecy about the nation of Egypt. When this prophecy was made (593-571 BC), and for hundreds and perhaps thousands of years before, Egypt was a large, rich, and great nation. Egypt was a paragon of progress, the nation where the most famous pyramids were designed and built. Egypt was a leader in mathematics, astronomy, and medicine (even brain surgery). God, through Ezekiel, foretold that after 40 years of desolation, Egypt would become a weak and base nation (Ezekiel 29), no longer ruled by a native prince (Ezekiel 30). This prophecy has been completely fulfilled.
Isaiah 13 contains a prophecy about the nation of Babylon. When this prophecy was made Babylon was the number one nation! In Isaiah 13 God, through Isaiah, foretold that Babylon would be destroyed and made desolate forever! The desolate ruins of Babylon are located in an area now inside the modern nation of Iraq. This prophecy has been completely fulfilled.

8.   <u>A great deal of the proof of the Bible lies in sources which are outside the Bible</u>. These sources deal with the fields of history and archaeology. This chapter 31, "Proof of the Bible," gives only the briefest of details. Brief details are given because *Learn What the Bible* Really *Says -- Fast!* is primarily about the Bible. *Learn What the Bible* Really *Says -- Fast!* is *not* primarily about history and archaeology. However, enough information is presented to enable you to research historical and archaeological works to prove that the claims made here are true.

<u>Summary</u>. 1. Proving the veracity of the Bible is an important matter. 2. The Bible proclaims itself to be the Word of God. 3. The Bible has internal proofs: Different men, writing at different locations and separated by hundreds or thousands of years, wrote the same particulars and details about the same subjects. Abundant internal proofs verify the Bible. 4. History proves the Bible. 5. Archaeology proves the Bible. 6. Fulfilled Bible prophecy proves the Bible. 7. Other examples of fulfilled Bible prophecy abound, such as Egypt and Babylon. 8. A great deal of the proof of the Bible lies in sources which are outside the Bible.

Bible Translations

CHAPTER 32
© 2005, Robert M. Kelley

Look up all Scriptures in your own Bible. Read and/or write the Scriptures on paper. Writing Scriptures on paper slows down your mind and causes the Bible verses to be more deeply burned into your mind.

All Scripture is inspired and true. However, you cannot learn everything at once. Therefore, the two most important Scriptures on this subject are in **bold** type and the next six most important Scriptures on this subject are underlined.

----

1.   In the twentieth century more than 50 English language Bible translations were made. Which should you use? Most Bible students do not have access to the Bible in its original languages. Most Bible students use Bible translations: translations from the original Bible languages and intermediate languages into English. In translation a literary work is converted from its source language to a destination language. Many translations of the Bible are available. Which should you use?

2.   The Bible which is inspired consists of the original utterances, both spoken and written. The Old Testament was originally written in Hebrew, except for the book of Daniel, which was written in Chaldee.
(Daniel was of royal lineage of the House of Judah. He was a captive in King Nebuchadnezzar's palace in the capital city of Babylon. Chaldee was the language of the Babylonians. Therefore Daniel wrote in Chaldee.)
The New Testament was originally written in Aramaic. For millennia the common language of Israelites and Jews was Hebrew. However, after the captivity, Aramaic, a sister language of Hebrew, became the common language of the Jews. Aramaic was the language of Palestine, the Fertile Crescent, and the Near East. It was the language of Jerusalem, Damascus, and Antioch. Aramaic was Paul's native language. When Josephus wrote *Wars of the Jews* (to the Jews) he wrote it in Aramaic. Hebrew was the Jews' religious language; Aramaic was the Jews' common language.
Jesus taught in Aramaic; his spoken words were written in Aramaic. An example is Jesus' near-last words on the cross:
   "And about the ninth hour Jesus cried with a loud voice, saying, Eli, Eli, lama sabachthani? that is to say, My God, my God, why hast thou forsaken me?" (**Matthew 27:46** *KJV*)
Matthew quoted Jesus' direct words which were in Aramaic.
Decades later, when the Christian church had grown beyond the Aramaic-speaking world into the Greek-speaking world and God called large numbers of Greek-speaking converts, the original inspired Aramaic was translated into Greek.

It is said that the Bible is inspired by God. (To be exact the Holy Spirit inspired the Bible.) The question is, "Exactly what Bible has been inspired by the Holy Spirit?" The answer is, "The original utterances as originally spoken and first written were inspired by the Holy Spirit." The Holy-Spirit-inspired Bible consists of the Old Testament in Hebrew (except for Daniel which was inspired in Chaldee) and the New Testament in Aramaic.

3.   All of the English language Bibles which are available today are Bible translations. The Old Testament was translated from the inspired Hebrew into English. (The book of Daniel was first translated from the inspired Chaldee into Hebrew.)
The New Testament translation story is more complicated. There were two main churches in early Christian times: the Eastern Church with its headquarters in Constantinople, and the Western Church with its headquarters in Rome. The Eastern Church has always used the New Testament in the original Aramaic. Most of the English language Bible translations available today have come from the Western Church, which preserved the New Testament in Greek. Therefore most English language New Testament versions are the result of two translations: (a) Aramaic was translated into Greek, and (b) Greek was translated into English.
(The earliest English language versions were derived, in part, from Jerome's Latin Vulgate and the Septuagint -- the Old Testament translated from Hebrew into Greek.)

4.   No Bible translation is inspired. Some people are shocked by this statement. The Bible in its original languages was inspired by the Holy Spirit. All Bible translations have been made by human beings. Human beings make mistakes. Consider the large size of a Bible translation project: The *KJV* has 66 books, 1,189 chapters, 31,102 verses, 773,693 words, and 3,566,480 letters. Human beings simply make mistakes. In addition, consider the nature of translation: When making the transition from a word in the source language to a word in the destination language, the best choices are not always immediately clear. If translation were as simple as there being a single direct-correlation word in the destination language for every word in the source language, then even computers could translate! In reality, for every source word in its context at least several destination words are possible. Thus translation is an art, not a science. (Therefore computers with application software programs cannot be validly used for translation!)

5.   All Bible translations contain errors. Most people do not have a working knowledge of Biblical Hebrew and Aramaic. Therefore the only Bibles which are available are translations. Since all translations are made by fallible human beings, all Bible translations contain errors.
In Luke 2 an angel visited shepherds who were watching their sheep at night:
    "And suddenly there was with the angel a multitude of the heavenly host praising God, and saying,
    Glory to God in the highest, and on earth peace, good will toward men."

(<u>Luke 2:13-14</u> *KJV*)

However, compare the *KJV* rendering with the *NIV* rendering:

> "Suddenly a great company of the heavenly host appeared with the angel, praising God and saying,
>> 'Glory to God in the highest,
>>> and on earth peace to men on whom his favor rests.'"

(<u>Luke 2:13-14</u> *NIV*)

The *KJV* portrays the heavenly host (of angels) saying that mankind on Earth is now experiencing peace and good will. With King Herod ruling there was hardly peace and good will. In fact, two years later Herod butchered a number of two-year-old-and-younger boys in this same village of Bethlehem. (For more on the life of King Herod, see chapter 21, "This is Satan's World.") The *KJV* rendering is inconsistent with what was happening. The *NIV* states that the only men who have peace are those to whom God has granted favor. In this case the *NIV* is correct and the *KJV* is in *error*.

6.   <u>Some errors were made when the New Testament was translated from Aramaic to Greek</u>. An example of an Aramaic-to-Greek translation error is this verse:

> "And again I say unto you, It is easier for a camel to go through the eye of a needle, than for a rich man to enter into the kingdom of God."

(<u>Matthew 19:24</u> *KJV*)

The correct rendering of this verse is given by George M. Lamsa in his translation:

> "Again I say to you, It is easier for a rope [margin: The Aramaic word *gamla* means *rope* and *camel*] to go through the eye of a needle, than for a rich man to enter into the kingdom of God." (Matthew 19:24 *Lamsa*)

(Note: The George M. Lamsa Bible contains the only New Testament version available today in which the original Aramaic was translated into English -- a single translation. All other New Testament versions are the result of two translations: (a) Aramaic was translated into Greek. (b) Greek was translated into English.)

Those who translated the New Testament from Aramaic to Greek *erred*. These translators chose the Greek word for camel instead of the Greek word for rope. Because almost all English-language New Testament versions are translations from Greek manuscripts, this error has been perpetuated in almost all English-language New Testament versions. The original Aramaic -- the original source inspired by the Holy Spirit -- shows that Jesus said "rope." "Rope" makes much more sense than "camel."

7.   <u>Some translation errors were made because the translators were ignorant of idioms</u>. An idiom is an expression which has a meaning different from its literal meaning. An example is the American English idiom, "food for thought." The meaning of "food for thought" is "something to think about." "Food for thought" has *nothing* to do with food. However, if one is determined to make a *literal* translation and is ignorant of idioms, one would search for the destination word for the source word "food." <u>A literal translation of an idiom does *not* convey</u>

its meaning.

Bible readers are often confused by the literal translation of idioms.

> "And if thy right eye offend thee [margin: Or, *do cause thee to offend*], pluck it out, and cast it from thee..." (Matthew 5:29 *KJV*)

The *KJV* reader normally assumes that this verse is about you gouging out your eye. However, the *Lamsa* marginal note on this verse is:

> "Aramaic idiom: *stop envying*."

The original, in idiom format, simply means, "Stop envying."

> "And if thy right hand offend thee, cut it off, and cast it from thee..." (Matthew 5:30 *KJV*)

The *KJV* reader normally assumes that this verse is about you amputating your hand. However, the *Lamsa* marginal note on this verse is:

> "An Aramaic idiom, meaning *stop stealing*."

The original, in idiom format, simply means "Stop stealing."

> "But I say unto you, That ye resist not evil: but whosoever shall smite thee on thy right cheek, turn to him the other also." (Matthew 5:39 *KJV*)

The *KJV* reader normally assumes that this verse is about one who seeks God becoming a punching bag, letting anyone beat you. However, the *Lamsa* marginal note on this verse is:

> "'Turn your cheek' is an Aramaic idiom meaning, 'Do not start a quarrel or a fight.'"

The original, in idiom format, simply means "Don't start quarrels or fights."

> "And another of his disciples said unto him, Lord, suffer me first to go and bury my father." (Matthew 8:21 *KJV*)

The *KJV* reader normally assumes that Jesus is saying that one who seeks God should not even attend a parent's funeral service. However, the *Lamsa* marginal note on this verse is:

> "Aramaic idiom: *take care of my father*."

George Lamsa explains that "bury my father" is an Aramaic idiom, which means being the primary care provider for your parent until your parent dies. "Bury my father" could take decades. A task which could take decades obviously prevented this man from becoming one of Jesus' personal, traveling disciples.

Some translation errors have occurred because the translator or translators was or were ignorant of source language idioms.

Consider the hundreds of millions of people who have been confused by reading the above quoted verses in the *King James Version*.

8.   The errors which exist in most Bible translations are not significant. One can list thousands of errors in dozens of English Bible translations. However, the good news is that the sum total of errors in most translations is not significant. That is, most Bible translations are faithful renderings of the original, inspired texts. As a general rule, most English Bible translations are reliable reproductions of the original versions.

Many people are concerned when they discover one word which they feel is improperly rendered in a translation. However, I believe that God communicates in ideas, not words. My belief is substantiated by these facts. The original Bible source languages have been translated into over 1,000 destination languages. God knew that man would make translations from the original, source languages. Therefore the Bible is composed of God's ideas, not God's words. Words are used to convey the ideas. God's ideas come through in almost all Bible translations. If God communicated only in words, then in order to understand God's inspired Bible every person worldwide would have to read the Bible in the original Hebrew (Old Testament) and Aramaic (New Testament) only.

9.   <u>Even though most Bible translations are good, a few are bad</u>. I have just said that most Bible translations are reliable. However, there are a few Bible translations that are just plain *bad*. Most apples are good; however, there are a few rotten apples. <u>The *Living Bible* is bad</u>. In the 1950s Kenneth N. Taylor desired a Bible in plain English. To create such a plain English Bible, Taylor took the *American Standard Version (ASV)* of 1901 and created, in his own words, a simple English rendering. Taylor called his new work the *Living Bible (LB)*, which was completed in 1971. Taylor did not create a translation. A translation is a conversion from a source language to a destination language. Taylor simply rephrased the English of the *ASV*. Taylor created what is known as a paraphrase. A *translator* is under the obligation to be totally true to the original, source language. A *paraphraser* is under no such obligation. Therefore the *LB* has many renderings which are inconsistent with the original languages. I used to call the *LB* "Living Lies." However, the *LB* was very popular. It sold over 40 million copies. Many readers say, "It's so clear!" I say, "It may be clear, but is it the Bible?"

10.   <u>The *Contemporary English Version (CEV)* is bad</u>. The *CEV* was created by Barclay M. Newman of the American Bible Society. Newman explains his creation of the *CEV* in the book, *Creating & Crafting the Contemporary English Version: A New Approach to Bible Translation*. Newman's goals were laudable. He desired to make a very readable English Bible translation. Unfortunately, creating and crafting got the upper hand over translating. The *CEV* is very readable and formatted very well. However, the renderings are so far from the original that one must ask if the *CEV* is the Bible. I read a lot of Bible translations. In fact, reading and studying Bible translations is one of my life-long hobbies. The *CEV* is the only Bible translation which I failed to read to the end. I put it down three times; the third time I stopped reading at Jeremiah 9:24. There are many errors in the *CEV*; it would take volumes to document all of them. I will discuss only three passages. These three passages are sufficient to raise troubling questions about the "creating & crafting" of the *CEV*. Here are three *CEV* passages containing errors.
In I Samuel 25:18 Abigail prepares "two jars of wine." Most other translations (including the *NIV, RSV, NRSV, NEB, REB*) render this phrase "two skins of wine." This error bugs me because it appears that Newman can't believe that wineskins were in use at this time. Is the evolution belief in play here?
Psalm 107 is one of my favorite Psalms. This Psalm encourages people to praise God for what He has done for others. Each section shows how God has saved others. The Psalmist reiterates the acts of God for others and enjoins the reader

to worship God. However, Newman has really butchered this Psalm. Newman begins each section with "Some of you..." (verses 4, 10, 17, 23). Newman has changed from the third person to the second person (from *they, them* (*KJV*) to *you*). Apparently the reason Newman did this was to avoid sexist pronouns (one of his social engineering agendas in creating the *CEV*?). Newman's social engineering totally changes the meaning of Psalm 107. All of the actions described in Psalm 107 did *not* happen to the audience or reader(s).

Jeremiah 9:23-24 has always been one of my favorite Scriptures. I have memorized these two verses. When reading these two verses in the *CEV* I did not even recognize them! First, God talks about three men, not one. Second, worshipping God is not the same as understanding and knowing God. Third, God does *not* show kindness, justice and mercy "to everyone on earth." (God has a Master Plan, and therefore calls people at different times, not all at the same time. In addition, God does, at times, treat the righteous differently from the wicked.)

In addition to these three passages, throughout the Bible Newman has shortened verses and chapters, leaving out the translation of many source words.

After reading Jeremiah 9:24, I concluded that life is too short to waste time on a non-Bible "Bible."

Each person has his or her own opinion of "rotten apple" translations. However, you should insure that your opinion is based on Bible facts.

11.   The *King James Version (KJV)* has been the dominant English Bible translation. No discussion of Bible translations would be complete without recognition of the role of the *KJV*. The history of Bible translations will not be reviewed here. Many books are available to tell this exciting story. In the last almost 400 years the *KJV* has been the dominant translation. (However, in recent years the *NIV* has out-sold the *KJV*.) The *KJV* was created in 1611 AD by the authority of James I of England (formerly James VI of Scotland). (This was an amazing turn of events since earlier English kings put anyone to death who dared to make an English translation.) The *KJV* has had a long tenure. Revisions were made in 1885 (*English Revised Version*), 1901 (*American Standard Version*), 1952 (*Revised Standard Version*), and 1989 (*New Revised Standard Version*). *KJV* lovers claim that the *KJV* is a majestic display of the English language. It was. Today many ministers and even some popular television evangelists still preach from the *KJV*. (One enthusiastic but uninformed Christian once said, "If the *KJV* was good enough for the apostle Paul, it is good enough for me!") Alternatives to the *KJV* were slow in coming. Ferrar Fenton completed his translation in 1903. Edgar J. Goodspeed and J.M. Powis Smith completed *The Complete Bible: An American Translation* in 1935. Major competitors to the *KJV* were the *Revised Standard Version* (1952), the *New English Bible* (1970), the *New International Version* (1978), and the *New Revised Standard Version* (1989). In addition, many individual scholars have made translations (e.g., *A New Translation of the Bible Containing the Old and New Testaments* by James Moffatt in 1926).

12.   Some people worship the *KJV*. I have met people who have absolutely

made an idol of the *KJV*. Recently I was talking to a minister. I had intended to show him the *KJV* error of Matthew 19:24, discussed above. As I began to speak he cut me short: "There are *no* errors in the *King James Version*!" It *is* possible that there could be a Bible translation with no errors, one that was inspired by the Holy Spirit. However, the *KJV* has many well-documented errors. The Holy Spirit does *not* inspire error! If a literary work has many errors, it obviously was not inspired by the Holy Spirit.

The *KJV* was, in its day, a great translation. However, the current year is 2005 AD, and the *KJV* is 394 years old. The English language has changed a lot in 394 years. (This subject is expanded on below.) There is *no* reason for "The *KJV* is God's Inspired Word" automobile bumper stickers. Some people worship the *KJV* more than God! Where would Christianity be if some Christians worshipped God as much as they worship the *KJV*?

13.   <u>Those who worship the *KJV* today would have rejected it in 1611 AD</u>. When the *KJV* was first published in 1611 AD many Christians flatly rejected it. The *KJV* was the "new-fangled" Bible translation. (Doesn't everyone know that whatever is new is not as good as the old? In addition, the *KJV* was created by *modern* Bible scholars!) When the *KJV* was first published in 1611 AD many Christians wanted to stay with "God's Bible," the *Geneva Bible*! (Did *Geneva Bible* owners have bumper stickers on their carriages and ox carts which said, "The Geneva Bible is God's Inspired Word!"?) In actual fact the *KJV* was superior to the *Geneva Bible* in several ways. More and better scholars were involved, better manuscripts were used, and a better translation method was employed. Nevertheless initial *KJV* acceptance was slow. Fifty years passed before there were as many *KJV* Bibles as *Geneva Bibles*. The same people who cling to the *KJV* today would have utterly rejected it when it was first published in 1611 AD!

14.   <u>The desire for newer translations came about because of English usage changes since the *King James Version*</u>. English usage, 1611 AD vintage, is obsolete today.

We don't say "thou" and "thee." We don't end verbs with "th" and "est." We don't use words like "behooved" and "peradventure."

In addition, hundreds of words in the *KJV* have changed meaning in the last 394 years. In 1611 AD if you wanted to say "conduct" you used the word "conversation." If you wanted to say "spirit" you used the word "ghost." If you wanted to say "precede" you used the word "prevent."

(An expanded explanation of the English usage changes since the *King James Version* can be found in the Preface of the *Revised Standard Version*.)

English vocabulary and usage have changed so much in the last 394 years that the *KJV* is practically incomprehensible to modern English readers. (For those to whom English is a second language, the *KJV* is essentially incomprehensible.)

15.   <u>Many people compare modern Bible translations with the *KJV*</u>. Because the *KJV* was an early popular translation and modern translations were made later, people tend to compare modern translation renderings with *KJV* renderings. I, like many Christians, began my spiritual journey reading and

studying the *KJV*. Later, when modern translations were published, I would purchase them, read them, and compare their renderings with the "inspired" *KJV*. To determine which rendering was most faithful to the original -- the modern rendering or the *KJV* rendering -- I would use Hebrew and Greek dictionaries and look up the actual Hebrew or Greek word(s). I would compare the Hebrew & Greek with each translation. In 90% of cases I found the modern translation to be more accurate; in 10% of cases I found the *KJV* to be more accurate. I was so used to the *KJV* rendering that I tended to regard any different rendering as "inaccurate." If you have been using a particular translation for a long time, then familiarity will tend to lead to the belief that anything *different* is "wrong."

16.   <u>Bible translations are imperfect tools</u>. The only Bibles available are Bible translations. All Bible translations contain errors. In this life human beings will never have perfect knowledge of God. As Paul says:
    "For we know in part, and we prophesy in part."
    "For now we see through a glass darkly [margin: Gr. *in a riddle*]..."
    (I Corinthians 13:9, 12 *KJV)*
In this life human beings will never have *all* the answers. The Bible translations available to human beings are imperfect. <u>However, they are quite adequate to enable human beings to be successful in the New Covenant</u>.

17.   <u>New Covenant success is not a matter of which Bible translation is used</u>. The way some people talk about Bible translations, one can believe that success in the New Covenant depends on which Bible translation one uses.
When Jesus Christ returns to Earth at the seventh trumpet and Christians are resurrected (dead Christians first, then live Christians) with wonderful, eternal-life spirit bodies (as described in I Corinthians 15), amazing discoveries will be made: Some used the *Geneva Bible*, the *King James Version*, the *Revised Standard Version*, the *New English Bible*, the *New International Version*, etc. Some used only scraps of paper on which were written a few Bible verses. Some memorized Bible verses from someone else's Bible or portion thereof. It will be discovered that New Covenant success was achieved in spite of the Bible translation used!
(Since about 33 AD most people have had few, if any, choices. Essentially only people living since 1900 AD have had *any* choices.)

18.   <u>Which Bible translations to use is a personal decision</u>. The use of any single Bible translation will not get one into the Kingdom of God. The non-use of any single Bible translation will not keep one out of the Kingdom of God. Using any single Bible translation will make one neither righteous nor evil. You should use translations with which you feel comfortable. I recommend using several Bible translations. A rendering which is confusing in one translation can be better understood by comparing it to the non-confusing rendering in another translation.

<u>Summary</u>. 1. In the twentieth century more than 50 English language Bible

translations have been made. Which should you use? 2. The Bible which is inspired consists of the original utterances, both spoken and written. The Holy-Spirit-inspired Bible consists of the Old Testament in Hebrew (except for Daniel which was inspired in Chaldee) and the New Testament in Aramaic. 3. All of the English language Bibles which are available today are Bible translations. 4. No Bible translation is inspired. 5. All Bible translations contain errors. 6. Some errors were made when the New Testament was translated from Aramaic to Greek. 7. Some translation errors were made because the translators were ignorant of idioms. A literal translation of an idiom does *not* convey its meaning. Bible readers are often confused by the literal translation of idioms. Consider the hundreds of millions of people who have been confused by reading the above quoted verses in the *King James Version*! 8. The errors which exist in most Bible translations are not significant. Most English Bible translations are reliable reproductions of the original versions. God communicates in ideas, not words. 9. Even though most Bible translations are good, a few are bad. The *Living Bible* is bad. 10. The *Contemporary English Version (CEV)* is bad. 11. The *King James Version (KJV)* has been the dominant English Bible translation. 12. Some people worship the *KJV*. 13. Those who worship the *KJV* today would have rejected it in 1611 AD. 14. The desire for newer translations came about because of English usage changes since the *King James Version*. 15. Many people compare modern Bible translations with the *KJV*. 16. Bible translations are imperfect tools. However, they are quite adequate to enable human beings to be successful in the New Covenant. 17. New Covenant success is not a matter of which Bible translation is used. 18. Which Bible translations to use is a personal decision.

Subject Index

Scripture Index

Note:
1.   Only Scriptures quoted (in whole or in part) in idention format are listed.
Scriptures mentioned or quoted, but not quoted in idention format, are *not* listed.

<u>Old Testament</u>

Genesis
1:2	91	1:21, 24	139	1:26-27	58
1:28	150	2:2-3	58	2:7	139
2:15	151	3:3	140	3:4	141
3:19	139	5:24	121	7:11-12	127
9:4	140	18:1-2	105	19:1	105

Exodus
20:2-3	83	24:4	18	24:7-8	18
25:18-20	109				

Numbers
20:7-8	178	20:9-11	178	20:12	179
20:24	179	23:19	79		

Deuteronomy
4:35	83	4:39	83	6:4	83
17:18-20	4	32:39	83	32:48-52	179
34:10-12	179				

Judges
2:1	105	13:3	105	14:19	92
15:14-15	92	15:14-19	180		

I Samuel
10:6	92	10:10	92	11:6	92
15:29	79	16:13	92	16:14	92

II Samuel
7:11-13	41	7:16	42

II Kings
2:1, 11	121	16:5	145

I Chronicles

29:11 ---------------- 42

II Chronicles
21:12 ---------------- 126

Job
1:10 ---------------- 112

Psalms

2:6 ---------------- 42	2:8-9 ---------------- 42	5:6 ---------------- 79
12:2 ---------------- 80	16:10 ---------------- 134	31:5 ---------------- 75
31:18 ---------------- 79	40:11 ---------------- 77	43:3 ---------------- 75
51:6 ---------------- 75	51:11 ---------------- 92	89:35-37 ------- 42
116:11 ---------------- 80	119:30 ---------------- 76	144:8 ---------------- 80
145:11-13 ------- 42	146:4 ---------------- 140	

Proverbs

6:16, 17 ------- 79	12:22 ---------------- 79	17:4 ---------------- 79
19:9 ---------------- 79	19:22 ---------------- 80	23:23 ---------------- 75
26:28 ---------------- 80	29:12 ---------------- 80	

Ecclesiastes

3:19 ---------------- 140	9:5 ---------------- 140	9:10 ---------------- 140

Isaiah

2:2-4 ---------------- 156	9:6-7 ---------------- 43	11:1-5 ---------------- 156
11:6-9 ---------------- 158	11:11-12 ------- 160	13:10 ---------------- 127
14:12 ---------------- 127	14:12-15 ------- 107	32:7 ---------------- 81
35:1-2 ---------------- 157	35:5-6 ---------------- 159	35:6 ---------------- 157
40:3-4 ---------------- 157	40:8 ---------------- 84	40:9-10 ------- 156
40:13-14 ------- 85	40:21-24 ------- 85	40:25-26 ------- 85
41:17-18 ------- 157	41:19 ---------------- 158	41:21-23 ------- 86, 144
43:10 ---------------- 83	44:6 ---------------- 83	44:24 ---------------- 83
45:19 ---------------- 75	49:8 ---------------- 63	57:4 ---------------- 80
59:3 ---------------- 80	59:4 ---------------- 80	59:8 ---------------- 117
59:14-15 ------- 76	65:17 ---------------- 54	65:17-20 ------- 71
65:25 ---------------- 158	66:22 ---------------- 72	

Jeremiah

5:3 ---------------- 75	7:28 ---------------- 76	9:5 ---------------- 76
23:14 ---------------- 80	31:12 ---------------- 158	31:31 ---------------- 93
31:31-33 ------- 21	31:33 ---------------- 60, 93	32:37 ---------------- 160
43:2 ---------------- 80		

Ezekiel

13:19 ---------------- 80	13:22 ---------------- 81	18:4 ---------------- 140
18:20 ---------------- 140	18:23 ---------------- 135	18:32 ---------------- 135

Bible Study Notes

Subject_____   Date_____

Bible Study Notes

Subject_____   Date_____

_____

Bible Study Notes

Subject_____   Date_____

_____

Bible Study Notes

Subject_____   Date_____

_____

Bible Study Notes

Subject_____   Date_____

Bible Study Notes

Subject_____ Date_____

Bible Study Notes

Subject_____   Date_____

_____

Bible Study Notes

Subject_____   Date_____

Bible Study Notes

Subject_____ Date_____
_____

Bible Study Notes

Subject_____   Date_____
_____

Did you benefit from using *Learn What the Bible* Really *Says -- Fast!* ?

Would you like others to:
√   Quickly master the Bible?
√   Discover the answers to life's most
     important questions?
√   Become spiritually strengthened?
√   Become closer to God?

You can obtain **additional** copies of
Learn What the Bible Really *Says --
Fast!* for:
√   Friends
√   Relatives
√   Neighbors

See the next page

For information on *Learn What the Bible* Really *Says -- Fast!*

By telephone:
Call:
800-652-1415 (toll-free)
937-298-6132 (local)

By internet:
Visit our website:
www.kelleybiblebooks.com

By mail:
Write:
Kelley Bible Books
P.O. Box 293125
Kettering, Ohio 45429-9125

To Order
Learn What the Bible Really *Says -- Fast!*

By telephone:
    Call the 800# at the website
    Have your credit card ready

By mail:
    Fill-in and mail this form (or form
    copy) with check or money order

Name_____

Address_____

City_____   State_____   Zip Code_____

Telephone No. (in case there are questions)_____

Please send me _____ copies of *Learn What the Bible* Really *Says -- Fast!* @ $23.95 per copy .... $ _____

7-1/2% Sales Tax (Ohio residents only) @ $1.80 per book .... _____

Packing and Shipping:
    U.S. Postal Service Media Class rate:
        $5.00 for first book, $2.00 each for additional books ..... _____

Total (enclosed check or money order for this amount) .... $ _____

Mail form (or form copy) with check or money order to:
Kelley Bible Books, P.O. Box 293125, Kettering, Ohio 45429-9125